Eight Generations

The Story of Our Family

by

Dennis Ford

EIGHT GENERATIONS
THE STORY OF OUR FAMILY

iUniverse books may be ordered through booksellers or by contacting:

iUniverse
1663 Liberty Drive
Bloomington, IN 47403
www.iuniverse.com
844-349-9409

ISBN: 978-1-4502-9901-5 (sc)
ISBN: 978-1-4502-9902-2 (hc)
ISBN: 978-1-4502-9903-9 (e)

Print information available on the last page.

iUniverse rev. date: 10/31/2020

The cover photograph is of the site of the Forde
farm in Derrynacong, County Mayo.
The house stood between the trees.

to the people who come after us

TABLE OF CONTENTS

Chapter One ~ Two Memories 1

Chapter Two ~ Erin—Patrick Forde & Bridget Freeman 6

Chapter Three ~ Erin—Patrick Hunt & Bridget Fitzmaurice 21

Chapter Four ~ Erin—Martin Griffin & Catherine Connell 30

Chapter Five ~ Erin—John Allen & Johanna Linnane...................... 42

Chapter Six ~ Lietuva—Juozas Bielawski & Petronele Falkewicz 61

Chapter Seven ~ Lietuva—Jonas Milosz & Magdalena Asakewicz 70

Chapter Eight ~ Lietuva—Tomas Storta & Agota Karuzas 78

Chapter Nine ~ Lietuva—Motiejus Juchnewicz & Kristina Blazys....... 83

Chapter Ten ~ Erin—Thomas Forde and Mary Hunt...................... 88

Chapter Eleven ~ Erin—Denis Griffin & Ellen Allen 103

Chapter Twelve ~ Lietuva—Mykolas Bielawski & Ursula Milosz....... 113

Chapter Thirteen ~ Lietuva—Franciszk Storta & Rozalia Juchnewicz 118

Chapter Fourteen ~ America—Patrick Ford & Catherine Griffin 134

Chapter Fifteen ~ America—Pawel Bielawski & Zofia Storta 151

Chapter Sixteen ~ Joseph Thomas Ford 168

Chapter Seventeen ~ Sophia Bielawska Ford.................................... 189

Chapter Eighteen ~ The Strange Case of Honest Den Ford 203

Chapter Nineteen ~ Felicia Ford.. 218

Chapter Twenty ~ Kathleen Ford Pecoraro 227

Chapter Twenty One ~ How We Did This Research....................... 235

End Notes... 243

Maps 58

Photographs 125

Chapter One

~

Two Memories

Family history involves memory. We recollect the names of the people of the past. Some of these people we knew. Some we knew about. Some come as surprises when we discover them. We recollect their dates and times, the places they lived, and the manner of their lives. We also recollect the particulars of our own lives, much of which are forgotten as we rush pell-mell through the hectic present.

The story of our family begins with two memories. I believe the first is the earliest memory of my life. The second is the memory of the first day I deliberately set out to recover our family history.

I'm three years old, maybe three-and-a-half. We enter *Cocci* (Aunt) Blanche's apartment on 8th St. in Jersey City. There are other people present, but I don't see them. Pawel Bielawski, my grandfather, is in the room. He wears a white short and is smiling. He has eyeglasses on. I'm told not to jump on him, as he is old and sickly, but I disobey. I run to him. He bends and picks me up. There's a sense of happiness.

I'm told that my grandfather—*Dziadek* in Polish and pronounced "ja-deck"—had a fondness for me. Maybe he was a kindly—fatherly—man. Maybe he thought that I would be the last baby born in his life. Maybe he recognized talent in preschoolers. My mother related how he held me as a baby and rocked me in his arms and how he doted over me with particular concern when I came down with whooping cough at six months of age. She said *Dziadek* rushed and checked on me whenever I whooped. It's sad to think I don't have any other memories of him. But the memory I have is a good one to start life with.

The personality theorist Alfred Adler placed great store in the importance of early memories. He believed they were retained because they had relevance for our current life style and because they indicated the trajectory of our lives. It doesn't take a credentialed Adlerian to connect this memory with my adult life. I like to think I'm a friendly person, empathetic and connected with others. And I like to think I'm a guileless person, "decent and ordinary", as I expressed elsewhere.

The memory of my grandfather plainly prefigures what I did for a chunk of my life. I spent the second half of the 1990s and the years 2009 – 2010 in pursuit of family history in the broadest sense. I've traveled thousands of miles to the old countries of Erin and Lietuva. I've reviewed hundreds of miles of microfilm. I've written to phone directories of resources. I've spent a fortune I could otherwise have applied to carousing—in recollecting the story of our family I've literally been jumping into my grandparents' arms.

It is 40 years later. I vividly recall the first day I hunted our family history. I had been thrown out of Kennedy assassination research for suggesting the Warren Commission had it right. It was an ignominious conclusion to a once bright career of chasing conspiracies and quite disconcerting at the time. I had spent a lot of time and money researching just who killed President Kennedy. In retrospect getting my passport rescinded from conspiracy land was the best thing that happened. I wish it had happened earlier. I looked for a new project that could occupy me and in which I could utilize the skills I honed sleuthing after the real assassins. I had used the New York City Public Library at 42nd St. and Fifth Ave. and the Mormon Family History Library at 65th St. and Columbus Ave. For some reason I decided to visit the National Archives. I had never been there and I was curious what it was like. I heard they had copies of the 1920 Federal Census. That seemed a sensible place to start.

I set out to New York City on a wickedly cold day in the winter of 1994 - 95 to visit the Archives. I was so poorly prepared I didn't know where the Archives were. I thought they were in a Federal building on Broadway near Duane and Reade Sts. in Lower Manhattan—the correct address was Varick and Houston Sts. I entered the building, rode the elevator to an upper story—security was nonexistent in that period—and found out I was in the wrong place by several frozen miles.

I had a rough idea of the location of Varick and Houston Sts., but it was horrendously cold. It was a hurting cold able to douse the barely struck fires of genealogy circulating in a chilled bloodstream. I can't honestly say what kept me walking. It may have been the idea that I had taken a day off from work. It may have been that I had run out of vacation days and needed to put this particular day to profitable use. It may have been too cold to turn back—I was somewhere between subway stations. I found the building before I froze and copied the Census. I also found out that the Archives had photocopies of the logs of the steamships on which our grandparents traveled to America. I thought I could learn the names of the ships our grandparents immigrated on. That sounded like an interesting follow-up project.

I didn't stop following up for the next five years.

On one of my visits to the Family History Library I spoke with a Mormon who said he intended to trace his ancestry to the Apostolic Succession. I haven't met him since, so I don't know if he was successful. Probably, he's hard at work somewhere in the Dark Ages. *Eight Generations* is more modest in scope. It traces our family history from my great-great-grandparents forwards in time to my great nephews. This is eight generations and more than two hundred years. In a few family lines on the Polish side it's nine generations, but eight seemed a nice even number in which to frame the story. It doesn't lead to an upper room in Jerusalem, but it goes back far enough. And it's not bad considering we come, I'm not ashamed to say, from peasant stock. There are no kings or queens, nor even a duke or duchess, in the story, only a chronology of princely people.

The names of my paternal great-great-grandparents are Patrick Forde and Bridget Freeman of Derrynacong, County Mayo, Ireland, Patrick Hunt and Bridget Fitzmaurice of Laughil, County Roscommon, Martin Griffin and Catherine Connell of Ballyegan, County Kerry, and John Allen and Johanna Linnane of Trippul West, County Kerry. The names of my maternal great-great-grandparents are Juozas Bielawski and Petronele Falkewicz of Kalniskes, Lithuania, Jonas Milosz and Magdalena Asakewicz of Malakonys, and Tomas Storta and Agota Karuzas and Motiejus Juchnewicz and Kristina Blazys of Girdziunai. In the text that follows the names of our direct ancestors and blood relatives are indicated in boldface in their initial appearances. Tangential and explanatory information lies in end notes. For the record, the names of my great nephews are Shane, Evan, and Alex York, Anthony and Dante Paradiso, and Jack Jones.

Eight Generations is organized in chronological order. The next four chapters document my Irish great-great-grandparents. The next four chapters take us to the Wilenska District in Southeastern Lithuania to document my Polish great-great-grandparents. We return to Ireland to the lives of my great-grandparents. It's back to Lithuania to my Polish great-grandparents. We then board steamships with my grandparents and cross the ocean to America. My parents are next, then myself, modestly, to be sure, and my sisters and their families. The last chapter describes how and where we did this research.

We're dealing with a large and uneven body of research on sixteen family lines. We have more information on certain families than on others. This owes to the luck of finding records and to the motivation of record keepers. It also owes to the presence of informants—in some lines we were very lucky, in other lines, not so lucky. I truly regret coming to genealogy so late, when a lot of the older people had gone to their just rewards. I should have spent less time measuring trajectories in Dealey Plaza.

Bernie Freeman was a friend from the period of my active research. Bernie's family hailed from the same vicinity of Eastern County Mayo as our Freeman ancestor, so we may have been distantly related—the operative word is "distantly". Tragically, Bernie died soon after we met. He was an elderly man of the old school. I believe at one point he was a teacher of Latin, so he was really old school.

Many people are not interested in family history and are suspicious of people who are. Bernie wasn't like that. Bernie related how happy he had been to read my file on the Freeman families of Annagh Parish—his ancestors were included in the file. He said it had been the desire of his immigrant mother that all his people should be "brought together".

"Bring them together," Bernie's mother instructed. That's what I've tried to do in *Eight Generations*. I wanted to collect—to recollect—in one place what we knew and what we learned about the many people who were part of our family's history in Erin and in Lietuva and in America. I was in position to do this research. I had the time. I was in the right place—it was a short hop on the IRT train from where I worked at the Barnes & Noble Sale Annex at 18th St. and Fifth Ave. to the depositories uptown. I knew how to do research and to use archival resources. I had the leisure to be able to travel and to engage in correspondence. I had the means. I had the motivation. I had the obsession. The obligation was entirely on me. I didn't want to shirk it, I couldn't shirk it. Within weeks of that shivery walk the quest to find where I came from was burning tenaciously.

It was a sacred trust and honor to document the details of family history and the history of the obscure places where our ancestors lived—they are places enmeshed in the general history of the time. We can study the events of history through the humble vantages of the townlands and villages and cities where our ancestors lived.

I've often thought about these people of the past. What did they look like? What kind of people were they? Were they decent and ordinary or indecent and extraordinary? How did they live? What were the particulars of their lives? What did they do on a daily basis? What was their routine? What did they believe? What did they believe in? What did they talk about? What would we have talked about if we met? What would they understand of my life? What kind of person would they judge me to be? What would they think of the people of my time?

The answers to these questions are conjectures. At best, they are informed guesses derived from scattered contemporary accounts, from scholarship, and from the creative imagination. In a physical sense the world of our ancestors is simple to comprehend. In a psychological sense their world is entirely removed from the spaces we inhabit. Our psychological and personal states are completely different, yet that doesn't impede an understanding of the manner of their existence. Nor does it impede an appreciation of the intrinsic value of lives widely separated in place and time.

The disparity is nearly as great in genetics as in the social-cultural history. From the perspective of *Eight Generations* 16 individuals were involved in creating me. Sixty-four individuals were involved in creating my great nephews—this is one half of their ancestry. This genetic diversity is so great we might expect it to exist among strangers. Yet these people are family. They are in my blood as I might be said to have been in theirs. If one of them had said "No" to the matchmaker or if one had missed the horse-and-buggy ride to the wedding, I might be someone else. The fact that I'm not inspires a debt of gratitude.

Chapter Two

~

Erin—Patrick Forde & Bridget Freeman

My Irish paternal great-great grandparents are **Patrick Forde** and **Bridget Freeman** of Derrynacong townland, Annagh Parish, County Mayo, and **Patrick Hunt** and **Bridget Fitzmaurice** of Laughil townland, Kiltullagh Parish, County Roscommon. This chapter pursues the family of Pat Forde and Bridget Freeman. The following chapter sets out the family of Pat Hunt and Bridget Fitzmaurice.

The later history of the Forde family is well documented, but the lives of Pat Forde and Bridget Freeman are poorly documented beyond land records. They married in 1852 or earlier, but no record has been located in the church registers. This may indicate they married in Annagh Parish—the register commenced in 1853—or in Aghamore Parish—this register commenced in 1864. There is no record of their marriage in the adjoining Parishes of Bekan in Mayo—the register started in 1832—or in Kiltullagh Parish in Roscommon—this register started in 1839.

There is no surprise in the fact that their baptisms were not recorded, as they were born before 1832. Since there are no baptism records we have no information about the parents or siblings of Pat Forde and Bridget Freeman.

What comes as a surprise is that no death records are extant. This is one of the two great mysteries in the Forde family. (The other, detailed in Chapter Ten, concerns the fate of Mary Ellen Forde.) If Pat and Bridget Forde died before 1864, when civil records of baptisms, marriages, and deaths commenced in Catholic Ireland, there would be no record. Unlike parishes in Lithuania, death records and burials were not recorded in

Irish parish books. If they died after 1864 a family member was obligated to report the death within six months. The mystery lies in the fact that the farm was in the hands of the Forde family continuously. If Pat and Bridget Forde died before 1864 their children would have been too young to run the farm. Viscount Dillon, the landlord, and his agents would have evicted any family who could not afford the rent. Someone kept the farm going and paid the rent until 1884 when my great-grandfather Tom Forde married and took over the property.

I believe that person was Bridget Freeman. I had originally believed that Bridget died at a young age. I now believe she survived to 1887 or later. Through the miracle of Google Books I found in May 2010 a listing for Bridget Forde of Derrynacong in a book published in 1889 entitled *Parliamentary Papers, House of Commons and Command, Volume 63* [1]. Bridget and a few other residents in Derrynacong successfully petitioned for a reduction in rent. Tom Forde was married and in residence in Derrynacong in that year, so it was unlikely Bridget was a sister. The only person who trumped a married son was the mother. This is not a perfect scenario, as there is no death record for her and Bridget was not listed in the Closed Valuation books (see below). Bridget was not included in the 1901 Census, so she appears to have died in the period 1887 – 1900.

According to the marriage record of his son, Pat Forde was deceased before May 1884. It's not possible to say when or where he died. It may be his death occurred in Derrynacong and went unrecorded, like Bridget's. He may have died in the Lancashire vicinity of England, where he went as a yearly migratory laborer. Or he may have died in transit to England or in some other part of Ireland. The place and year is not known and it is too difficult and too expensive to find out—consider that 54 individuals named "Patrick Forde" died in Ireland in the period 1864 – 1884.

And it is not possible to say which family resided in Derrynacong at the time of the marriage. Usually, the bride moved into the groom's home as part of the dowry, but sometimes the groom "married into" the bride's home. This "reverse dowry" happened three times in our family's story (Pat Hunt, Martin Griffin, and Denis Griffin). It may have happened with Pat Forde, but there are no records to indicate this.

Pat Forde and Bridget Freeman had the following known children. It is possible other children were born before Annagh Parish records commenced.

Michael Forde was baptized by Fr. T. Gibbon on 12 June 1853. Godparents were John Kelly (or Tully) and Catherine Dyer. No other information is available on the life of Michael Forde. It is not uncommon in genealogy that the only indication a person was born and breathed for whatever length of life is a single record in a Parish book.

Thomas Forde, my great-grandfather, was born on 4 July 1856 and baptized by Fr. William Scully on July 7. Tom's godparents were Henry and Anne Hamrock of Leow townland, Annagh Parish. Tom married Mary Hunt on 7 May 1884. He died, aged 82, on or about 30 May 1939. Tom's life and family are detailed in Chapter Ten.

Hubert Forde was baptized 11 June 1858. His godmother was Mary Hunt. We are not sure of the priest. No other information is available on the life of Hubert Forde. A man named Hubert Forde served as godfather to Agnes, Tom's daughter, in 1903. Now, Hubert is an unusual name in Annagh Parish. We like to think the man baptized in 1858 is the same Hubert who stood as Agnes's godfather, but we can't say for certain. No census record clearly identifies Hubert in Ireland or in England. Incredibly enough, there was a second Hubert Forde at the same time period in Eastern County Mayo. This Hubert was the son of Pat and Anne Forde of Larganboy townland in Bekan Parish.

The likeliest origin of the English surname *Forde* derives from the Irish *Mac Giollarnath*, which is a version of *Mac Giolla na Naomh*. This translates as "son of the servant of the saint." In a process I don't understand Forde derives from the "*ath*" in the name, which translates as "ford", as of a river. In Ireland the name was written variously as "Forde" and as "Ford"—there was no consistency. In America it became "Ford", as in the case of my grandfather, who left the "e" in Ellis Island.

Our Forde sept (clan) originated in antiquity in southwestern Galway on the coast of Galway Bay. A portion of this sept has been in Eastern County Mayo since before the Norman Invasion. *The Annals of the Four Masters*, an important trove of history and genealogy, records the death in battle of a *Giolla na Naomh* in nearby Clooncrim townland in County Roscommon in 1464. This *Giolla na Naomh* was allied with a Flynn from Kiltullagh Parish—they are described as brothers-in-law. Their opponent in the skirmish was Philip MacCostello, father of the man who donated the land for the Abbey in Ballyhaunis.

The Forde surname was strongly localized in Bekan Parish. There are 18 Forde males listed in Griffith's 1856 Valuation of Bekan Parish, the majority in the townlands of Larganboy and Reask. Four Fordes are listed in Annagh Parish in 1856. Of course, there were a lot more Fordes in residence in Bekan and Annagh Parishes in the nineteenth century—the name becomes less frequent in County Roscommon. My file listing Forde baptisms and marriages in the vicinity of Ballyhaunis runs to 32 pages.

In a similarly incalculable fashion the surname *Freeman* was an Anglized form of *O Saorthaigh*, which translates as "laborer". There was an alternate derivation for Freeman used by the priest in the Annagh Parish books of the 1850s and 1860s. This was the surname "*Seery*". The surname Freeman was uncommon in Annagh and Bekan Parish. It was more strongly localized in the townlands of Aghamore Parish to the north [2].

People generally married at the same economic level, small farmers marrying small farmers and laborers marrying laborers. People generally married within a limited geographical extent—in social psychology this is called "proximity". But it's important to recognize that borders exist on paper more than they do in actuality. Marriages across Parish and county borders were quite common. For a few shillings paid to the Parish priest a fellow could cross a "border", get a bride, and hurry home before the *good people* were notified.

Pat and Bridget Forde resided in Derrynacong townland—this is our Forde ancestral home. Derrynacong derives from the Irish *Doire na cong*, which translates as "thin strip of oak". Derrynacong is located a few miles to the north of the market town of Ballyhaunis. It is in Annagh Civil Parish, Claremorris Poor Law Union, County Mayo [3].

Pat Forde was the only one of our Irish ancestors listed in Griffith's 1856 Valuation. (Our other great-great-grandparents were either too young to hold property or resided with relatives.) Griffith's was a country-wide effort directed by Richard Griffith to rate properties for tax purposes. It described the size and tax rate for each farm and for each structure on the farm. It also described the landlord and occupier for each property—only the head-of-household was named. It serves as a mid-nineteenth census substitute—a fire in Dublin in 1922 destroyed census information other than statistical summaries. In most places in the West of Ireland census data listing entire families starts in 1901.

In 1856 Pat Forde held property in rundale in Derrynacong with John Fitzmaurice, Pat Fitzmaurice, and William Quin (Quinn). The total acreage was 54 acres, two roods, and 25 perches. An acre is 4,840 square yards, a rood is one-fourth of an acre (1,210 yards), and a perch is one-fortieth of an acre (30 yards). Pat Ford's tax rate on the farm was one pound and 15 shillings. The tax rate on the house was five shillings. The total tax assessment of the nineteen farms in Derrynacong at that period was 40 pounds, six shillings, and ten pence [4].

Pat Forde held additional land in Derrynacong with John Fitzmaurice, Pat Fitzmaurice, and a second Pat Fitzmaurice (specified as "widow"). This was nine acres, two roods, and four perches. Pat Forde's tax rate on this parcel was assessed at 11 shillings. Griffith's does not specify this parcel as bog, which would have been a valuable commodity—bog was cut, dried, and used in place of wood for warmth and cooking.

The landlord in Derrynacong and in much of Annagh Parish was the Viscount Dillon. The Dillons were absentee landlords who lived in England and who come down in history as benevolent types. The nineteenth century Fordes paid rent to the 15th Viscount, Dominick Geoffrey, the 16th, Arthur Edmond, and the 17th, Harold Arthur, who sold their holdings to the Irish Land Commission at the turn of the twentieth century (see Chapter Ten).

Rundale was an agricultural system practiced in the West of Ireland in the eighteenth and nineteenth centuries. It was a type of collective farming that usually involved extended families. Land was allocated on the basis of need—farmers got strips of good soil, bad soil, and bog depending on family size and resources. Periodically, the land would be reallocated as families grew or dwindled. The rundale members were responsible as a group for paying the rent to the landlord. The senior person collected the rent from all parties and paid the landlord's agent—in our case it was John Fitzmaurice, who was listed first.

Each party's holding included a cultivated infield—this was a vegetable garden and a potato patch—and a pastoral outfield. The size of the infield was strictly determined by the amount of manure available—this meant the number of cows and pigs available for this onerous duty. The rest of the townland was broken into bog and marginal land communally shared.

Rundale was a workable system of land demarcation, but it came under pressure from two sources in the first half of the nineteenth century—the exploding population and the conversion of pasture into potato gardens. Once the blight struck in 1845 the rundale system collapsed and was replaced in most townlands by individual holdings.

Very few native Irish owned their farms—the term for ownership is "in fee". The "forty shades of green" were owned by absentee upper-crust British and Irish landlords like the Dillons who leased the land to individual farmers through a complex layering of middlemen and agents. The leases could be "at will" or yearly or "for life". The latter involved identifying three individuals whose life spans defined the length of the lease. The death of the longest-lived of the three terminated the lease.

In Mayo, Roscommon, and Kerry most farms were "small" and worked by families—they were between five and twenty acres. This size amounted to sustenance farming. Pat Forde and Pat Hunt were small farmers. Larger farmers subleased small plots of land to agricultural laborers, who raised potatoes on the plots and worked on the larger farm. Martin Griffin and John Allen were agricultural laborers. This category of laborer was at the bottom of the food chain. Their existence was insecure from season-to-season. Their potatoes failed, the large farm went belly up, rival laborers volunteered to work for less—any number of events could put families on the road looking for work.

We don't know the relationships among the rundale partners. Any marriages occurred before Parish records were kept. And we don't know the relationship of John and Pat Fitzmaurice of Derrynacong to Bridget Fitzmaurice of Laughil. It is one of the joys of family history to relate that descendents of Pat Forde and William Quinn remain in contact in the twenty first century. Kathleen Fitzharris of Derrynacong was the great-granddaughter of William Quinn. Kathleen was instrumental in filling out the Forde family history—a full family history of Derrynacong was cut short by her death in 1997. We had the pleasure of corresponding with Kathleen and meeting her in 1996. I stay in touch her son Patrick, who lives on the West Coast of America. It is a delightful surprise that two great-great grandsons of rundale partners, separated by time and vast distances, remain in touch more than a century and a half after Griffith's Valuation.

At some point shortly after Griffith's Valuation was conducted the rundale partnerships in Derrynacong were broken up. Property was distributed along the British and American lines of individually held—not owned—farms. Pat Forde got #7—this is the ancestral Forde farm.

The rent on this property was four pounds, five shillings, in 1887. We can assume it was the same or similar in the 1850s. (The rent was reduced to two pounds, 13 shillings, and six pence, in November 1887). Rent was paid by raising and selling pigs and cattle and by money earned in the annual summer migration as harvestmen to the Lancashire region of England.

Property #7 is 17 acres, three roods, and 16 perches. (After 1901 the size of the farm increased slightly to 18 acres and 29 perches.) This is approximately one-third mile long and a tenth-of-a-mile wide. Land was valued at two pounds, 15 shillings. The house was valued at five shillings. Immediate neighbors were William Quinn and Michael Kedian. From notations in the Closed Valuation Books it's clear attempts were made to apportion individual holdings in accordance with the size of holdings listed in Griffith's [5].

The Forde farm can be precisely mapped from 1858 to the present day. It can be observed on Google Earth, as, indeed, all the holdings in Derrynacong can. Google shows that the land is virtually the same in 2010 as it was in 1856—a rugged mixture of woods and pasture, with more cows than people in residence.

Derrynacong was beautifully mapped in color in 1858 by Lord Dillon's agents. Property #7 consisted of nine acres, three roods, and 27 perches of arable land, one acre, three roods, and ten perches of bottom land, one acre and 16 perches of reclaimable land, and four acres and 19 perches of bog. None of the land was described as "reclaimed".

The properties in Derrynacong were precisely mapped on the Ordnance Survey Maps (#93) periodically updated through the centuries. The original survey dates to 1838—surveyors literally walked the countryside measuring distances with chains.

The townland system extends far back in history. (A map dated 1683 names a number of townlands adjacent to Derrynacong.) Market towns gradually arose to accommodate the farmers' trade and needs. The market town in Eastern County Mayo is Ballyhaunis, which held cattle fairs at the intersection of Main and Knox Sts. on June 1, July 2, September 22, and October 29. Photographs taken in the early twentieth century show that these fairs were busy and bustling events. Ballyhaunis also held the local police station and the post office. By the 1860s mercantile establishments sold boots, clothing, and alcoholic beverages, including Jameson, Guinness, and Hennessy cognac.

The most famous site in Ballyhaunis is St. Mary's Abbey, established by the Augustinian friars around 1430. Built on the grounds of a Norman manor house, the Abbey survived the Cromwellian outrages of the seventeenth century. The Abbey closed as a functioning church in June 2002 when the Augustinians ran out of friars.

The cemetery on the Abbey grounds was the only consecrated burial place in Annagh Parish for centuries. A small section contains prominent headstones. Thousands lie buried in unmarked graves on the eastern hill. Any of our Forde and Freeman ancestors who died before the 1880s would have been buried there. Perhaps that is where Pat and Bridget sleep.

In 1882 a new cemetery—called, sensibly enough, the New Cemetery—opened a few miles to the south. The story has it that the New Cemetery remained vacant for some years because no one wanted to be the first person interred.

Samuel Lewis's 1837 *Topographical Dictionary*—this is a listing of market towns and Parishes—gave the population of Annagh Parish as 6,885. The *Dictionary* described eight schools in the Parish, with 390 boys and 230 girls in attendance. In the nineteenth century there were a number of educational options. Itinerant teachers set up "hedge schools" and taught classes for a small fee. These hedge schools arose from the excessive laws directed against the Catholic peasantry in the earlier centuries. They literally were held in the hedges—in the backwoods and countryside. In the 1830s there was a well-attended—and quite publicly functioning—hedge school on Main St. in Ballyhaunis.

There were, in addition, "national schools" in which a secular education was taught in English to children of every religion. These schools were sponsored by the landlords and local gentry, with a pittance from the peasants. Teachers were paid eight pounds a year—about the same as a harvestman in Lancashire.

Finally, there were Catholic schools that combined secular subjects with religious training. Archbishops in the Tuam diocese where Annagh and Kiltullagh Parishes are located tended to be forward-looking clerics who favored the national school system. The exception was the reactionary Archbishop John MacHale (1791-1881, archbishop from 1834). Ever the conservative—MacHale opposed the Land League of the 1880s—MacHale wanted Catholic children to be taught only in Catholic schools.

Life in Derrynacong, as throughout the West of Ireland, was harsh and grim. It was a feudal existence in which the only escape was through emigration. The British authorities were cruel and unforgiving—a man could be deported to Botany Bay for stealing a sheep. Medicine did not exist—the common cold could turn deadly. Life revolved around the farm. The work was back-breaking, the conditions primitive. The Catholic Church, personified in the ferocious Archbishop MacHale, dominated daily existence with suffocating authority.

James MacParlan provided a description of life in County Mayo in 1802. He found agriculture to be in a "very backward state." Farms ran from two to twenty acres. Implements were of an "inferior kind." He judged the land—"soil" and "surface" were written as "foil and furface"—served best for pasturage. The only crops were potatoes and oats. Barley was forbidden, as it could be malted and turned into *poteen*. Dietary staples were potatoes, oaten bread, milk, cabbage, and a type of porridge. There was no green food in winter. Daily wages ran eight pence [6].

Alexis de Tocqueville toured Ireland in the 1830s. He reported that small farmers such as Pat Forde lived in single-room huts built of sun-dried mud and stones. The roofs were sown of thatch. There were no windows or chimneys. Smoke left by the open door. (Sixty years later J.M. Synge wrote that inflamed eyes were common among the peasants because of poor ventilation.) Animals lived inside the house. There were dung heaps at the door.

Asenath Nicholson was a religious lady from Chelsea, Vermont, who traveled throughout Ireland gently proselytizing on behalf of Protestantism. In *Ireland's Welcome to the Stranger* she provided a first-hand account of conditions in the West of Ireland in the immediate years before the Famine. In July 1844 she saw a sight that would become tragically common in two years—a man was starving to death in a region of plenty. Nicholson described the people as living in abject poverty and without work. Beggars were everywhere. Nicholson plainly saw one of the root causes of this extreme poverty—the peasants were "oppressed to death by the English."

Pat Forde and Bridget Freeman—as did all our Irish great-great-grandparents—lived through the most calamitous event in Irish history. This is the Great Famine that resulted from the blight that destroyed the potato harvest in the 1840s. The Famine is more correctly called "The Great Hunger"—*An Gorta Mor*—as there was no shortage of food. People starved while other cash crops were sent to overseas markets.

The numbers are startling—we are not talking of a nation in Africa or Asia, but of a country a brief boat ride across the sea from the then dominant power in the world. One million Irish people died in this period. Another million left hearth and home and emigrated. The peasants who stayed suffered the most immense hardships, living in the midst of grief and partings made in coffins and in coffin ships. The spiritual and psychological effects must have been devastating.

The Great Hunger originated in the unique world of nineteenth century Ireland and in the malignant non-response of the British government. Nineteenth century Ireland was essentially a world of sustenance farming. More than 300,000 agricultural laborers lived on farms of five acres or less. This life style was made possible by the potato, which disturbed the balance between tillage and pasture. The potato was nutritious and substituted for other sources of food. The potato could grow almost anywhere. The first half of the nineteeth century saw the large-scale conversion of pasture into smaller and smaller fields of potatoes. Hinterland that would not normally be used for crops was converted to potato cultivation. By 1845 one third of all tilled land was potato. This bloom of tubers occurred mostly in the poorest sections of the country. The fact that the potato grew so abundantly and served as the primary source of food led to increasing subdivision of the land and to an explosion in population. By 1845 Ireland was a country of nearly eight million souls. Landlords looked the other way, as they collected rent from these barely inhabitable scratches of soil.

Three million people relied on the lumper potato as the main source of food. It literally was breakfast, lunch, and dinner. It was also food for the pigs, who grew fat on pratties and were sold to pay the rent.

Seven pounds of potatoes could provide all the calories a grown man required on a daily basis. This is something like 20 potatoes. This mound of potatoes wasn't all hard-boiled. It included mashed potatoes, chips, even a kind of pattie or latke. Overall, the diet of our Irish ancestors was bland. They ate little meat or bread. Eggs were rarely consumed. Fish products were seasonal and salted for preservation. Small farmers would have had a few additional vegetables like cabbage and onions to supplement the ubiquitous lumper. Milk was heavily consumed. Nicholson reported heavy use of tobacco. Father Mathew's famous campaigns for drinkers to take "the pledge" suggested *poteen* was also heavily consumed.

Potatoes were easier to grow than grains and they were hardy. One good acre of potato harvest yielded seven tons on average. This was enough to feed six people for several months.

There are downsides to potato cultivation. Potatoes have a short shelf life compared to cereals. Planting took place in late February or early March. Harvested in autumn, potatoes lasted only till early summer. In summer cereals replaced potatoes. The large-scale and year-round conversion to cereals never happened during the Famine, since small farmers and landless laborers had no money to purchase seeds.

Planting potatoes is no easy chore. In East Mayo the process involved three people. The first person used a spade to bore a hole in the soil. The second dropped the seed potato in and added a bullet of fertilizer. The third patched up the hole. The field where this took place was called a "lazy bed". The soil was raised into straight ridges separated by trenches a few feet wide.

There's a cautionary tale they tell in logic class about the dangers of induction and prediction. This is the tale of the turkey that gets well fed every day of the year. The turkey wakes up on a certain Thursday morning in late November expecting the usual hearty meal—and spends the rest of the day headless on a platter. The lives of our ancestors weren't as comfy or as predictable as the life that turkey experienced. Pat Forde and Bridget Freeman lived hard and uncertain lives, as did the rest of them. Hunger was a fact of life—the Famine worsened an already bad situation. The prolific potato combined with the prolific subdivision of the land into smaller and smaller holdings complicated an already dicey situation—it was diciest for the people least able to ride out the bad times.

And one day in the midst of their wrenching poverty they awoke to find the potatoes had turned black.

The start of the Famine can be dated to late August 1845. In the span of a few weeks one third of the potato crop was destroyed. The culprit was a mold named *phytopthora infestans*. Borne on the poisoned winds, the mold returned for the next three years. Three quarters of the 1846 crops was destroyed, leading to "Black '47". In 1847 the blight receded and there was an average yield, although the total acreage given to potatoes had been reduced. In 1848 the blight returned and a third of the crops was ruined [7].

All our Irish great-great-grandparents lived through this grim period— if they didn't, someone else would be writing this. In age they were adolescents and young adults. Probably, that was the best age to experience the scourges of hunger and disease—like all pestilences, the Famine struck hardest at the youngest and oldest. We can't say what the effects were. Three great-great grandparents lived to respectable ages, so they survived physically. We can't say how the Famine affected them psychologically or how it turned them as personalities. We can say that none became psychologically disordered. None became criminals. Nor can we say what their economic status was before the Famine. Pat Forde emerged into the 1850s as a small farmer. The others emerged as landless laborers. Perhaps the others were small farmers before the blight changed the color of the land. We can't—and ought not—speculate that any of them escaped the virulence of that period or that they lived elsewhere than in mud huts speckled with manure.

Derrynacong lost twenty percent of its population in the period 1841-1851. So did Annagh and Bekan Parishes. The Mayo *Constitution* reported on 11 January 1848 that five people died of starvation in Bekan Parish. On 29 February 1848 the *Constitution* reported that two people died of starvation in Ballyhaunis. There persists to this day a memory that three bodies were found near the Hunt farm in Laughil. Letters from Fr. Eugene Coyne, the Annagh Parish priest, reported that the situation was grim. Fr. Coyne wrote on 9 March 1849 that the people "are now in a most wretched state without food or seed." In the same letter he mentions that a woman was found dead of starvation. Charles Strickland, Viscount Dillon's agent, reported that nearly half the tenants on Dillon's land had nothing to eat other than corn donated from overseas. A traveler wrote that conditions were as bad in Ballyhaunis as in Skibberin in County Cork, which is considered the Bowling Green of famine desperation [8].

The effects of prolonged malnutrition are vitamin deficiencies like scurvy, eye diseases, and suppressed immune systems. The latter made individuals susceptible to infectious diseases. In fact, far more people died of infectious diseases than starved to death. There were plagues of typhus, smallpox, cholera, and "relapsing fever", a generic term for any number of conditions. Scurvy (vitamin C deficiency) can lead to swollen joints and to gum disease. Psychologically, it leads to tiredness and to depression. Babies and toddlers were at especial risk, given their lack of immunity. They were also at risk for stunted intellectual development. The brain grows at a phenomenal rate in the first few years of life. Food deprivation—and intellectual food deprivation in families disrupted by sickness and death—can lead to faulty development of the brain. It is a pernicious and little known side effect of famine that the youngest children are at risk for reduced intelligence and mental retardation.

The response of our ancestors to the Famine must have been bewilderment and horror. In a season the world had come apart. Literally, the color of the landscape changed. Families were broken up. Houses were broken up by "crowbar brigades" who evicted families. People were leaving the ancestral farms. Mothers and fathers and brothers and sisters were dying of the most dread diseases. Bodies were found on the roadways. Walking skeletons were observed. People dropped to the turf and were seen to eat grass in their hunger. They had no understanding of what befell them or how to stop it. They had no knowledge of germs or how insects such as lice and fleas spread disease—microorganisms weren't observed until the 1880s. There was no work. There was nothing to eat. They did not know where their next meal was coming from [9].

And they were harassed by the British.

The British aristocrats knew nothing of welfare or of an organized response to crises, as modern nations exhibit when catastrophes occur. They also knew nothing of kindness or compassion. We must be clear that the British response to the Famine was inadequate, cruel, and malignant. The government took the harshest position. No one was to prosper from the Famine. No one was to be fed for free. No one was to get a hand out. This malicious policy derived from an unrelenting laissez-faire economic policy. The policy also derived from a pathological dislike of the Irish. The British aristocracy believed Irish landlords were incompetent. They saw Irish peasants as ignorant and indolent. They believed that the peasants would use the Famine as an excuse to get on the government dole. They also believed that the peasants were uninterested in improving their situation. They believed the peasants were happy living from year to year on land they did nothing to reclaim.

The aristocrats made what social psychologists call "the fundamental attribution error". They looked to the personalities of the peasants to explain the predicament they were in rather than to the situation the peasants faced. Sure, some peasants were indolent and manipulative. The majority of peasants were locked in an untenable situation. If they improved the land by reclamation and by better crop management, their rent was raised. If they did little or no improvements, the rent stayed the same. For paying less rent to absentee landlords they were called lazy. A lady from Vermont clearly understood this in her jaunts across Ireland. Members of the great washed classes in Parliament did not.

The initial response of the British government was to buy corn and oatmeal from overseas and sell it at cost to local "relief committees" who purchased it from funds collected locally. Distribution of "Peel's brimstone"—named after Prime Minister Robert Peel and, yes, his name was "Peel"—was insufficient to relieve hunger. Daily distribution was limited to one pound per family per day.

I obtained from the National Archives in Ireland a copy of a flyer published on 1 June 1846 by the Castlerea Relief Committee—this is the Poor Law Union in which Laughil lies. The flyer was intended for landlords and for gentry with means. The flyer suggested that circulars be distributed "stating the alarming destitution already existing" and asking for "aid for the relief of the poor." The flyer noted that "at least one third and in some cases one half of their principal article of consumption had been lost by disease." The Castlerea Committee practiced its own form of laissez-faire as the flyer stated they wanted to "avoid giving gratuitous relief, by giving employment to the able-bodied and by keeping food at such a price as to be within reach of the poor."

In June 1846 the British made the harsh and horrendous decision that the care of the indigent poor was to be borne completely by the Irish gentry. The burden fell on the recently established "workhouse" system—this term is an euphemism for "poorhouse". Workhouses served as dormitories for the indigent, as day care for the children, as food kitchens for the starving, and as hospitals for the sick. The workhouses soon became houses of death—in some the death rate for admissions was 25%. There were so many deaths, re-useable coffins with bottoms that dropped open become the custom.

Initially, "relief"—an euphemism for "food"—was to be given only to the "impotent poor". Able-bodied poor people received relief only if they paid for it or if they were destitute. To help the Irish along the route to destitution the Gregory Clause of 1847 was adopted. Tenants qualified for relief only if they held a quarter acre or less of land. The Gregory Clause led to a horrible choice. Farmers could give up their land and receive relief or they could eke it out under uncertain conditions. Many chose the later, as the clause was amended in May 1848 to provide relief to the wives and children of "obstinate" farmers. In his 1849 letter Fr. Coyne referred to farmers "not giving up their land lest (as they say) they would never have their own fireside again."

A system of "outdoor relief" similar to the 1930s WPA in America was started in 1847 so people could pay for their food. People were paid nine pence a day to work on road projects and public works. On 7 November 1847 there were 1,097 males, 66 women, and 47 children on "outdoor relief" in the Barony of Costello where Mayo and Roscommon are located. In February 1848 there were one half million people building bridges, cutting roads, or chipping rocks. It is certain that some or all of our ancestors were on "outdoor relief".

Temporary soup kitchens were established in the first half of 1847 to assist the collapsing workhouse system. The kitchens served "Soyer's Soup", named after a contemporary chef. The soup consisted of barley and onions cooked in beef stock and served with bread. It's estimated the soup provided half of adult daily requirements. Before the soup kitchens terminated in the summer of 1847 as many as three million people were sipping this inadequate broth.

The loss of the potato harvest had a cascade effect through the rural world. Large farmers could not employ agricultural laborers in the same numbers. Small farmers had only vegetable gardens by which to survive. People ran out of money. Credit was not extended. Debts were called in. There was no work. There were no potatoes to buy. Prices rose sharply. And other crops and cattle were being shipped overseas, quite as if nothing was amiss.

The class of agricultural laborers was especially hard hit by the Famine. The number of landless laborers shrunk from 50% of the Mayo and Roscommon population in 1841 to 10% in 1851. The percentage fell in Kerry in that decade from 50% to 20%. This loss of population has to be placed in the context of what this shrinkage implies. One million people went to their particular judgments in the afterlife. Another million got out and sailed to New York City.

The decline in laborers occurred through death and emigration and by the consolidation of farms—this consolidation was helped immensely by the Gregory Clause. There was a slow return of the land from potato tillage to pasture and to the raising of cattle. The excessive subdivision of farms among siblings ended. The first child who married "got the farm". Everyone else emigrated.

People farming virtually by hand. People escaping on wooden vessels propelled by sails. People watching helplessly as their fields turned black. People dying of plagues of infectious diseases. People so hungry they ate grass. Huts of dried mud. Pigs living in kitchens. Dung heaps smoking in doorways. This sounds like another world—it sounds like something completely out of our experience. Yet I am only one person removed from *An Gorta Mor*. I knew my grandparents and my grandparents knew people who experienced the Famine. They would have heard stories about the terrible events that happened. They would have seen the effects of the Famine in the faces and habits of the old people who survived. Something that sounds incomparably distant was only a conversation away.

Chapter Three

~

Erin—Patrick Hunt & Bridget Fitzmaurice

In the previous chapter we reviewed the lives of our Mayo great-great-grandparents. In this chapter we cross the border—no great journey—into County Roscommon and gather what is known of **Patrick Hunt** and **Bridget Fitzmaurice**, our other Irish paternal great-great-grandparents.

Pat Hunt married Bridget Fitzmaurice—the name is sometimes written as it is pronounced, Fitzmorris—on 1 February 1853 in Kiltullagh Parish in County Roscommon. The witnesses were Peter Fitzmaurice and Bridget Loftus. The priest was either Fr. William Feeney or Fr. Pat McLoughlin. They resided after the marriage in the townland of Laughil, which is located in the hills that border County Mayo.

Pat Hunt was from Annagh Parish in County Mayo, so he "married into" the Fitzmaurice holding. He paid three shillings to the Annagh priest to be "released" to marry in a different Parish. They paid one pound four shillings for the wedding [10].

Pat Hunt was likely the son of **Hugh Hunt** and **Mary Kelly**. For the briefest period in the 1820s the Tuam archdiocese collected marriage records from all parishes, providing a few tantalizing entries for lucky family historians. The register recorded the marriage of Hugh Hunt and Mary Kelly of Annagh Parish on 27 February 1823. Witnesses were Michael and Hugh Kelly. The priest was Fr. Michael McManus. Pat Hunt and Bridget Fitzmaurice named their first son Hugh, an uncommon name in that place and period. If they held to the tradition of naming the first son after the paternal grandparent Pat Hunt's father was named Hugh—of course, there could have been another Hugh Hunt of Annagh Parish lost to history [11].

Pat Hunt's death was reported to the civil authorities as occurring on 27 April 1884. This was two weeks before the marriage of his daughter Mary to Tom Forde—it must have been an unhappy time. Pat's age was given as 53, which makes 1831 the year of his birth. The cause of death was "dropsy", which can be understood as edema, indicating possible heart problems. He was under a physician's care for two months. The informant was Catherine Fitzmaurice, who was likely Bridget's sister. The place of burial was likely in the Parish cemetery at Garranlahan.

Like Pat Hunt's, Bridget Fitzmaurice's baptism occurred before Parish records were kept. Her age was given as 75 on the 1901 Census of Ireland and as 86 on the 1911 Census. This indicates that she was born around 1825 – 1830. The advanced years noted on the census are possible. The Fitzmaurices of East Mayo were a long-lived family, regularly surviving into their eighties.

Bridget's death was reported as occurring on 7 September 1917. Her age was given as 71—probably 91 was meant. The cause of death was "senile decay", an euphemism in civil records for the vicissitudes of old age. The informant was her son Patrick. At the time of death Bridget resided with Pat and his family in the townland of Milltown in County Roscommon. Bridget was buried with the Hunt family in Ballintober, a headstone's throw from the great ruins of a castle belonging to the O'Connor Dons, historical overlords in that region of Roscommon. The age on the grave was 95, the date of death was 2 March 1914. These records are not correct—perhaps the monument was added later. There are no civil records that match the 1914 date.

Mrs. Josephine Keigher, Bridget's last surviving granddaughter, remembered that Bridget walked with a cane and that she smoked a pipe. (We had the pleasure of meeting Mrs. Keigher in 1998.) The 1901 Census indicated that Bridget spoke English and Irish and that she could not read.

We don't know who Bridget's parents were. Parish records allow us to identify a number of likely siblings. There is a marriage record dated 15 March 1840 for **Catherine Fitzmaurice** of Laughil and Hugh Murphy of Rabbitborough townland. Their witnesses were Thomas Waldron and Honor Murphy. **Margaret Fitzmaurice** of Laughil married Michael Hart in February 1841. Their witnesses were Thomas Hart and Mary Henaghen. A note in the Parish register indicated Michael was from Bekan Parish in Mayo. And Pat and Bridget Hunt lived on the same farm with **Patrick**

Fitzmaurice, who married Bridget Kyne (Coyne) on 28 January 1860. Their witnesses were Martin Flatley and Ellen Burke [12].

Weddings in that period were simple occurrences completely unlike modern extravagances. They were held in the bride's home. There was no Mass. The concept of a honeymoon was completely unknown. The ceremony was followed by a celebration similar to our modern reception. There were a number of customs in Irish weddings, some of which are on the ridiculous side. In one custom young men called "straw boys" disrupted the reception and demanded to dance with the bride. They wore masks and pointed caps of straw. In another custom the bride's mother-in-law broke a piece of cracker over the bride's head as she entered the house for the first time as a married woman. This was supposed to keep the peace—I'm not sure it did.

Later in the century when marriages were held in churches, there were processions back and forth. In Annagh and Kiltullagh Parishes torches were lit alongside the roads. There was a custom called the "bride's bottle". A whiskey bottle was given to the guest who arrived at the reception first. This custom looks as if it could have been dangerous.

Marriages were generally held in winter. They were forbidden to occur during Lent. Marriage generally involved people of equal social and economic levels. This was because marriage had an economic side involving dowries and the dispersal of land and unmarried siblings. As they are today, marriages were ordinarily "arranged" through the informal network of friends, relatives, and neighbors. Professional matchmakers existed, as in the novels of John B. Keane, but they generally acted like marriage agencies, matching people who, challenged in whatever ways, couldn't easily find mates.

The surname *Hunt* derives rather directly from the Irish *O Fiachna* meaning "hunt". In this region of Ireland the surname was strongly localized in Annagh Parish, especially in the vicinity of Derrynacong. The surname Fitzmaurice is Norman. It, too, is strongly localized in East Mayo. The Fitzmaurices in the vicinity of Ballyhaunis are believed to be descendents of a Norman warlord named Maurice de Prendergast (1125 - 1205), who hailed from the Pembrokeshire region of Wales and who came over with Strongbow in the invasion of the twelfth century. Specifically, our Fitzmaurices are descendents of his son Gerald McMaurice, who founded the line in East Mayo. In Irish the "Mc" or "Mac", meaning "son of", becomes "Fitz" [13].

Pat and Bridget Hunt had the following known children: Mary; Hugh, Patrick; Michael; and Thomas.

Mary Hunt, my great-grandmother, was baptized in Kiltullagh Parish on 20 August 1854. Her godparents were Pat Flynn and Bridget Hunt. The priest either Fr. William Feeney or Fr. Pat McLaughlin. Mary Hunt married Tom Forde of Derrynacong on 7 May 1884. Mary's death from tuberculosis was reported to civil authorities as occurring on 12 April 1897. Mary's life and family will be covered in Chapter Ten.

Hugh Hunt was baptized on 6 January 1858. The godparents were James Cox and Anne Dodd. The priest was not specified. Hugh was alive in 1888, when he served as a godfather to his sister's baby, but we have no information on his later life.

Patrick Hunt was baptized on 20 November 1859. His godparents were Patrick Fitzmaurice and Catherine Fitzmaurice. The priest was not specified. Patrick died 3 March 1923—this is the date on the stone in Ballintober cemetery.

Patrick married Celia Hussey of Clydagh townland, County Roscommon, on 8 February 1892. Witnesses were Nicholas Hussey and Ellen Hussey. The priest was not specified. Celia Hussey died 10 March 1928. Her age was given as 68. She was buried in the Hunt plot in Ballintober. (Her name appeared as Bridget on the 1901 Irish Census.) We don't know the names of her parents.

Patrick Hunt and Celia Hussey had the following known children: Bridget; Patrick; Mary; John; Andrew Hubert; Catherine; and Margaret. We know very little about their lives.

Bridget Hunt was baptized on 30 November 1892. Godparents were Thomas and Ellen Hussey. Bridget married Pat McLoughlin of Galway.

Patrick Hunt was baptized on 30 December 1893. Godparents were Andrew Corr and Mary Fitzmaurice. Patrick died at an advanced age on 12 December 1982. He was buried in Ballintober Cemetery. We had the pleasure of meeting his late son Terry in Ballyhaunis in 1996.

Mary Hunt was baptized on 21 September 1895. Her godparents were Michael Hussey and Catherine Winston. Mary immigrated to the United States at some point.

The 1901 Census listed **John Hunt** as her twin. The 1911 Census gave separate ages for them—15 for Mary, 10 for John—so their birth dates are not clear.

Andrew Hubert Hunt was on baptized on 4 September 1897. Godparents were Austin Winston and Bridget Casserly. Andrew immigrated to Australia, where he made a considerable amount of money. He may have returned to Ireland at some point later in his life.

Catherine Hunt was baptized 28 January 1899. Godparents were James Kilraine and Catherine Kilraine. Catherine married an Englishman—we shouldn't hold that against her.

Margaret Hunt was born c. 1903—she was listed in the 1911 Census as eight. No other information is available.

Michael Hunt, the third son of Pat Hunt and Bridget Fitzmaurice, was baptized 4 October 1862. The sponsor was Catherine Discon. The priest was not specified. Michael died in Milltown, aged 84, on 30 August 1947. The cause of death was given as cardiac failure. He was under doctor's care for eight months. We saw a photograph of Michael Hunt when we visited Ireland in 1996. Taken in his old age, he looked to be somewhat stocky. He was said to be tall in his younger years. He had white hair in the photograph and a full mustache that curved around his lips. He smoked a pipe and loved horses, according to his daughter, Josephine Keigher.

Michael Hunt married Bridget Ganley on 2 February 1890. The witnesses were Thomas Fitzmaurice and Kate Ganley. The priest was Fr. John McDermott. The place of the wedding was the Erritt Chapel in Loughglynn Parish, County Roscommon. Bridget's age was given as 19. Bridget was the daughter of Dominick Ganley and Catherine McNulty. At the time of the wedding she resided in Tully townland, Tibohine Parish, County Roscommon. According to Mrs. Keigher, Bridget died in 1919, but no civil record has been located.

Michael "married into" the Ganley household in Tully townland. At some point they moved to Milltown in Baslick Civil Parish in the Castlerea Union of County Roscommon.

Michael and Bridget had the following known children: Patrick Joseph; Mary; Dominick; Catherine; Rose Anne and Bridget Agnes, twins; Michael; Margaret; and Josephine.

Patrick Joseph Hunt was baptized on 31 December 1890. Godparents were Patrick Hunt and Catherine Waldron. The priest was not specified. Patrick was killed in action in or near the town of Proven, Belgium, in

World War One on 26 July 1917. He was the only person in our family group known to have died in the War to End Wars. Patrick was buried in Bleuet Farm Cemetery, Elverdinghe, in Belgium (plot 1-B-13).

Patrick enlisted in the Irish Guards on 7 August 1915. At the time he resided at Benington Bush Hotel in Liverpool. (There is a note—"Liverpool Coopers"—on the enlistment papers we obtained from the Irish Guards.) Patrick was described as 5'11 in height with a chest measurement of 39.5 inches and no distinctive marks. (On the family photograph we saw in Ireland he has dark hair and distinctively large ears—those ears look to run on the paternal side.) He was described as "fit for service" and in "need of dental work". He served as a private in the First Battalion (Reg. # 9486). After enduring a year of the unimaginable horrors of trench warfare Patrick died in an artillery attack with nine other soldiers. Two additional men later died of their wounds.

There were a number of Hunt family rumors about Pat's service. There must have been mixed feelings about his service in the English army on behalf of English imperialism—the World War was followed by the partition of Ireland and by the violence of the Black-and-Tans and of the Civil War. Mrs. Keigher remembered that her mother advised him to cut a finger off so he wouldn't have to serve. The family believed that he died on the last day of the war and that he volunteered for service while in America. Our research into the Fordes proved helpful to Mrs. Keigher, who wanted to learn the truth of Pat's service. Despite her great age, she traveled to Belgium in September 1998 to visit Patrick's grave and honor her brother across the distance of 80 years.

Mary Hunt was baptized on 31 July 1892. Godparents were Edward Quinn and Mary Flanagan. Mary immigrated to the United States.

Dominick Hunt was baptized 20 January 1894. Godparents were Patrick Waldron and Bridget Waldron. Dominick died 10 August 1979. Dominick married Bridget Dyer, who died 16 November 1987. They lived in Milltown and were buried in the Ballintober Cemetery. Dominick and Bridget were the parents of the late Pat Hunt of Carrick, County Roscommon. We met Pat and his wife Kathleen in 1996 and again in 1998. Both were quite hospitable and helpful in providing us with family details. We also met three of their children who were generous in recollecting stories of their Forde aunts.

Catherine Hunt was baptized 5 December 1896. Godparents were John McNulty and Catherine Ganley. Catherine did not marry. No other information is available.

Rose Anne Hunt and **Bridget Agnes Hunt**, twins, were born in 1900. Godparents are not known. Rose immigrated to the United States and married a man named George Brown. Bridget married a man named John Tom Fitzmaurice of Brackloon townland in Mayo. Bridget died in Ireland at an advanced age.

Michael Hunt was born circa 1905. He married a lady from County Wicklow. No other information is available.

Margaret Hunt was born circa 1907. She immigrated to America and married a man with the family name Devily. My father and I had the pleasure of meeting one of her children who resides on the New Jersey Shore.

Josephine Hunt was born 1912. Baptism information is not available. Josephine died 3 August 2000. She married Austin Keigher and resided in Ballyglass, Tulsk, County Roscommon. We had the pleasure of meeting Mrs. Keigher in Pat Hunt's home in Carrick in 1998. And we had the pleasure of meeting her three children, all of whom have been generous in relating their family history.

Thomas Hunt was the last child born to Pat Hunt and Bridget Fitzmaurice. He was baptized on 16 January 1870. Godparents were Timothy Flynn and Catherine Flynn. The civil record lists 6 January 1870 as his birthday—he's a rare Irish baby born before his baptism. Thomas was a change of life baby. His birth sets an upper limit of his mother's age. My grandmother had a change of life baby at age 44, so we can use that as an arbitrary upper limit to having children. This indicates that the earliest Bridget Fitzmaurice would have been born was 1826, a date that jives with the census records. There is no other information available on Thomas Hunt's life.

Pat and Bridget Hunt resided in Laughil townland after their marriage. They are not listed in Griffith's Valuation, which would indicate they lived with relatives. These relatives are not known, but the likeliest guesses are Pat Hart or Michael Hart. There is no record of Patrick Hart in the Kiltullagh Parish books, which commenced in 1839. There is a February 1841 marriage record between Michael Hart and Margaret Fitzmaurice. It may be that Michael married into the Fitzmaurice farm. He and Margaret disappear from the Closed Valuation books shortly after 1856.

Pat Hunt and his brother-in-law Pat Fitzmaurice replaced Pat Hart shortly after 1856. They resided on property 1-D—this was afterward numbered as #4. The Hunt portion was six acres, one rood, and eight perches. The land was valued at two pounds, the house at five shillings. The Fitzmaurice portion was three acres, five perches. Their land was valued at one pound, the house at five shillings.

Pat Hunt held his property in rundale with a small number of families. In 1901 the partners were Bridget Hunt, Patrick Fitzmaurice, William Forde, Michael Flynn, Timothy Flynn, Jr., and Stephen Grennan. The landlord was Roderick O'Connor, who was related to the O'Connor Dons of Castlerea and who was a professional artist. Rundale persisted in Laughil long after it ceased in other places. This may be attributable to the obscurity of the place or to the small size. Total acreage was only 81 acres.

In 1901 Bridget Hunt resided in Laughil with her son Patrick, his wife Celia, and their family. Their two-room house was built of stone or wood with a thatch roof. The 1901 Census listed three windows in the house—for some reason the Irish Census listed the number of windows in a dwelling. They had a cow house, piggery, and barn. Pat Fitzmaurice resided on property #5. His house was also of wood or stone with a thatch roof and two windows. Pat also has a barn. He was literate and described as a widower. He was the only person listed on the form. The members of his family have emigrated or died. His age was given as 70.

Sometime after 1901 the Hunts left Laughil and settled in Milltown. This move may have been a private family rearrangement or it may have been sponsored by the Congested Districts Board. This was a national effort to better utilize the land by sorting farms into productive size and by educating farmers.

Bridget Hunt's status improved at the end of her life. Her son Pat held the land in Milltown "in fee". It was a farm of 20 acres. The land must have been very good, as it was rated at thirteen pounds.

Laughil is the English version of the Irish *Leath Choill*, which means the "half wood". (The Parish priest often spelled it *Leachoil* in the registers.) We had the pleasure of visiting there in 1996. It is a lonely and beautiful place situated on a hill with a grand view of the surrounding valley. It's difficult to judge how far one can see or to discern distance, since there aren't a lot of trees, but somewhere in the valley is the church at Garranlahan. There's been a church in that location since 1441. The Franciscan order ministered there till 1814 when a new church called St. Patrick's—what else?—was built. The original church is believed to have stood on the grounds of the present-day cemetery. We visited the cemetery in 1996. It is an eerie place with broken tombstones and grave markers off kilter. A person almost has the urge to shove a stone over and have a look at the bones, but that would be disrespectful. It's likely Pat Hunt was buried here, maybe his daughter, Mary. And it would be disrespectful to the bones of strangers, too.

There are descendents of the original rundale partners in Laughil. In 1996 we visited the Fordes who reside there. They were a young couple with a baby. We were told that the Fordes of Derrynacong and Laughil were the same family, but we have not been able to document this in the Parish records. The connection must pre-date Famine times. Unfortunately, the couple in Laughil had no knowledge of nineteenth century genealogy. They extended the ancient virtue of hospitality. The evening we visited was cold—it was May, but it could have been November. We were in the hills in the Old Country and my hypothalamus was in working order. When they saw that I was shivering they offered me a hot toddy. This is tea brewed with whiskey mixed in the water. They must have gone light with the water. When I took a sip I instantly started sweating.

The chief town in the vicinity is Ballinlough, which lies near Carrick on Route 60. The yearly cattle fair was on 29 September. Issac Weld toured the West of Ireland and published *Statistical Survey of the County of Roscommon* in 1832. Weld reported that there were 44 cabins in Ballinlough, "none very good, none very bad." He also reported there were two schools "fully attended". Samuel Lewis's 1837 *Topographical Dictionary* gave the population of Kiltullagh Parish as 7,106 residents. Just to the north of Route 60 is Lough O'Flynn, which is named for one of the chief families in Kiltullagh. There is a small artificial island on the lake. If Medieval in origin this "crannog" would have served a defensive function. It is possible the island was built in Famine times as one of the public works projects.

Fr. O'Donovan wrote in his nineteenth century work *Letters Containing Information Relevant to the County of Roscommon* that there was a magical stone in a Kiltullagh graveyard that could never be moved. If the stone was in Garranlahan I would have wasted my time shifting gravestones. Fr. O'Donovan also wrote that a banshee is heard howling on the Lough whenever a Flynn dies. This must be a noisy place as there are a lot of Flynns nearby.

Chapter Four

~

Erin—Martin Griffin & Catherine Connell

My Irish maternal great-great-grandparents are **Martin Griffin** and
Catherine Connell of Ballyegan townland in Galey Parish, County Kerry,
and **John Allen** and **Johanna Linnane** of Trippul West townland in
Kilconly Parish, County Kerry. Both townlands are in the Listowel Union
of North Kerry. We examine the lives of Martin Griffin and Catherine
Connell in this chapter. The lives of John Allen and Johanna Linnane are
examined in the following chapter.

We did not have access to Parish records on the maternal side. Instead
we relied on civil records microfilmed by the Mormon Church and on
information provided by the Killarney Heritage Centre, which researched
Parish records on a pay-as-you-go basis. Ballybunion Parish records are
currently accessible on-line—they're free and beautifully indexed—but
this service was not available when we were active in the 1990s.

The Killarney Heritage Centre was unable to locate the marriage
record of Martin Griffin and Catherine Connell, but we found what we
believe is the Ballybunion Parish record of their marriage when we visited
the National Library in Dublin. The record, which is in Latin and barely
legible, lists a marriage between Martin Griffin and Catherine Connell.
"Of Gale" is specified next to Martin's name. (This is Galey Parish.)
Witnesses are — Sweeny—the personal name is not identifiable—and
Denis Connell. No priest was listed. The date looked to be 1 September
1852. The on-line record gives the name as "Maurice Griffin", but I wrote
"Martinis" when I copied the record in Dublin.

If accurate, the date 1852 is interesting. It is much earlier than we suspected and separated by seven years from the baptism record of their first known child in 1859. This is an excessively long period for peasants to go without making babies—it is the appointed function of peasants to make as many babies as possible. There are conjectures that can fill in the gap. There may have been a few miscarriages in those years. There may have been one or two children who died young—there would be no record of their deaths. A child may have survived whose name has not surfaced in any document. It is possible that the child may have been named "Edward". This is the personal name of Catherine Connell's likely father. As Martin "married into" her family it would have been appropriate for the firstborn son to carry the maternal grandfather's name. And a death notice was reported to civil authorities by Edward Griffin in 1868. Unfortunately, there is no Census information that identifies this person, so we can't be certain.

No baptism records have been located for Martin Griffin, but he would have been born before Parish registers commenced in Ballybunion Parish in 1832. Martin would have had siblings—being a peasant, probably a number of siblings—but none can be identified.

Martin Griffin's death record is extant. His death was reported to authorities as occurring on 22 January 1909. The place of death was Ballyegan. The cause given was "old age". Martin's age was given as 80, which is quite possible. The informant was his son-in-law John Lynch. Martin was buried in Galey Cemetery, which lies on the Listowel-Ballybunion Road. There is no stone.

According to the 1901 Census Martin resided with his daughter Kate and John Lynch in the townland of Inch East, which is adjacent to Ballyegan. His age was given as 63, which is not accurate, given the date of his baptism. He spoke Irish and English and could not read.

The Lynch holding was subleased from Michael Hanrahan of Listowel. The walls of the house were wood or mud. The roof was thatch. The house had two rooms and two windows in front.

The baptism record of Catherine Connell has not been located. It is likely that Catherine was the daughter of **Edmond Connell** and **Bridget Costello**. The Killarney Heritage Center was able to locate a number of records pertaining to this family. Unfortunately, Catherine's baptism was not among them [14].

Catherine's death record is extant. The date of death was given as 28 February 1876 in Ballyegan. The cause of death was typhoid fever. She received medical attention for one week. Her age was listed as 44. The informant was Martin Griffin. Like Martin, Catherine would have been buried in Galey Cemetery.

Typhoid fever hints at the pre-industrialized and pre-sanitized conditions our great-great-grandparents faced. Typhoid fever is pretty much unknown in the civilized world, but as many as 200,000 people die of it annually in the Third World. Typhoid fever is caused by the bacterium *Salmonella typho*. Infections occur when fecal matter gets into water used for drinking, washing, or bathing. Food products can be affected if handled by an infected person and contagion can occur directly between people. Symptoms include fever, pain, and loss of appetite. A rose-colored rash can break out. Mortality runs as high as 30% without antibiotics.

The surname *Griffin* derives from the Irish *O Griobhta*, meaning "Griffin-like". (No one in our family was known to have the head of an eagle or the body of a lion.) The name was strongly localized in Kilconly Parish in North Kerry. The personal name "Martin" must have had some relevance to families in this region. There were six individuals with this name in Kilconly Parish in the 1840s and '50s. Like the Fitzmaurices, the Griffins were a long-lived line, many living into their eighties and even older. My father and grandmother had a distinctive trait that may run in this line—we saw this same characteristic in Michael Lynch, who was descended from Martin and Catherine Griffin and who we met on our visit in 1996. This is a feature of light blue eyes set in pronounced lids under a prominent brow.

The surname Connell derives from *O Conaill*, meaning "friendship". The name occurs throughout Kerry and Munster province. Our Connell sept was localized around Ballydonohue townland.

My grandmother and her sisters had red hair, so there may be a Viking heritage in this side of the family. It is supposed that red hair in the Irish indicates a Viking ancestry. I don't know this for a fact, but I like to think it's true.

The Killarney Heritage Centre provided records on the known children of Martin Griffin and Catherine Connell: Denis; Honora; Bridget; Catherine; and Martin.

My great-grandfather **Denis Griffin** was baptized 5 October 1859. His godparents were Robert Connell and Bridget Griffin. Fr. J. Walsh presided. Denis married Ellen Allen of Trippul West townland on 26 April

1885 in the chapel in Ballydonohue. No civil record of his death has been located, but it occurred before 1908, when his family began immigrating to America. Denis's life and family will be described in Chapter 11.

Honora (Nora) Griffin was baptized 6 September 1862. Her godparents were John Griffin and Anne Griffin. The priest was Fr. J. O'Keeffe. According to the civil record, Nora died in Inch West townland, aged 86, on 24 June 1949. She was buried in Galey Cemetery. The informant was her daughter Hanna Enright.

Nora Griffin married John King of Affouley (Affoulia) townland in Galey Parish on 21 August 1887. (Affouley is adjacent to Ballyegan.) Witnesses were Ned Purtill and Kate Griffin. Fr. Mortimer O'Connor officiated. The civil record indicates Nora could not write—she signed her name with an "X". The rest of the wedding party were literate.

John King was the son of Pat King. Neither a baptism record nor his mother's name has been identified with certainty. John died in Inch townland on 8 August 1924. His age was given as 65. The cause of death was "chronic bronchitis". The informant was his daughter Nell [15].

In 1901 Nora and John King resided in the townland of Affouley. The 1911 Census finds them in Inch West. We have a smattering of knowledge on their children, the ages of which are confused. Michael and Joan Lynch of Affouley were helpful in sorting out the families of Nora and John King and Nora's sister Catherine. The known children of Nora and John were: Martin; John; Patrick; Catherine; Nora; Mary; Margaret; Bridget; Ellen; Julia; and Hanna.

Martin King appears to be the oldest. His age was given as 18 on the 1901 Census and as 25 on the 1911 Census. If correct, these ages indicate he was born a number of years before Nora and John married. (The marriage record does not describe John King as a widower.) We were told by the Lynches that Martin never married.

John King was described as 12 on the 1901 Census and as 20 on the 1911 Census. Like Martin, John did not marry. The Killarney Centre did not locate baptism records on either Martin or John.

Patrick King was baptized 11 February 1888, which made him the eldest child in the context of john and Nora's marriage. The godmother was Catherine Griffin—this was his aunt, not my grandmother. The priest was Fr. C. Godley. Like his brothers, Patrick never married. Strangely, he was not listed on ether the 1901 or the 1911 Census. We have no additional information on the lives of Martin, John, or Patrick.

Catherine King was baptized 3 April 1892. Her godmother was Catherine Houlihan. The priest was Fr. H. O'Sullivan. We have no information on her life.

Nora King was described as age six on the 1901 Census. The Killarney Centre did not provide a baptism record. Nora died 21 November 1985. Her age was given as 91. Nora married Patrick Walsh on 26 July 1936. Their witnesses were Mossie Neville and Kathleen Neville. Fr. C. Leary presided. Patrick Walsh was described in the marriage record as the son of Michael Walsh of Coolard townland. Patrick died 10 April 1986. His age was given as 83. The stone in Galey Cemetery listed their address as 42 O'Connell St. in Listowel. We have no information about their family, but it is unlikely they had children, given Nora's age at the time of the marriage.

Mary King was baptized 8 August 1896. Her godmother was Margaret King. The priest was Fr. P. Browne. We were told Mary never married.

Margaret King was described as a daughter of Nora and John King, but we have no baptism record and no Census records on either the 1901 or 1911 form. We were told by the Lynches that Margaret married a man named Neville and that their son died in June 1999, aged eighty five [16].

Bridget King was baptized 10 December 1898. The godmother was Helen King. The priest was Fr. G. Behan. Bridget died, aged 86, in 1985. Bridget was buried in Lisselton Cemetery. Bridget married Michael Lynch in the fall of 1920. Michael was the son of Jeremiah Lynch and Elizabeth Kennelly. (Bridget's aunt Catherine married a son of Jeremiah and Elizabeth, so there are two connections between these families.) Bridget and Michael had a large family. We had the honor of meeting their son Michael, his wife Joan, and Mrs. O'Shea, Joan's mother. We spent two very nice afternoons in their home in Affouley [17].

Ellen (Nell) King was listed as nine years on the 1911 Census. No baptism record is available. Nell married John King on 4 January 1927 in the Chapel at Ballydonohue. Their witnesses were James Buckley and Hanna King. Fr. Michael Fuller officiated. John King was described as the son of James King of Ballydonohue. No information is available on their lives.

Hanna King was born circa 1904. We do not have her baptism record. Hanna was listed as seven on the 1911 Census. She died 16 December 1970. She married Patrick Enright on 11 November 1939 in the Chapel at Ballybunion. They had at least one son. We have no other information on her life. Patrick Enright was the son of Thomas Enright of Ballydonohue.

This Enright family had some connection with Maurice Walsh, author of *The Quiet Man*. Patrick died 19 July 1959. His age was given as 57.

Julia King was born in 1906. We do not have the baptism record. Julia married Denis Reidy in the Chapel in Ballybunion on 12 February 1929. Their witnesses were Maurice O'Connor and Hanna King. Fr. Fuller officiated. Julie died 7 February 1978. She and Denis were buried in Galey Cemetery. On the stone is a notation for their daughter Joan, aged five, on 25 October 1931—the year does not appear to be correct. Perhaps it was five months rather than years.

Denis Reidy was the son of Denis Reidy and Anne Allen of Ballyegan. He was listed as a policeman on the marriage record. Denis was baptized 16 July 1893. He died 27 April 1972.

Bridget Griffin, the daughter of Martin Griffin and Catherine Connell, was baptized 2 September 1865. Her godparents were Dermot Murphy and Mary Quinlan. Fr. O'Connor presided. Bridget died in childhood, the date given as 26 January 1868. The cause of death was not specified. The informant was Edward Griffin.

Catherine Griffin was baptized 11 December 1867. Godparents were John Callaghan and Margaret Callaghan. The priest was Fr. O'Connor. The civil record gives the date of Catherine's death as 30 March 1942. Her age was 74. She died in the hospital in Listowel. Her residence was given as Ballyegan. She was buried in Lisselton Cemetery. There is no stone—it is the plot immediately behind the marked grave of Michael and her niece Bridget Lynch.

Catherine married John Lynch of Affouley on 18 February 1896. Witnesses were Edmond Purtill and Bridget Murphy. The priest was Fr. C. Counihan. After their marriage they resided in Affouley.

John Lynch was the son of Jeremiah Lynch and Elizabeth Kennelly. John was baptized on 24 April 1868. His godparents were Michael Farrell and Bridget Lynch. He died of cancer in Killarney on 20 January 1950. He was buried with Catherine in Lisselton Cemetery.

The known children of John and Catherine Lynch were: Jeremiah; John; Edward; Michael; and, possibly, Denis.

Jeremiah Lynch was baptized 12 September 1896. His godmother was Mary Lynch. The priest was Fr. Counihan. We were told that Jeremiah immigrated to England, but we have no information on his life.

John Lynch was baptized 21 May 1899. Godparents were John Purtill and Bridget Purtill. He died in New York City on 26 December 1981, aged 82. (His death certificate has 19 May 1899 as his birthday.) He was buried in the Nolan plot in Calvary Cemetery, Queens, New York (sect. 50, plot 35, #17).

At some point before 1924 John immigrated to America and married Mary Nolan. They lived in Astoria in New York City. They had children, one of whom became a priest—we have not been able to identify his name. John worked in the newspaper business in New York City. Mary Nolan was the daughter of Daniel Nolan. Her mother's name is not known. Mary died in May 1987. Her age was given as 77.

Edward Lynch was born and baptized on 12 December 1907. His godmother was Julia Purtill. The priest was Fr. J. Burke. He immigrated to England at some point, but he resided in Ballyegan in the 1930s.

Michael Lynch was born on 1 October 1909 in Ballyegan, according to the civil record. No baptism record has been located. He also immigrated to England. No other information is available on the lives of Edward and Michael.

We were told by Michael Lynch of Affouley that **Denis Lynch** was another son of John and Catherine Lynch, but we have not been able to find baptism or civil records. We were told that he married a lady named Kathleen Kelly, ran a machine shop on the Ballybunion Road in Inch, and died young.

Michael Lynch remembered that Catherine and her sister Nora were musically inclined—he would have known them as a teen. Across the distance of sixty years Mrs. O'Shea remembered Catherine and Nora as "very nice ladies".

Martin Griffin was the last known child of Martin Griffin and Catherine Connell. He was born on 10 February 1870 and baptized on February 12. The godmother was Bridget Purtill. The priest was Fr. J. Lawlor. Martin died of heart disease on 28 September 1931, aged 61, in New Haven, Connecticut. He was buried in St. Lawrence Cemetery in West Haven (sect. G, Ave. 13, lot 63). His occupation on the death certificate was "boilermaker".

Martin married Catherine Lovett on 20 November 1896 in the Church of the Sacred Heart in New Haven. Witnesses were John Lynch and Mary Lovett. The priest was Fr. McKeon. Martin resided at the time of marriage in New Haven, Catherine in "York City", very likely New York City.

Dennis Ford

Catherine Lovett was the daughter of William Lovett. It is possible that she was the sister of Pat Lovett who married Mary Allen in New Jersey (see Chapter Five). If that is the case her mother was Catherine Gallivan. Her baptism was 16 February 1871 in Coolkeragh townland in Galey Parish. Her godmother was Elizabeth Dillane. Catherine Lovett died of tuberculosis on 6 March 1920, aged 49. The death record gave the year of her birth as 1871. The 1900 Federal Census gave her birth as occurring in March 1874.

The 1900 Federal Census reported that Martin immigrated to America in 1896. In fact, there is a record of an individual by that name arriving in the port of New York on 29 June 1896 on the steamship *Adriatic*. However, the 1930 Federal Census listed 1890 as the year of immigration. And the 1910 Census listed 1895, so it's anyone's guess when Martin arrived in America. It is not known when Catherine immigrated. The 1900 Census reported the date as 1891.

The families from Ballybunion that emerged in Martin's generation generally immigrated to Hoboken, New Jersey, or to New York City. It's not clear why Martin resided in New Haven. The 1930 Census described him as a trucker for a steam railroad, so he may have gone where the tracks led. We've found indications that Galey Parish people immigrated to Connecticut rather than to New Jersey, so he may have gone where the people of his Parish went.

The known children of Martin Griffin and Catherine Lovett offer a sad tale of early deaths mostly due to tuberculosis. Their known children were: Catherine; William; Nora; Anna; Martin; Dennis; John Francis; Helen Teresa; and Edward Vincent.

Catherine Griffin was born 28 August 1897. She was baptized on September 2. Godparents were Patrick Reilly and Mary Dwyer. The priest was Fr. George Sinnot. Catherine never married. She died, aged 30, on 28 June 1928. She was buried with her parents and siblings in St. Lawrence Cemetery.

William Joseph Griffin was born 5 March 1899 and baptized on March 9. Godparents were Joseph McGovern and Johanna Lovett. Fr. Sinnott officiated. William never married. He died, aged 26, of tuberculosis in the Cedarcrest Sanitarium in Newington, CT, on 4 October 1926. William registered for the World War One draft in June 1918. On the register he was described as short and having a medium build with blue eyes and brown hair [18].

Nora Griffin died, aged 19, in April 1920. This is the only record we have of Nora's life.

Anna Griffin was born 6 August 1902. She died, aged 91, on 9 December 1993. Anna married Thomas Casey on 7 August 1924 in Sacred Heart Church. Witnesses were Hubert Cox and Marian Roler. Fr. W. Redding officiated. Thomas Casey was the son of Michael Casey and Jane McNamara. He was born 15 August 1903 and died 20 December 1977. We do not know if they had children. They resided in East Haven. They were buried in St. Lawrence Cemetery.

Martin Griffin was baptized 8 September 1904. Godparents were Pat Gallagher and Kathleen Colt. Martin died in young adulthood in June 1926.

Dennis Griffin was born 10 June 1906. His baptism record has not been located. He died in Hamden, CT, in February 1979. He married a lady named Mary Coden—the name is phonetic. Mary Coden was born 28 September 1909 and died 23 November 1997. Dennis and Mary had two daughters. Like his father, Dennis was described on the Federal 1930 Census as a trucker for a steam railroad.

John Francis Griffin was baptized 3 November 1908. Godparents were Patrick Lovett and Anna—the surname is not known. John Francis died in childhood in October 1911.

Helen Teresa Griffin was born 8 December 1910 and baptized on December 18. Her godparents were Patrick McKiernan and Julia Ryan. Helen died, aged 84, on 5 October 1995. She married a man named William Warner, but the date is not known. We do not have details of William's life or whether they had children. They resided in Hamden.

Edward Vincent Griffin was born 2 November 1913. He died of tuberculosis in Winchester Hospital in West Haven in the teenage years on 24 October 1931. The death record stated that he was under doctor's care for five years. His occupation was "bundle wrapper".

My great-great-grandfather Martin Griffin was an agricultural laborer. He survived the near extermination of that class in County Kerry after the Famine. We can't say what his family's status was before the Famine, but it was likely the same as after. He was not listed in Griffith's Valuation. Perhaps he was not married at the time. Edmond and Bridget Connell were not listed in Griffith's. A man named Robert Costello was listed as holding property #1b in Ballyegan. This is on the Affouley side of the townland and it is the same property Martin later held.

Martin Griffin makes a brief appearance in the Closed Valuation Books in the 1880s. He subleased land from Jeremiah Murphy, afterward from Maurice Murphy. They in turn leased land from Meade Dennis, the landlord. There was no rate for land—Martin didn't have any. His house was valued at five shillings. The house would have been wood or mud with a thatch roof.

We visited Ballyegan on our genealogical jaunts to Ireland. It is located midway on the Listowel – Ballybunion Road near a place called Galey Crossroads. The road is reputed to be the straightest in Ireland. The road was the site of the unusual monorail that ran the eight miles between Listowel and Ballybunion on a single track. Called the Lartique Railroad after its inventor, the line ran from 1888 – 1924. Passengers sat in basket-like cabins on either side of the single track. Our ancestors would have gotten off at Lisselton, the single stop on the line.

Galey Cemetery lies at this crossroad. Farther up the road is a holy well dedicated to St. Bartholomew. Holy wells are one of those strange Irish customs that bear an unholy resemblance to paganism. Visiting days were the last Saturday in April, the Saturday before St. John's Eve in mid-summer, and the Saturday before Michelmas in November. The ritual consisted of walking in a clockwise direction around the well while reciting nine decades of the rosary. The devotee would then sip the water and leave a piece of cloth on nearby trees. Legends associated with the well include a magical trout that appears whenever a wish is to be granted. The well was supposed to have changed locations when someone washed his clothes in it. The stream that feeds the well is supposed never to go dry. And water from the well is supposed never to boil.

In the nineteenth century Galey Parish was two-fifths bog. In the twentieth century it still looks two-fifths bog. There are signs warning of the dangers of bogs. I remember the word "death" was posted in one of the signs. The site where Martin and Catherine lived is inaccessible. We visited Jack Griffin's homestead on the other side of Ballyegan. Jack's descended from Patrick Griffin and Mary Barry who lived in Ballyegan at the same period as our Griffins. We're not related, but Jack has been quite helpful in supplying genealogical information. He's achieved some local fame as he farms in traditional ways. Jack's been the subject of two videos and the subject of poems by John Malachy Raftery.

The land of our Kerry ancestors borders the Atlantic Ocean. The mouth of the Shannon River is to the north of Ballybunion. So many tears have been shed singing of the Shannon a second river could be laid beside it. The Cashen River is to the south of Ballybunion. The Cashen is wide at this point and the view is scenic, as the Ballybunion side lies on cliffs high over the water. The cliffs run along the coast all the way to the Shannon. It is possible to walk along them for some distance. You have to be careful not to lean too far over, as the angry white ocean lashes the rocks ten dizzying stories below. The remnants of a medieval castle belonging to the Fitzmaurice sept—this is the Kerry branch descended from Maurice de Prendergast—stand at the verge of a cliff at the center of town. It's the emblem of Ballybunion, but all that's left of the castle is a lonely wall a few stories tall. The ruin faces the Atlantic from a cliff that juts onto the broad beach below—it's odd to see a wall poised at the edge of the vast sea.

World famous golf courses lie south of the castle remnant along the coast—the street is named Sandhill Road. If golfers slice the ball, they have to don wetsuits and jump into the sea. Aside one of the courses lies an antique cemetery that was in poor repair when we visited. If the ball slices in that direction, golfers have to dig among toppled headstones. Knockanore Mountain lies to the east of Ballybunion. This is a 665 foot lump that cuts the region in two. The mountain is so high and so out of proportion to the surrounding countryside only a wet shade of green can be discerned from the crown.

Listowel, the largest city in the vicinity, is eight miles inland. *Pigot's 1824 Guide* described Listowel as "a well-built little town ... pleasantly situated on a gentle declivity of the [river] Feale." Lewis's 1837 *Topographical Dictionary* gave the total number of houses as 273, "many of which are well-built ... There are two good hotels. Fairs are held on alternate Wednesdays and also on May 13, July 25, and October 28, chiefly for cattle, sheep, and goats ... behind the castle, in the river Feale, are the extensive flour mills of Messers. Leonard and Co., producing annually about 8,000 barrels ... The soil is remarkably fertile and the neighborhood is celebrated for producing wheat of superior quality." Lewis noted that there was a national school in town, two private schools, and sixty children in a Catholic school.

Listowel was described in *Slater's 1846 Directory* as a town with one fever hospital, two druggists, three bakeries, four blacksmiths, seven butchers, eleven linen drapers, and fourteen public houses. This pretty much describes Listowel today. The center of town is one long block crammed with restaurants, shops, and public houses—today, we call them "taverns".

North Kerry did not escape the horrors of the Famine. There are accounts of food riots in 1846. The workhouse stood at the western end of

Listowel. Nearby is *Teampaillon Ban*—the "little white chapel." The chapel stands at the entrance of a field where the nameless people who died in the workhouse were buried. A few benches are beside the chapel. Out of respect, no one walks on the field. There are no stones.

Chapter Five

~

Erin—John Allen & Johanna Linnane

Our second North Kerry great-great-grandparents are **John Allen** and **Johanna Linnane** of the townland of Trippul West, Kilconly Parish, in the Listowel Union of County Kerry. Their family history is extensively documented, as all but one of their children immigrated to New Jersey. We were fortunate to locate descendents of the child who stayed on Sandhill Road in Ballybunion. Their marriage record has not been located either by the Killarney Heritage Centre or by us when we inspected the microfilm of the Parish registers, but the event would have occurred in the mid-1850s.

We have the baptism record of John Allen—he is the single Irish great-great-grandparent whose baptism record is extant. John was the son of **Timothy Allen** and **Mary Gallivan**. He was baptized in Ballybunion Parish on 10 July 1833. Godparents were Patrick Allen and Juliana Connor. The priest was Fr. F. Enright. His family resided in the townland of Tulla More, which is adjacent to Trippul West where he lived as an adult. The name was recorded as "Allin", which is phonetic and how the priest wrote it.

There is no record of the fates of Timothy and Mary. They were not listed in Griffith's Valuation in 1852. Perhaps they resided with relatives. Perhaps they did not survive the Famine. The Killarney Centre found records for two of John's siblings. **Dermot Allen** was baptized on 22 May 1835. His godparents were Patrick Ferris and Catherine Gallivan. **Bridget Allen** was baptized on 10 January 1838. Her godmother was Bridget Gallivan. We found a third sibling—**Michael Allen**—on the church records available on-line. Michael was baptized 30 June 1831. His godparents were J. Moore and M. Dillane. The townland was Shrone, which is on the other side of Knockanore Mountain.

John Allen's death was reported to the civil authorities as occurring on 18 December 1912. He died in Cunighatuscane Hospital in Listowel. Cause of death was cancer of the lip—perhaps it was skin cancer. He was under doctor's care for two years. His age was given as 87—in fact, he was 79. His place of residence was Trippul. The informant was Timothy Walshe of the hospital. We don't know where he was buried, but Kilconly Cemetery was the likeliest place.

The baptism record of Johanna Linnane has not surfaced, but we know her parents were **Timothy Linnane** and **Ellen Keeffe** and that they resided in nearby Lacka townland. Neither Timothy nor Ellen was listed in Griffith's Valuation.

We were lucky to gather this information because **Mary Linnane**, Johanna's sister, immigrated to America and resided with her nephews John and Pat Allen in Hoboken. The 1900 Federal Census clearly gives her birth date—February 1843. Using this information, the Killarney Heritage Center found Mary's baptism record. She was baptized on 6 February 1843. Her godmother was Ellen Courtney. We don't know when Mary immigrated, but it was before 1895, as she was listed on the New Jersey Census of that year. On the Census her surname was spelled the way it likely sounded, "Leynert". Mary never married. She died 13 November 1906 and was buried in Holy Name Cemetery in Jersey City.

The Killarney Centre did not locate Johanna Linnane's baptism record, but it found records for two siblings. **Thomas Linnane** was baptized on 8 September 1836 or 1837. His godmother was Cecilia Sullivan—it may be Gallivan. The townland was Keelomeero, which is adjacent to Lacka. **Patrick Linnane** was baptized 24 July 1845. His godparents were James Hennessy and Sara Linnane. Nothing is known of the lives of Thomas and Patrick. A fourth sibling of Johanna's was likely **John Linnane**, who was baptized on 21 June 1832 (godmother Mary Ruddle) and who married Mary Lovett. Their children immigrated to Hoboken.

The Killarney Centre did not find the baptism record of **Timothy Linnane**, who was likely another brother. My grandmother was very close to Timothy's son, who also immigrated to Hoboken [19].

Johanna Linnane's death was reported to civil authorities as occurring on 18 March 1896. The cause of death was consumption (tuberculosis). She was described as a "laborer's wife" and as 59 years of age—this puts her birth around 1836-37. She was under doctor's care for five years. The informant was her husband John Allen. She was likely buried in Kilconly Cemetery.

The majority of Allens in Ireland are of English or Scottish ancestry. If Scottish, Allen derives from the MacAilin family of the Campbell clan. They came to the West of Ireland in the seventeenth century—in fact, a man named Edward Allen was listed in Penders 1639 Census as residing in Ballybunion. In the 1850s the Allen families were localized in a swath of townlands from Trippul and Tulla More on the north side of Knockanore Mountain to Affouley on the south side.

The surname *Gallivan*—or Galvin—derives from the Irish *O Gaelbhain*, meaning "bright white". The *O* signifies "son", so this would refer to an individual described as "son of bright white". Maybe we're descended from an archangel—that would give the Mormons something to consider. The surname is localized in the same swath that contains the Allen name—from the Shannon across Knockanore Mountain towards the Cashen River.

The surname *Linnane* is spelled a bewildering number of ways and with any number of "n's", "i's", and "e's". The likeliest origin of the name derives from *O Leannain*, meaning "little cloak". We can only wonder what being the "son of little cloak" meant. In America Linnane became "Leonard". There was a prominent family of millers and engineers in Listowel named Leonard. Perhaps the American version was taken from this family. The Linnane families were scattered throughout North Kerry, especially in Lisselton Parish where Lacka townland is located.

The surname *Keeffe* derives in some mysterious way from the Irish *O Caoimh*. The word translates as "son of kind" or "son of gentle". "Kind" and "gentle" are adjectives—perhaps we need to add a noun like "one" or "man". The name also derives from a person named Caoimh who was believed to have lived in the eleventh century and to have been descended from an early King of Munster—we may be royalty after all! The surname is not unusual in North Kerry, but it is not especially common in the immediate vicinity of Ballybunion.

The known children of John Allen and Johanna Linnane were: Timothy; Ellen; John; Mary; Henry; Patrick; and Johanna.

Timothy Allen was born in the time period 1856 – 1860. His baptism record has not been located. Timothy died on 5 July 1940 according to civil records. He was buried in Killehenny Cemetery, which lies on Sandhill

Road adjacent to the golf courses. There is a prominent monument in the cemetery to him and his family.

Timothy married Johanna Purtill on 14 February 1885. Witnesses were Bartl. Flahive and Mary Flahive. Fr. Mortimer O'Connor presided. Johanna's parents were Thomas Purtill of Ballybunion and Elizabeth Gallivan of Lixnaw Parish. Johanna was called the "Rose of Tulla More". She died 20 February 1948 [20].

Timothy became a ticket agent and station master in Ballybunion for the Lartique Railroad. He was also an agent for the Cunard Line. He may have been a schoolmaster in the townland of Rahavanig at one point. He "married into" the Purtill home. Afterward they resided in Gortnaskeha townland and in Listowel. In 1901 and afterward they resided in Ballybunion.

Timothy and Johanna Purtill had twelve children. Eleven were alive in 1911. Information was obtained from the Killarney Centre. Death dates derive from the monument in Killehenny Cemetery. We were fortunate to make the acquaintance of Thomas Allen, Jr. and his wife Helen, who received us hospitably in their home on Sandhill Road in 1998 and who shared family stories.

Thomas Allen was baptized 3 March 1886. The godmother was Elizabeth Mulvihill, the priest was Fr. Charles Godley. Tom married Mary Halpin of Finuge Parish. They had three children, including Tom and Evelyn, who we met in 1998. We were told that Thomas worked as a golf pro for many years. He had a problem with his foot that caused him to walk with a limp. He served as an intelligence agent for the IRA in Ballybunion. He was arrested once and warned by a friendly officer not "to go out the back door", as he would be shot under the pretense that he was trying to escape.

Mary Teresa Allen was baptized 15 October 1887. Her godmother was Janet Hanrahan. Fr. Godley officiated. We have no information on her life.

Timothy Allen was born circa 1888-89. No baptism record has been found. He died 4 December 1959, aged 70. He married Bridget O'Callaghan, who died 30 March 1970. They had at least one son and daughter. Timothy and Bridget were buried in Killehenny Cemetery. Timothy was reputed to have had a bad temper. He challenged a British policeman to a fight when he saw him taking advantage of a local man.

John Joseph Allen was baptized 20 July 1890. His godmother was Catherine Purtill. Fr. Godley officiated. Joseph—he appears to have used this name—never married. He worked as a ticket taker on the Lartique Railroad.

Elizabeth (Lil) Allen was baptized 6 December 1891. Her godmother was Mary Stack. Fr. Godley officiated. Elizabeth never married. She died 11 July 1952.

Joanna (Hanna) Allen was baptized 25 June 1893. Her godmother was Mary Walsh. Fr. M. O'Shea officiated. Joanna married a man named Keane in England, but no other information is available.

Catherine Allen was baptized 16 February 1896. Her godparents were Patrick Hayes and Elizabeth Purtill. Fr. M. O'Brien officiated. She was listed as Kathleen on the 1911 Irish census.

Christiana (Chris) Allen was baptized 20 June 1897. Her godparents were Thomas Allen and Elizabeth Purtill. Fr. P. Courtney officiated. Chris was an expert golfer who won a number of tournament trophies. Chris died 27 December 1955.

Patrick John Allen was baptized 26 June 1901. His godparents were Michael Kirby and Teresa Dee. Fr. G. Byrne officiated. Patrick died on 15 June 1989. He married Kathleen McCarthy, who died 30 January 1990. Her age was given as 88 years. They had at least two sons. They are buried in St. John's Cemetery in Ballybunion. Pat was a school teacher. Tom Allen recollected in 1998 that Pat told him that, as a boy, he brought cigarettes and whiskey to "the man in the bog"—possibly this was John Allen.

Francis Allen was baptized on 28 January 1903. His godparents were Pat Allen and Catherine Purtill. Fr. E. Crowley officiated. Francis married a lady named Beatrice Duggan of Tipperary and worked on the railroad. They may have eloped to America around 1928, but we do not have the full story. Francis was supposed to immigrate earlier, but his mother burned the ticket his uncle sent from Hoboken. They lived in New York. Francis may have died in March 1970. There is a record in the Social Society Death Index for a person of his name born on 27 January 1903.

Gerard Allen was born around 1906. No baptism record was located. Gerard was a person with Down Syndrome. He survived into adulthood, but no other information is available.

Anne Allen was listed on the 1911 Census as sixteen years of age, but no other information is available. Her baptism record has not been located.

Ellen Allen, my great-grandmother, was baptized 14 January 1858. Her godmother was Ellen Linnane. The priest was Fr. J. Walsh. Ellen married Denis Griffin on 26 April 1885. She immigrated to the United

States in June 1912. Ellen died in New York City on 15 September 1919. She was buried in Holy Name Cemetery in Jersey City. Ellen's life and family will be described in Chapter 11.

John Allen was born in the time period 1859 – 1862. His baptism record has not been located. The 1900 Federal Census listed his birth as occurring in June 1859. The 1915 New Jersey Census listed his birth as June 1862. His age was given as 69 years on the 1930 Federal Census, so the year would be 1861. His death record (his sister Mary was the informant) gave an exact date—18 June 1860.

John never married. The 1900 Federal Census gives the year of immigration as 1889 and described John as naturalized. He was described as a factory worker on that census. In 1900 he resided at 221 Clinton St. in Hoboken with his aunt Mary Leonard and a man named Thomas Sheehy. The 1910 Federal Census described John as an "engineer", which probably means railroad engineer. He lived with his sister Mary Lovett and her family in the 1920s. The 1930 Census described him as a "watchman in the courts". The Census also stated that he immigrated in 1890 and was naturalized.

John died around 70 years of age on 11 January 1931. He had been under treatment for a year. At the time of death he resided with his sister Mary at 735 Park Ave. in Hoboken. He was buried in the Lovett plot in Holy Cross Cemetery in North Arlington, New Jersey (Sect. 7 - B -7).

John's nieces Rita Nelson and Kitty Fleming remembered that John was a short man and that he had a full handlebar mustache.

Mary Allen was baptized 17 September 1865. Her godparents were John Walsh and Ellen Walsh. The priest was Fr. J. O'Keeffe. Mary was one of those Irish babies baptized before she was born—the civil record listed her birth date as 23 November 1865.

Mary Allen died 9 September 1949, aged 83. She resided at the time of death at 419 Garden St. in Hoboken. She was described as a resident of the United States for 55 years, which puts her immigration in 1894. (The 1910 Census gives the year as 1890, the 1930 Census as 1891.) She was buried in the Lovett plot in Holy Cross Cemetery.

Mary married Patrick Lovett on 28 July 1895 in the Church of Our Lady of Grace in Hoboken. The witnesses were John Allen and Mary O'Connor. Fr. James Kelly officiated.

Pat Lovett's parents were William Lovett and Catherine Gallivan of the townland of Coolkeragh in Galey Parish, County Kerry. He was baptized on 23 March 1867. His godparents were Thomas Lovett and Honora Pierse [21].

With Mary Allen and Pat Lovett we can see a pattern where a small number of families, born in the same general vicinity in Ireland, immigrated to the same American city, inter-married there, and served as witnesses in weddings and as godparents in baptisms. We see that a Lovett marries a Griffin, a Lovett marries an Allen, and an Allen marries a Griffin. The Allens, Lovetts, Keanes, Leonards, and Fords remained close throughout the twentieth century. A limited geographical destination may have played a role—nearly everyone lived in the "Mile Square" city of Hoboken—but these families were cemented through sacramental events as well. We also see in the Allens and in the other families a type of immigration called "chain immigration". All—or most—members of a family immigrate to the same city one at a time. The people who come to "Amerikay" save up and send money or tickets for the younger siblings to follow. This pattern generally involved siblings. In the case of the Allens and the Griffins it involved uncles sending for nephews and nieces.

Pat Lovett died 9 April 1925, aged 62. On the death certificate he was described as a railroad worker. He and Mary resided at that time at 124 Bloomfield St., Hoboken. He may have had a handlebar mustache.

The 1930 Census listed Pat and Mary and their family as residing at 735 Park Avenue in Hoboken. The rent was $51.00 a month.

Mary Allen and Pat Lovett had the following known children: William; Johanna; John; Timothy; Thomas; and Catherine. Except for William's, all baptisms took place in Our Lady of Grace Church.

William Joseph Lovett was born 29 June 1896 in New Haven, CT. He was baptized July 2. His godparents were Martin Griffin and Mary Leonard. The fact that a man named Martin Griffin served as godparent virtually clinches the possibility that Pat and Catherine Lovett were siblings. Friends may serve as witnesses in Irish weddings, but care was taken that relatives and in-laws serve as godparents, especially for the older children.

William died, aged 32, on 10 February 1929. He was described as a "foreman, publishing house" on the death record. He resided at 218 Willow Ave. in Hoboken at the time of death. He was under treatment for three months. Rita Nelson and Kitty Fleming recollected that he had a heart condition. He was buried in the Lovett plot in Holy Cross Cemetery.

William registered for the World War One draft on 5 June 1918. He indicated he worked for the W.J. Thompson Co. on West 43rd St. in New York City. He was described as having blue eyes and blond hair.

Rita Nelson and Kitty Fleming remembered William as tall and thin and of a nervous temperament. He worked in the same company as his uncle Pat Allen. One day he had an argument with Pat, who called him a "son of a bitch". He threw an object at Pat for that remark and quit. He told his mother about what happened, saying, "You know what that makes you." The story has a happy ending—Pat Allen apologized and William returned to work.

William was the only sibling to marry. He married a lady named Mary Costello. We have not located the marriage record. Mary Costello was born in 1897. She died in 1972. Later in life she married a man with the wonderful name of Harry Twible. William and Mary had two children [22].

Johanna Lovett was born and baptized on 9 September 1897. Her godparents were Pat Allen and Mary Ferris. The priest was Fr. George Browne. She died 31 December 1956. She resided at 927 Washington St. in Hoboken at the time of death. Johanna was described as a clerk for International Paper Co. She was buried in the Lovett plot in Holy Cross Cemetery.

John Lovett was born 12 August 1899. He was baptized on August 13. The godparents were John and Johanna Allen. Fr. Robert Freeman officiated. John died in childhood in February 1910. He was buried in the Allen plot in Holy Name Cemetery.

Timothy Lovett was born 23 April 1901. He was baptized April 28. His godparents were John Keane and Margaret Enright. Fr. Freeman officiated. Timothy died 20 March 1933 in the New Jersey State Sanitarium for Tuberculosis in Lebanon. He was described as a "railway clerk". (The 1930 Census has him as a "chief clerk" for a steam railroad.) He was under doctor's care for a year and a half. He was buried in the Lovett plot in Holy Cross Cemetery.

Thomas Lovett was born 8 April 1903. He was baptized April 19. His godparents were Maurice Quinlan and Hanna Lovett. Fr. Freeman officiated. He died 25 June 1985, aged 82. My father recollected that Tom was a well-liked local figure with modest habits. He worked for the Railway Express Co. He was buried in the Lovett plot at Holy Cross Cemetery.

Catherine Mary ("Kitty") Lovett was born 21 July 1905. She was baptized on July 31. Her godparents were James Hickey and Mary Guider.

Fr. Fitzpatrick presided. Kitty never married. She died 16 July 1986, aged 80. She was buried in the Lovett plot in Holy Cross Cemetery. She resided with her brother in Hoboken. She had on the door to their apartment a notice that read—*America, Lovett or leave it.* Kitty worked for the city of Hoboken and was a politically "connected" person. She worked in some capacity with Selective Service during World War Two.

Henry Allen, the third son of John Allen and Johanna Linnane, was baptized in Ballybunion Parish on 12 May 1868. His godparents were Martin Kennelly and Anne Mahoney. The priest was Fr. C. Mahoney. The informant was Martin Costello of Tullaghboy townland. Henry died, aged 44, on 5 January 1912 in Hoboken. At the time of death he resided at 105 Harrison St. He was under treatment for two weeks. He was buried in Holy Name Cemetery.

Henry married Margaret Campen in Our Lady of Grace Church in Hoboken on 5 April 1896. Witnesses were Michael Gillen and Catherine Gallivan. The priest was Fr. James Kelly. Margaret was the daughter of John Campen and Mary Guider. The civil record of their marriage reported that Margaret and her parents were born in New Jersey. It appears she and Henry did not have children.

The 1900 Federal Census reported that Henry immigrated to America in 1892 and that he was not naturalized. He was described as a dock worker. Margaret's birth date was given as March 1868. She's called "Maggie" on the Census. The 1910 Federal Census listed Henry in residence at 217 Clinton St. He was described as married, but Margaret was not listed with him.

Patrick Allen, the fourth son of John Allen and Johanna Linnane, was baptized on 12 February 1871. His godmother was Mary Walsh. Fr. C. Murphy officiated. The civil record of his birth gave 1 March as his birth date. Patrick died in Teaneck, NJ, on 21 November 1952. He was 81. He was buried in St. Joseph's Cemetery in Hackensack, NJ (section C or D - 27 - P341).

According to Pat's obituary he emigrated in 1891. There is an emigration record for Patrick Allen, aged 19, arriving in New York harbor on the steamship *Campania*. The date is 11 May 1891. He was accompanied on the boat by Thomas McCarthy. This is the likely record, as there are a lot of connections between Pat and Thomas [23].

Pat Allen married Mary Ferris on 12 April 1896 in Our Lady of Grace Church. Witnesses were Thomas McCarthy and Mary Leonard.

Fr. George Browne officiated. Pat resided at 115 Willow Ave. at the time of the marriage. His occupation was given as "conductor".

Mary Ferris was the daughter of Edmond Ferris and Nora Moran of Laheseragh townland in North Kerry—the townland is on Knockanore Mountain about halfway between Trippul and Ballyegan. Mary was baptized in Ballybunion Parish on 15 December 1872. Her godmother was Mary Callaghan. Mary died in a nursing home in Saddle River, NJ, on 29 March 1968, aged 95 years. At the time of death she resided in Bogota, NJ. We can't identify when Mary immigrated [24].

Pat and Mary Allen had a large family. Their known children were: John Patrick; Edward; Josephine; Margaret; Raymond; Lillian; Walter; Helen; and Mildred.

John Patrick Allen was born 15 January 1897 and baptized on January 24 in Our Lady of Grace Church. His godparents were Martin and Ellen McNamara. The priest was Fr. Browne. John Patrick died as a baby six weeks later on March 5. He was buried in Holy Name Cemetery.

Edward Allen was born 9 June 1898 and was baptized on June 12. John and Johanna Allen were the godparents. Fr. George Fitzpatrick was the priest. He married Agnes Donohue on 23 July 1919 in Our Lady of Grace Church. Edward Ferris and Catherine Donohue were the witnesses. Fr. E. Murphy presided. Agnes was the daughter of Daniel Donohue and Catherine Schaffhauser. Edward and Agnes had five children. Edward worked as a lithographer in New York City. Kitty Fleming remembered that he was a heavyset man. He died before May 1967.

Josephine Allen was born 15 September 1900. We do not have her baptism record. Josephine died 4 July 1979 in Tucson, Arizona. We don't know where she's buried. Josephine married Frank Gonzales, who was born in Hoboken around 1898 and died in February 1960. He was buried in St. Joseph's Cemetery in Hackensack. Josephine and Frank had three children. They worked for a period of time for Bergen County, NJ.

Margaret Allen was born 18 November 1901. She was baptized on December 1. Her godparents were Michael Callahan and Mary Ferris. The priest was Fr. Connell. Margaret died 3 May 1967. She was buried in St. Joseph's Cemetery. She married a man named Michael Shea. They had one daughter.

Raymond Allen was born 17 December 1905, according to the civil record. We do not have his baptism record. Raymond died suddenly in Asbury Park, NJ, on 25 July 1958. He was buried in St. Joseph's Cemetery (R-15-18). At the time of death he resided in Teaneck. He worked as an expeditor for Wright Aeronautical Corp. Raymond married Josephine Murphy of Jersey City on 11 August 1925. The Church has not been identified. Josephine was the daughter of Joseph Murphy and Marie Gangloff. She was born 14 November 1903 and died 3 March 1988. She worked as a telephone operator for Curtis-Wright Corp. They had six children, including a child named Constance Marie, who died 21 February 1929 at the age of two. Constance was buried with her uncles in Holy Name Cemetery in Jersey City. She was called "Bunny". Across a distance of nearly 60 years Kitty Fleming remembered that Bunny had blond hair and was very pretty.

Lillian Allen was born 11 January 1908. This is a civil record, we do not have her baptism record. Lillian died in January 1976 in Goshen, NY. She married a man named Jack Nutley, who may have worked in Geismer's Clothing store in Hoboken—Geismer's was an upscale store that also sold the green uniforms we wore in Our Lady of Grace grammar school. They had seven children.

Walter Leonard Allen was born 4 January 1910. He was baptized in Our Lady of Grace Church on January 16. His godparents were John Dee and Ellen Carmody. The priest was Fr. Devlin. Walter died of a heart attack on 21 October 1954. He was buried in the McLaughlin plot in Holy Name Cemetery. At the time of death he resided in North Bergen. Walter worked in a paper manufacturing plant. He married Margaret E. McLaughlin. We don't know her parents with certainty or when they married. Margaret died 13 July 1977. Her age on the headstone was given as 66 years. She and Walter had two children.

Helen Allen was born 26 February 1912. She was baptized in Our Lady of Grace Church on March 12. Her godparents were John Griffin and my grandmother Catherine Griffin. We do not have her death record. She married a man named Henry Syversen on 16 August 1947. They did not have children. We don't have records for Henry Syversen. Helen was sickly and may have had some psychological trouble. She may also have had Parkinson's Disease.

Mildred Allen was born 25 September 1915. She was baptized in Our Lady of Grace Church on October 3. Her godparents were Martin and Mary Sheehy. The priest was not specified. Mildred died in April 1997. We do not have the civil record or the place of burial. She married Robert Bund in St. Joseph's Church in West New York on 9 April 1939. The witnesses were Warren Bund and Helen Allen. The priest was Fr. J. A. McHale. She and Robert had two children. Mildred married a second time. This was to Thomas Hughes circa 1967. They lived in Washington, NY.

Robert Bund was born in the Bronx, NY, on 6 June 1914. His parents were George Bund and Florence Rumline or Romlein. He worked as a butcher. He died by suicide in Bergen Pines County Hospital on 6 January 1957. He was buried in the Allen plot in St. Joseph's Cemetery. At the time of death he and Mildred resided in Hillsdale, NJ.

Rita Nelson and Kitty Fleming remembered that their Uncle Pat Allen was a strong personality with a bad temper who was the "big wheel" in the family. He worked in a publishing or paper company. Later in life he owned a tavern in Teaneck named "Three Barons". Despite being a Catholic he joined a Masonic Lodge to increase business.

Lillian Rauh, Pat's granddaughter, remembered that Pat was a dominant personality. He appeared to have been stern with his children. At family gatherings he always entered a room first. He never allowed his children to have more than one drink in his presence. His children played musical instruments—Walter the violin and his daughters the piano.

According to Lillian he initially worked as an elevator operator. He worked in (or managed) a company that published a magazine called *Gentle Woman*. He had red hair that turned white as he aged. Several of his children were reported as having red or auburn hair, notably Josephine and Mildred.

Pat resided with his brother John and his aunt Mary Leonard in Hoboken in 1895. According to the 1900 Federal Census he and Mary Ferris resided at 515 Grand St. in Hoboken. The 1910 Census placed them at 616 Park Ave. Pat was described as employed in publishing. The 1920 Census found Pat and his family at 705 Park Ave. in Hoboken. The 1930 Federal Census found them at 78 28th St. in North Bergen, NJ. They own the house, valued at $6,500. Pat was described as a "publisher".

Johanna Allen was the last known child of John Allen and Johanna Linnane. She was baptized 19 April 1874 in Ballybunion Parish. Her godmother was Mary Costello. The priest was Fr. Mortimer O'Connor. The civil record of her birth listed the date of birth as May 20. Johanna died in Hoboken on 14 October 1939, aged 65. She was buried in Holy Name Cemetery (block K, Sect. DB, grave 61, no headstone). At the time of death she resided at 614 Garden St. in Hoboken. She was under doctor's care for two years.

My father recollected that my grandfather Pat Ford liked Johanna best of all his wife's relatives. At her funeral he knelt and kissed the ground. This odd behavior may have represented some obscure Irish custom.

Johanna married John Keane on 25 January 1902 in Our Lady of Grace Church. Witnesses were Edward Ferris and Catherine Keane. The priest was Fr. G. Fitzpatrick. John Keane was baptized 20 April 1877. His godmother was Bridget McGrath. His family lived in Shanganagh townland in the civil Parish of Moyarta in the Kilrush Union of County Clare (the Catholic Parish was Carrigaholt). His parents were Lawrence Keane and Margaret Behan. John worked as a longshoreman on the local docks, possibly for the Holland American line. John died 23 March 1951. He was buried with Johanna in Holy Name Cemetery. His daughters Rita Nelson and Kitty Fleming remembered that he came from a family that had artistic talent. He was very religious. He stopped in church every day and prayed the rosary out loud on his knees. His family had to walk around him as he prayed [25].

We do not know when Johanna emigrated. There is a record for a person of her name, aged 21, arriving in the port of New York on the steamship *Majestic* on 13 April 1898. Unfortunately, the dates do not correspond. There are three individuals named John Keane arriving in New York in the same period—we can't say which became Johanna's husband.

The known children of Johanna Allen and John Keane were: Lawrence; John; Margaret; Joanna; Ellen Margaret and Mary, twins; Thomas; Katherine; and Rita. All baptisms occurred in Our Lady of Grace Church.

Lawrence Keane was born on 25 October 1902. He was baptized on November 2. His godparents were Edward Ferris and Catherine Kane. (The surname in the record is written Kane, but the name is pronounced "Keen".) The priest was not indicated. Lawrence died 3 July 1904. He was buried in Holy Name Cemetery.

Margaret Keane was born on 17 June 1904. She was baptized on June 19. Her godparents were John Allen and Nora Callan. Fr. O'Neill presided. Margaret worked for a time in the Hoboken Public Library. She was a tall lady. Margaret never married—my father recollected that his mother suspected Margaret had a crush on Pat Ford. Margaret died in 1954.

John Keane was born on 30 January 1906 and baptized on February 11. His godparents were Thomas Keane and Mary Lovett. The priest was Fr. Devlin. John died as a baby on 5 April 1906. He was buried in Holy Name Cemetery.

Joanna Keane was born on 11 February 1907. She was baptized on February 17. Her godparents were Patrick and Mary Allen. Fr. O'Neill presided. Johanna worked for many years for the Cosmopolitan Shipping Co. She never married. She died in 1983. We don't know where Margaret and Joanna were buried.

Ellen Margaret Keane was born on 2 August 1909 and baptized on August 8. Her godparents were William Lovett and Ellen Carmody. The priest was not named. It's likely Ellen died 5 September 1910. There is a burial record in the Keane plot for "Helen", aged one year. If this is the same individual, she was a twin. There is a record in the grave for **Mary Keane**, died 5 October 1909 at age two months. We have no baptism record for Mary.

Thomas Joseph Keane was born on 13 December 1911. He was baptized December 31. His godparents were John and Kathleen McMahon. Thomas died 9 May 1981. He was buried in Holy Name Cemetery (block H, sect. BC, grave 27). At the time of his death, Thomas resided in North Bergen. He worked for the Black Diamond steamship line and for Ferguson Furniture.

Thomas married Olga Gabrielson on 14 October 1939 in Our Lady of Grace Church. The witnesses were Edward Holmell and Anna Gabrielson. The priest was Fr. Francis X. Coyle. Sadly, this was the same day his mother died. We were told by his sisters that he wanted to put the wedding off, but his family advised he should go ahead and marry despite the tragedy. Olga was the daughter of John Gabrielson and Alava Olsen. She was from Brooklyn, NY. She was born 2 July 1911 and died in December 1975. It is not known if they had children.

Katherine "Kitty" Keane was born on 6 February 1914. She was baptized on March 8. Her godparents were Martin Mahoney and Johanna Lovett. The priest was not named. Kitty worked as a telephone operator in Maxwell House in Hoboken. She died at an advanced age on 27 June 2003. Kitty married Phil Fleming in Our Lady of Grace Church on 6 August 1944. Phil was the son of Dennis Fleming and Rose Burke. He was born 5 June 1914 and died in March 1979. He worked as a Hoboken fireman for twenty years and may have risen to the rank of captain. They had two children.

Rita Mary Keane was born on 1 April 1918 and baptized on April 14. Her godparents were Timothy Lovett and Nora Clohessy. Rita married John Nelson, Jr. in Our Lady of Grace Church on 1 April 1942 or 1943. Fr. Quinn presided. John Nelson was the son of John Nelson and Rose

McCourt. He was born 8 July 1915 and died in February 1974. They had two children. The last of her generation, Rita Nelson is alive at the time of this writing (December 2010).

In the 1920 Census John and Johanna resided at 819 Park Ave. in Hoboken. In the 1930 Census they resided at 614 Garden St. John was described as a foreman on the docks. The record is uncertain, but it appears they owned their home, listed at $11,500.

Like Martin Griffin, my great-great grandfather John Allen was an agricultural laborer. We can't say what his family's status was before the Famine, but it was likely the same as after. John was not listed in Griffith's 1852 Valuation of Kerry. Patrick Allen of Tulla More was listed—perhaps he was John's brother. John makes only two appearances in the Closed Valuation Books. His family occupied property 6A—later it became 5A— in Trippul West. (Trippul translates as "cluster" or "bunch"—of what, we can't say.) He had no land. His house was valued at five shillings. Probably, the house was made of wood or mud with a thatch roof. A 1902 note in the Closed Valuation books indicates "land in Trippul East". John leased the land from William Townsend and Jackson Gun. They, in turn, leased the land from Trinity College, which owned vast tracks of North Kerry.

According to the 1901 Census of Ireland John Allen resided with his daughter Ellen and son-in-law Denis Griffin. His age was given as 70. He was described as unable to write. He was bilingual in English and Irish. In the 1911 Census his age was given as 84. He was described as an "old age pensioner" and as being able to read and write. He signed the census in remarkably clear script.

We visited Trippul in 1996. But there really is nothing to visit. The road divides a flat parcel of land. Knockanore Mountain is visible in the distance. A large squat building is astride the road. I believe the building served as a creamery in years past. Property 5A is inaccessible. It's on the south side of the road, but there is no footpath and there would be no measure of distance to indicate how far we needed to walk. In the nineteenth century the land was excessively subdivided among agricultural laborers. The Ordnance Survey Map (#25) shows a maze of small holdings. The Closed Valuation Books reveal constant reconfiguring of holders.

Kilconly Parish commences at the Atlantic cliffs and runs inland toward Knockanore Mountain. The land has a distinctively "shore" look. It's flat with white roads and thick shrubbery bordering grasslands reserved for cows. The northernmost tip of Kilconly opens to the mouth of the

Shannon River. County Clare is visible across the water. It is an impressive view and one lauded in poetry and song. Lewis's 1837 *Dictionary* claimed 1,660 inhabitants. There was a public school with 100 pupils at that period with two additional schools for 130 children. There was a small school in Trippul in the 1820s. Classes were in a "mud and sods" building. The instructor was Patrick Crawley. The "London Hibernian and Kildare-place Society" sponsored the school.

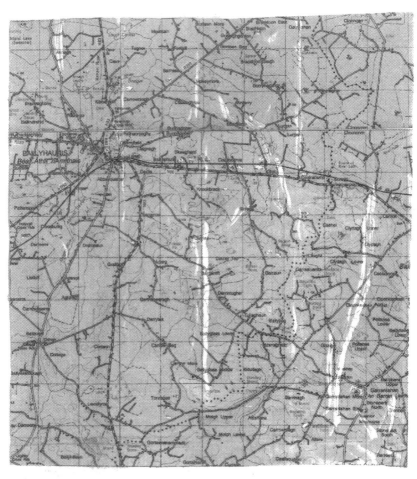

Ordnance
Survey
Ireland

Irish maps by permission of Ordnance Survey Ireland
Ordnance Survey Ireland Permit No. 8730
Ordnance Survey Ireland/Government of Ireland

DERRYNACONG -- Annagh Parish, County Mayo

LAUGHIL -- Kiltullagh Parish, County Roscommon

dotted line to center / right of map is county border

Derrynacong and Laughil

North Kerry

Trippul townland, Kilconly Parish

Ballyegan townland, Galey Parish

Shannon River

Atlantic Ocean

BALLYBUNNION

Ordnance Survey *Ireland*

Trippul and Ballyegan

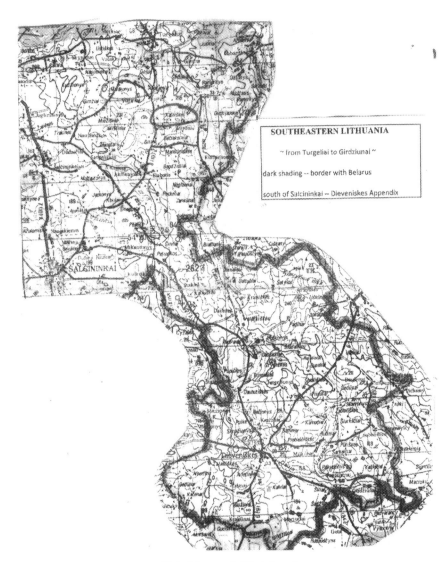

Kalniskes and Girdziunai

Chapter Six

~

Lietuva—Juozas Bielawski & Petronele Falkewicz

My Polish great-great-grandparents on the paternal side are **Juozas (Josef) Bielawski** and **Petronele Falkewicz** of Kalniskes village and **Jonas (John) Milosz** and **Magdalena Asakewicz** of Malakonys village. Both villages are located in Turgeliai Catholic Parish in Southeastern Lithuania approximately 20 miles south of Vilnius. The villages are about a mile or two apart. In this chapter we examine the lives of Juozas and Petronele. The next chapter details what we've learned of Jonas and Magdalena. In the following chapters we proceed to the very border of Lithuania and examine the lives of our Polish maternal great-great-grandparents.

We were fortunate to meet my mother's cousins still in residence in the ancestral villages, but most of the records in these chapters were supplied by the Archive in Vilnius. The Archive did a wonderful job researching our family histories, but the glaciers penguins huddle on melt at a faster pace. Some of our requests took six years to answer. We had no choice in this. We didn't have the luxury of examining microfilms at Family History Libraries. Even if we did, the records are in handwritten Polish and Russian, often in badly handwritten Polish and Russian. Unfortunately, census schedules and land records—these are very useful in Irish research—are unavailable in Lithuania. A favorable aspect of Lithuanian Parish records is that they go back farther in time than Irish Parish records. This came as a surprise, considering the devastation wrought by two World Wars and by the stupefaction of communism.

A word about names. The original Parish records were written by Polish and Russian speaking priests. Often the surnames—even the personal names—varied in spelling. There was no attempt to be consistent. The registers were interpreted by archivists who were barely literate in English and who translated names into a Lithuanian format. This presented a problem in re-translating the names back into a Polish format, as our ancestors were not Balts, but Slavs. I opted to translate the names into Polish as best I could—the Baltic "—ius" surname ending became the Polish "–wicz" and I did not identify women by their marital status as is done in Lithuania. I did, however, identify gender at the ending of surnames by the use of "—ski" for males and "—ska" for females. When the surnames looked too odd, I indicated this with a question mark. Except for a few, I left the personal names in Lithuanian. This may seem an unusual choice, but it was how I dealt with the names for the last fifteen years and how I always identified individuals.

Juozas Bielawski and Petronele Falkewicz married on 3 February 1846 in Tabariskes Parish. (Tabariskes Parish is immediately to the east and north of Turgeliai Parish, which is where they lived as adults.) Their witnesses were Baltramiejus Klimas, Andrius Klimas, and Jurgis Aleknawicz. The priest was Fr. Antanas Sakalauskas. Both Juozas and Petronele were from Zaltuny village, which is adjacent to Kalniskes to the southeast.

Juozas Bielawski was born on 16 March 1822 in Zaltuny village. He was the son of **Antanas Bielawski** and **Marijona Semaskas**—they were born in the eighteenth century. Juozas was baptized in Tabariskes Parish on March 17 by Fr. Paulius Vormilita. (Unlike Irish babies, Polish babies are not baptized before they are born.) His godparents were Jurgis Zienaiuskas and Ona Laucas (Lauciute in Lithuanian). He was the second in his family named Juozas.

Juozas died of consumption on 4 May 1864—this was the day before the Battle of the Wilderness in the American Civil War. He resided in Kalniskes at the time of death and was buried on May 6 in Zaltuny Cemetery.

The Vilnius Archive did not locate their marriage record, but found a number of records of the children of Antanas Bielawski and Marijona Semaskas. Their known children were: Rozalia; Marijona; Juozas; Jurgis; Juozas again; and Agota. All baptisms were in Tabariskes Parish.

Rozalia Bielawska was born on 12 September 1804 in Zaltuny. She was baptized on September 18 by Fr. Mykolas Gutauskas. Her godparents were Tomas Buinickis and Marijona Belkawicz.

There was a second Bielawski in residence in Kalniskes at the same time as Juozas in the mid-nineteenth century. This was Rozalia Bielawska, wife of Jonas Bogusas and grandparent of Marijona Satkewicz who married my great-grandmother's brother in 1870 (see Chapter Seven). We can't be certain, but it is likely this Rozalia was Juozas's sister. We have a death record for the widow Rozalia Bogusas. She died "of fever" on 10 November 1850. Her age was 50 years. She left the children Motiejus, Ona, and Marijona.

The Vilnius Archive found a record for Marijona Bielawska, who was the illegitimate daughter of Rozalia Bielawska. She was born in Pamerionys—probably Pamerkys—village on 30 March 1832 and baptized by Fr. Juozas Giniotas in Turgeliai Church on April 3. Godparents were the nobles Stanislav Balcewicz and Petronele Markewicz.

Marijona Bielawska, the daughter of Antanas Bielawski and Marijona Semaskas, was born 26 September 1812 in Zaltuny. Fr. Eustachijus Pacewicz baptized her on October 4. Her godparents were Simonas Bielawski and Kristina Galechrewicz (?). The difference of eight years between the births of Rozalia and Marijona may indicate that additional children were born whose names have not survived.

The first **Juozas Bielawski** was born on 3 July 1815 in Zaltuny. Fr. Kazimier Kojakauskas baptized him on July 4. His godparents were Simonas Chmieliuskas and Agota Wasilewska. We do not have his death record.

Jurgis (George) Bielawski was born 16 March 1818 in Zaltuny. Fr. Pacewicz baptized him on March 24. Godparents were Simonas Armelewicz and Ona Klimasauska.

Agota Bielawska was born 29 March 1825 in Zaltuny. Fr. Baltramiejus Klumbawicz baptized her on March 30. Godparents were Jurgis Zurauskas and Ona Lavicas. Agota appears to have been alive in 1884, when an individual of this name served as godparent to my great-grandfather's brother.

Antanas Bielawski and Marijona Semaskas and the other members of their generation witnessed one of the great catastrophes in Lithuanian history—Napoleon's arrival and subsequent return to Vilnius in his 1812 Moscow campaign. Napoleon's massive army—the largest even seen in Europe till that time—arrived in Vilnius in late June 1812. In some quarters he was hailed as a hero. Lithuanian royalty believed he intended to liberate them from the Russians. In fact, he intended to place Lithuania under the domination of France.

Napoleon's arrival in Vilnius presaged the disasters he faced in the East. Massive thunderstorms broke out, miring his supply lines. There were large-scale defections in the ranks, numbering up to 50,000 soldiers who evaporated into the countryside and who came into violent conflict with the peasantry. Napoleon's army was so vast it could not be quartered in one place and made overwhelming demands on local supplies. Public buildings and churches were seized and put to military use. Napoleon also made demands on the citizenry. He ordered Lithuanian fodder to fill the gaps in his army. Each nobleman had to supply a certain number of men between the ages of 18 and 34.

Six months later in December Napoleon's broken army, reduced by several hundred thousand, staggered back to Vilnius, causing further chaos. Discipline had broken down and marauding bands of soldiers stormed through the city. Disease broke out, leading to the deaths of thousands. Thousands more froze to death. The situation became unmanageable—makeshift hospitals used corpses to insulate the windows and keep the cold out. In January 1813 frozen corpses were piled stories high outside buildings. The corpses banged like boards in the wind.

Petronele Falkewicz was the daughter of **Motiejus (Matthew) Falkewicz** and **Felicijona** (or **Apolonija**) **Ziemenas**. She was born 18 March 1827 in Pamerkys village, which is located to the immediate north of Zaltuny. She was baptized in Turgeliai church by Fr. Eustachijus Sutkewicz on March 21. Her godparents were Matausas Cernius and Kotryna Bizunas. We do not have her death record—it was after 1864.

Her parents Motiejus Falkewicz and Felicijona Ziemenas married in Turgeliai church on 28 August 1822. Fr. Atanazijus Ignatawicz officiated. Their witnesses were Motiejus Fedarawicz and Motiejus Prokopawicz. The church record reported that Motiejus was a widower. We do not have information about his first marriage. Both bride and groom were from Pamerkys village. The church registry does not indicate the names of their parents.

The Turgeliai Parish book reports the death of Apolonija Falkewicz in Pamerkys village on 18 October 1842. Her age was given as 35 years, but she was likely a few years older. The cause of death was "the brain disease", whatever this may be. She was buried by Fr. Mykolas Skrabauskas on October 20. The Parish record is hopelessly muddled. Her first name is different than the name in the marriage record and her maiden name is given as Kizine (?), but she is likely Petronele's mother, as the record states she left the widower Motiejus and the daughter Petronele.

Felicijona's family name was given variously as "Ziemenas" and as "Zenkewicz". In Petronele's marriage record the name was given as "Palciauska"! Even the relatively simple name "Falkewicz" was spelled variously as "Falkawska" and as "Falkauskas". Whatever it's true form, the name, like Bielawski, was quite common in the Turgeliai vicinity.

We don't know what the name "Falkewicz" translates as. The name "Bielawski" means "of the white place". It is a relatively common Polish name and can be found throughout Lithuania and Poland. The Lithuanian version is "Bieliauskas". Generally, the name derives from a locality, but the possibility that there was a low-order nobleman named Bielawski in Turgeliai Parish can't be excluded. Peasants sometimes assumed the names of local nobility.

We had an interesting experience on our visit to Lithuania in 2000. Mecislav Bieliauskas took us to the site of Zaltuny Cemetery (see Chapter 12). The Cemetery is long gone. The grounds are a vacant grassy field at the outskirts of the ruins of a creamery set off a well-maintained road. The only indications that the field held human remains were two headstones lying flat in the tall grass. It took a little effort for our party to find the stones. We made the search in a pouring rain.

The Polish wake resembles the Irish wake, but without the reputation. The body was usually waked in the home for two days. The family was expected to provide food and drink for the visitors. As in Ireland, wakes played an important social role. People from the countryside gathered and exchanged news and gossip. Distant relatives became re-acquainted. Speeches were made and lamentations uttered. After the burial the family held a dinner. This is a custom that persists to our own time.

The Lithuanians had a custom of collecting tears and placing them in vials that were buried with the dead person. The more grief, the more vials, and the greater the love demonstrated. The vials would be shown to the Ferryman on the way to the afterlife as a sign of the importance of the deceased. If the deceased had a lot of vials he might get a window seat. If he had a few he traveled steerage. If he had none, he got put to work in the coal house.

We've encountered tuberculosis several times in our history—we'll encounter it again. Perhaps it is time to more fully describe the "captain of the deaths of men", as Bunyan called it. Tuberculosis was a common and often fatal malady in previous decades in the industrialized nations—into the 1920s thousands of Americans died of it. To this day tuberculosis remains a ferocious killer in the developing nations of Africa and Asia. The culprit is a bacterium that mostly affects the lungs. The germs can be eaten or drunk, as in milk, but the usual means of infection is by inhalation. The bacteria become surrounded by waxy clusters of cells called "tubercules" secreted by the body in self-defense. If the tubercules open, the germs can affect other organ systems. Symptoms include fevers, coughing, chest pains, shortness of breath, and bleeding. The course of the disease is very variable—many people carry the tubercules their entire lives without incident. Cures became available only when antibiotics were developed. One of the first cures—streptomycin—was developed at Rutgers University in New Jersey.

Records have been located for five children of Juozas and Petronele Falkewicz. The children were: Antanas; Marijona; Mykolas; Kazimier; and Juozas. We can be fairly certain this is the complete family group as the five were listed in Juozas's death notice. All baptisms were in Turgeliai Parish.

Antanas Bielawski was born on 1 February 1849 and baptized on February 6. His godparents were Juozas Kadzewicz and Agota Bielawska. The priest was Fr. Antanas Sabaliawski. The village was given as Bagdziuliai, which is to the immediate south of Kalniskes.

Marijona Bielawska was born on 10 June 1852 in Bagdziuliai. She was baptized by Fr. Aleksandras Eidzetowicz on June 15. Her godparents were Juozas Lechnowicz and Anna Lechnowicz. She was alive in 1884, when she served as my grandfather's godmother. We have no other information on the lives of Antanas and Marijona.

Mykolas (Michael) Bielawski, my great-grandfather, was born on 29 September 1856 in Kalniskes village. He was baptized 14 October by Fr. Mackewicz. His godparents were Steponas Valeika and Marijona Liniauskas. Mykolas married Ursula Milosz on 15 February 1881. We were told by his daughter that he died in 1916. Details of his life will be narrated in Chapter 15.

Kazimier Bielawski was born 26 February 1859 in Kalniskes village. He was baptized March 4 by Fr. Mykolas Mironowicz. His godparents were Juozas Olechnowicz and Terese, the wife of Juozas Bagdzuilis. The latter way of writing the names of married woman was quite common in the Parish books. It was slightly sexist, to be sure, but slightly useful in developing family connections.

Juozas Bielawski, the fifth and last child, was born 1 March 1864 in Kalniskes village. He was baptized March 6 by Fr. Mironowicz. The godparents were Aleksandras Olechnowicz and Ona, wife of Mykolas Olechnowicz. This was three months before his father passed away. We have no information on the lives of Kazimier and Juozas.

The Polish did not adhere to rigid naming customs as did the Irish. The baby could be named after a grandparent or a relative. It was also the custom to christen the baby with the name of the saint on whose feast day the baptism fell. Relatives usually served as godparents, especially for the first few babies.

There were any number of superstitions associated with the christening. The godmother could not be pregnant—this would bring bad luck. A gold coin was placed inside the diaper—presumably, it was retrieved at a later point. My Aunt Blanche placed my sister Kathleen on the floor immediately after her baptism. I don't know the significance of this, but I don't think we wanted to find out what followed if the custom wasn't met.

We visited Kalniskes in 1997 and again in 2000. We were graciously received by my mother's cousin Michail Bielawski and his lovely wife Helene—our trips are described in *Genealogical Jaunts*. We didn't get to see much of Kalniskes and there didn't appear much to see. As with the townland in Erin, the village—*kaimas* in Lithuanian—is merely a scattering of farms without any central organization and nearly without any central road. On our first visit we literally drove across an open field to get to Michail's homestead. The word "Kalniskes" means "hilly" or "hill"—with the exception of one minor elevation, there didn't appear to be any hills in sight. This was once a province of Russia and the terrain resembles what we expect of Russia—dense forest interspersed with patches of groves and grassland. Indistinct views of Kalniskes and our other ancestral villages are available on *Google Lithuania*.

Mykolas lived in a different section of Kalniskes than his grandson Michail. We were taken to the site in 2000. It appeared to be a grove or orchard of some kind. The specific site pointed out to us was heavily overgrown with shrubbery—this vacant parcel of nature is our ancestral home in Kalniskes.

The village life of our Polish ancestors resembled that of our Irish people. The peasants were dependent on one another. There were considerable social obligations among villagers. Probably, everyone was distantly related. If not related, then bound through the Church and through shared farm labor.

The Lithuanian system resembled rundale in a number of ways. Families lived in clustered houses. The houses were usually small and built of logs with thatched roofs. Land was allotted in a three-tier system. Families got one parcel for personal use. The size of this parcel depended on the size of the family and could be adjusted as conditions changed. Potatoes, cabbages, and cucumbers were the usual vegetables. Our Polish ancestors consumed a nearly vegetarian diet. Meat was rarely eaten. As in Ireland, cows and pigs were raised for profit. Rainwater was the only means of irrigation. There were no bricks of bog to cut into fuel. Wood was used for fuel and it was readily available in the vast forests.

The other parcels were communally farmed. One parcel was reserved for pasturage—an important role for this parcel was to catch the manure used in tillage. The other parcel was used to farm grains like rye, wheat, and barley.

There was another way peasant life in Lithuania resembled peasant life in Ireland. Our Polish "rural persons" lived in a repressive society. They had minimal legal rights or resources. They did not own the land. They could make no changes to the land. They owed the nobility services, such as sharing in farming or transporting crops. They could not better themselves in socioeconomic status. They could not travel freely. They were frozen in place with little hope of bettering their situations or making independent lives for themselves.

This probably did not affect our ancestors, but Tsar Nicholas I instituted severe repressions of Lithuanian life in the middle of the nineteenth century. Russian became the official language. It was a crime to publish books or newspapers in Lithuanian. It was no longer possible to use Lithuanian in schools. Russian culture was declared to be the official culture. Leaving aside the aggressive effort to convert Catholics to the Orthodox faith, this could be said to be a premature version of what was attempted in the Soviet era.

We see one obvious change in this repression of language. The Parish registers copied by the Vilnius Archive change from Polish to Russian at this time period.

There was a large-scale and politically diffuse revolt in 1863, but it is doubtful our ancestors were involved in it. The revolt did establish a few reforms, including eased travel restrictions. And the revolt was severely suppressed. There were hundreds, if not thousands, of public hangings in the Old Town in Vilnius as a reprisal.

We visited the Church of the Assumption of the Virgin Mary in Turgeliai, the Parish of our Bielawski and Milosz ancestors. This is a ponderous red brick church that stands imposingly at a confluence of roads. There is a life-sized statue of Jesus behind the church. The appearance of the statue is startling, as it is in bright life-like colors. The Parish cemetery is located behind the church. This is a crowded and confused place as the paths fall and rise in a patternless, apparently unplanned, manner. In places we stood elevated over a vast array of stones and crosses. In other places we were in a pit surrounded by the markers of dead people. The effect was somewhat eerie—the mood wasn't helped by the drenching rain the day we visited.

There has been a church at this site since 1511. The first church, made of wood, burned in 1729. It was replaced by a second wood building that stood until 1836. Under the guidance of Fr. Mironowicz that church was demolished and replaced by a stone building with a vaulted ceiling. A rectory was constructed nearby in 1855. Additional buildings were added in 1884 under the sponsorship of Fr. Kiprijonas Zebrowski, a priest of some note. In 1895 – 1905 the church was rebuilt and expanded. Side aisles were added and the roof was raised. A new entrance was built. Two square towers were added. The church survived World War Two, but renovations had to be made in the 1950s.

Chapter Seven

~

Lietuva—Jonas Milosz & Magdalena Asakewicz

Our second Polish great-great-grandparents on the paternal side are **Jonas Milosz** and **Magdalena Asakewicz** of Malakonys village in Turgeliai Parish. The surname Milosz is pronounced "Me-wosh". Asakewicz is pronounced "A-sa-kay-vitch." We have a lot of details on these families and can trace our ancestry through nine generations on the Asakewicz side. We haven't reached the San people—we haven't even reached the Apostolic Succession—but this is impressive, considering the peasant stock of our ancestors, the events in Europe that destroyed so many things, and the fact that we didn't have a single piece of information when we started.

Jonas and Magdalena were married in Turgeliai church by Fr. Mykolas Skraubawski on 15 November 1842. Their witnesses were Jonas Dulkis, Juozas Dulkis, Jonas Petkewicz, and others. Jonas was described as 23 years of age, Magdalena as 18. Both were from Malakonys village, which is located a mile or two to the north of Kalniskes. The marriage record gave the name of Jonas's father as **Juozas Milosz**. His mother's personal name was **Viktorija**. Unfortunately, her family name was not indicated.

There is a baptism record extant in Turgeliai Parish for an individual named Jonas Milosz. He was born 9 December 1816 and baptized December 11. His godparents were Antanas Jurewicz and Teresa Pilecka. The priest was Fr. Policarp Hermanas. The village was not indicated. His parents were **Jurgis**—not Juozas—**Milosz** and **Viktorija Petrusewicz**. It's likely, but we can't say for sure that the Jonas Milosz born in 1816 was the same person who married Magdalena Asakewicz. The priest may have made a mistake, writing "Juozas" for "Jurgis" (George). We've discovered priests made a lot of mistakes in the Parish books—only the head priest at Rome is infallible and maybe not about this. There was a second Milosz family in residence in Malakonys in the early years of the nineteenth century. A man named **Juozas Milosz** was married to **Justina Prokopawicz**—no record has been located for a son named "Jonas" in their family. The surnames Petrusewicz and Prokopawicz appear as godparents in our Milosz family. The fact that we can't identify with certainty the maternal line Jonas descended from—Petrusewicz or Prokopawicz—makes it impossible to identify siblings.

The death record of Jonas Milosz exists. He died of pneumonia in Malakonys village on 26 June 1869. He was buried in Turgeliai Cemetery by Fr. Jonas Barkauski on June 28. His age was given as 48 years—if he was born in 1816, his age would be 54. The death record stated that he left the widow Magdalena, the sons Motiejus, Kazimier, and Tomas, and the daughters Ursula, Regina, and Tekle.

Magdalena Asakewicz was the daughter of **Jokubas (Jacob) Asakewicz** and **Kristina Vaiciulewicz**. She was born 8 July 1824 in Malakonys and baptized July 19 by Fr. Simon Vysniauski. Her godparents were Ludvikas Usinawicz and Anna Prokopawicz.

Magdalena died in Malakonys "of old age" on 4 February 1899. Her age was 74. She was buried in Turgeliai Cemetery—the date was not specified. The priest was Fr. P. Sepeckis. She left the sons Motiejus and Kazimier.

We have records for two of Magdalena'a siblings. **Marijona Asakewicz** was born 5 April 1826 in Malakonys village. She was baptized in Turgeliai Parish on April 11 by Fr. Eustachijus Sutkewicz. Her godparents were Jonas Dulka and Elzbieta Dulka.

Laurynas Asakewicz was born 27 July 1831 in Malakonys village. He was baptized in Turgeliai Parish on August 2. The priest was Juozas Gineta. His godparents were Petras Slenkawicz and Marijona Kasneriene. At some point Laurynas married Anele Limosa. A son, Felix, was born 14 November 1865. We have no other information on the lives of Marijona and Laurynas.

The Vilnius Archive located records pertaining to Magdalena's parents. Jokubas Asakewicz and Kristina Vaiciulewicz married on 16 September 1823 in Turgeliai Parish. Their witnesses were Tomas Dulka and Jonas Kazlauski. The priest was Fr. Karol Mikalauski. Both were described as residing in Kazimierskes village, which is located to the immediate west of Malakonys.

Jokubas Asakewicz was the son of **Petras Asakewicz** and **Kotryna Scerba**—they are my great-great-great-great-grandparents—at this level we need exponents to keep track of the generations. Jokubas was born 2 July 1802 in Valakininkai village, which is located to the immediate north of Malakonys. He was baptized July 6 in Turgeliai Parish. His godparents were Jonas Scerba and Kotryna Sveiskovska. The priest was Fr. Brunas Bernackis.

Jokubas Asakewicz died in Malakonys "of fever" on 15 August 1842. He was buried on August 17 in Turgeliai Cemetery. The priest was Fr. Michail Skrabawski. Jokubas was 39 years of age. He left the widow Kristina, the son Laurynas, and the daughter Marijona. Magdalena was not named. He died three months before her wedding.

Petras Asakewicz and Kotryna Scerba married on 18 February 1798 in Turgeliai Parish. Their witnesses were Simonas Tribockis and Petras Satkewicz. The priest was Stanislav Venslauskas. The village was not indicated. Petras and Kotryna were born during the American Revolution or prior. I'm happy to say that we have pushed our ancestry into the eighteenth century. This record encompasses nine generations in our family's history.

The Archive located records for three siblings of Jokubas—these are the known children of Petras Asakewicz and Kotryna Scerba.

Simonas Asakewicz was born 7 October 1809 in Valakininkai village. He was baptized October 10 by Fr. Leonas Puzyna. His godparents were Kazimier Drozda and Marijona Markewicz.

Viktorija-Tekle Asakewicz was born 16 April 1812 in Pavlovas village. She was baptized April 18 by Fr. Jokubas Koralewicz. Her godparents were Tedeusz Delkewicz and Antanina Petrowska.

Feliks Asakewicz was born 16 November 1814 in Dobranovina village. He was baptized November 19 by Fr. Zacharius Bablauski. His godparents were Jonas Zyla and Marijona Talkewicz. Dobranovina and Pavlovas villages are to the immediate east of Malakonys.

Kristina Vaiciulewicz was the daughter of **Jurgis Vaiciulewicz** and **Viktorija Rybacanas**—in Lithuanian it's Rybacankaite. She was born in Bajorai village on 16 December 1800. Bajorai village is to the immediate east of Malakonys. She was baptized in Turgeliai Parish by Fr. Silvestras Rozewicz on the same day. Her godparents were Jonas Zenkewicz and

Kristina Sabotas. As with Petras Asakewicz and Kotryna Scerba, identifying Kristina's parents carries us nine generations back from my great nephews. Their marriage record was not found, but it was in the 1790s.

Kristina's death record is extant. Kristina died in Malakonys "of inflammation" on 24 March 1850. She was buried on March 26 by Fr. Antanas Sabaliawski. Kristina's age was given as 50 years. She left the son Laurynas and the daughters Marijona and Magdalena.

Kristina's mother Viktorija Vaiciulewicz died on 3 March 1806 in Bajorai village. No information as to the cause was given. Her age was listed as 30 years. She was buried in Turgeliai cemetery. If accurate, Viktorija was born before the American Revolution.

Jurgis Vaiciulewicz remarried after Viktorija died. This was to Marijona Dulka on 4 November 1806 in Turgeliai Parish. The priest was Fr. Kajetonas Keleris. The witnesses were Jonas Serba (Scerba?) and Tomas Dulka. This marriage may explain the many instances that members of the Dulka family served as witnesses and as godparents to Jurgis's descendents.

Jurgis Vaiciulewicz died "of the old age" on 13 January 1831 in Bajorai village. He was buried "in the village cemetery" by Fr. Vladislovas Drukteinis on January 15. He age was given as 80 years, which places his birth in the 1750s and is likely an exaggeration. He left the widow Marijona and the sons Matausas, Kazimier, and Motiejus.

Marijona Vaiciulewicz died "of the fever" on 13 March 1847 in Bajorai village. She was buried by Fr. Mykolas Grabowickis on March 15. Her age was given as 80 years, which places her birth in the 1760s. Her three sons survived her.

The Vilnius Archive found records for two siblings of Kristina. They are the children of Jurgis Vaiciulewicz and Viktorija Rybacanas.

Agota Vaiciulewicz was born on 31 December 1798 in Bajorai village. She was baptized by Fr. Franciszk Alsauskas on the same day. Her godparents were Jurgis Karazinas and Kristina Prokopawicz.

Kotryna Vaiciulewicz was born on 21 September 1805 in Bajorai village. Fr. Feliksas Cieskauskas baptized her in Turgeliai church on September 22. The godparents were Jurgis Sobatas and Ona Dulkas.

Petras Asakewicz and Jurgis Vaiciulewicz and their wives lived through a tumultuous period in Lithuanian history. Under the enlightened leadership of King Stanislaw Augustus Poniatowski the Commonwealth of Poland and Lithuania produced the first written constitution in Europe. Published in 1791, the constitution was modeled on the American constitution. It established separation of powers and sovereignty for the nobles and bourgeois classes. (The peasant class was excluded—we might expect this.) Reactionaries in Europe saw the constitution as a threat to monarchies. Catherine the Great of Russia invaded Poland and took over a sizeable chunk of territory. Tadeusz Kosciuzko, a hero of the American Revolution, led an insurrection in 1794. His defeat led to the "partition" of Poland and Lithuania in 1795. They disappeared as independent countries and became provinces of Russia, Austria, and Prussia. Lithuania fell to the Russian sphere. A century of repression followed. Lithuania emerged briefly as an independent country after World War One, but in a truncated form as Poland, its former ally, invaded Vilnius and claimed the eastern half of the country. Lithuania disappeared again after World War Two, enduring four decades of Soviet stupefaction. Lithuania did not regain its 1795 borders and recover as an independent nation until the Soviet Union broke up in 1991.

We have a large number of records for the children of Jonas Milosz and Magdalena Asakewicz. All births were in Malakonys village. All baptisms were in Turgeliai Parish. Their children were: Ona; Motiejus; Kazimier; Tomas; Marijona; Ursula; Kristina; and Tekle.

Ona Milosz was born on 26 November 1843. She was baptized on December 5 by Fr. Mykolas Skrabawski. Her godparents were Juozas Milosz and Kristina, wife of Juozas Dulkis. Anna died in childhood in Malakonys on 5 July 1845. She was buried on July 7 in Turgeliai Cemetery by Fr. Zigmantis Monkewicz.

Motiejus Milosz was born 6 January 1847. He was baptized by Fr. Skrabawski on January 12. His godparents were Jurgis Prokopawicz and Marijona, wife of Petras Prokopawicz. Motiejus died of pneumonia in Malakonys on 7 March 1907. He was sixty years of age. He was buried in Turgeliai Cemetery by Fr. Steponas Verzbauskas. He was survived by his widow Marijona and son Martynas.

Motiejus married Marijona Satkewicz in Turgeliai on 5 July 1870. The witnesses were Jonas Butkewicz, Andrius Klimasawski, and Motiejus Karpawicz. Fr. Jeronimas Grigarawicz presided.

Marijona was the daughter of Jokubas Satkewicz and Ona Bogusas and the granddaughter of Jonas Bogusas and Rozalia Bielawska of Kalniskes village. Marijona was born 27 November 1850 in Kalniskes. She was baptized December 3 by Fr. Antanas Sabaliauski. Her godparents were Alexandras Juchnewicz and Agota Bielawska. We don't know when

Marijona died, but it was after Motiejus. We don't know what the relationships were among Rozalia, Agota, and Juozas Bielawski, but it's likely they were siblings.

Motiejus and Marijona had one known child, **Martynas**, who died circa 1934. (We don't know when he was born.) Martynas had eight children, one of whom we met on our 2000 visit to Malakonys. This is how the encounter is described in *Genealogical Jaunts*:

> "Despite being closer to civilization, as we understand the word, Malakonys looked in poorer repair than Girdziunai. The houses were dilapidated and none that I saw was painted. Hens ran everywhere and a truck with a cow pulled up as we arrived. Nothing in the surrounding countryside looked to be under cultivation other than small vegetable gardens at the sides of the houses.
>
> "Emilia [our guide] asked a tall young lady tending one of these gardens if she knew anyone by the family name of Milosz. The young lady replied that her mother was named Milosz and that she would run to get her mother. Which she did on the instant, leaving a toddler to cry insistently for 'Mama'.
>
> "Presently, two middle-aged ladies appeared, one of whom was the mother. We started to make inquiries, when they said they would get their father. Which they did on the instant. They returned with a gentleman of eighty-nine years. Which he looked. He was short and somewhat stocky. He had bright blue eyes and thick white hair. He walked with a cane and his right arm shook dramatically [26]."

Kazimier Milosz, the son of Jonas Milosz and Magdalena Asakewicz, was born on 6 March 1850. He was baptized on March 19 by Fr. Sabaliauski. His godparents were Kazimier Daskewicz and Justina Jankelewicz. Kazimier died "of inflammation" in Malakonys on 8 January 1911. He was sixty years of age. He was buried in Turgeliai Cemetery by Fr. J. Jankauski. The date was not given. His son Antanas was listed as his survivor.

Kazimier married Viktorija Vilkinis on 1 June 1873. Their witnesses were Mykolas Kisielius (?), Laurynas Prokopawicz, Jonas Satkewicz and others. Fr. Bonaventuras Voisiata (?) presided.

Viktorija was the daughter of Juozas Vilkinis and Marijona Kuralawicz. Her age on the marriage register was 19, so she would have been born circa 1854. Viktorija died "of inflammation" in Malakonys on 24 August 1909. She was survived by Kazimier and by their son Antanas. Her age was given as 59.

Kazimier and Viktorija Milosz had the following known children: Stanislaw; Juozas; Terese; Antanas; Jonas; Mykolas; and Povilas. All births were in Malakonys. All baptisms and burials were in Turgeliai Parish. We know nothing of their lives.

Stanislav Milosz was born on 4 November 1874. He was baptized by Fr. Dilkewicz on November 10. His godparents were Stanislav Satkewicz and Ona, the wife of Jonas Grebstunas. Stanislav died on 10 February 1875 at three months of age.

Juozas Milosz was born on 20 March 1876. He was baptized by Fr. Voisiata on March 25. His godparents were Stanislav Satkewicz and Elena Bisauskas. Juozas died "of the spasms" in childhood on 14 February 1880.

Terese Milosz was born on 19 August 1879. She was baptized by Fr. Sakauskas on September 2. Godparents were Mykolas Satkewicz and my great-grandmother Ursula Milosz. Terese died in childhood on 28 May 1882.

Antanas Milosz was born on 1 October 1882. He was baptized by Fr. Zebrowski on October 24. Godparents were Laurynas Prokopawicz and Ona Jankauskas. Antanas was alive in 1911.

Jonas Milosz was born on 5 September 1885. He was baptized by Fr. Zebrowski on September 9. The godparents were Tomas Stolenkawski and Regina, the wife of Antanas Dulke. Jonas died "of the measles" in childhood on 21 January 1892.

Mykolas Milosz was born on 26 September 1888. He was baptized by Fr. Zebrowski on October 23. Godparents were my great-grandfather Mykolas Bielawski and Marijona, the wife of Mykolas Dulke.

Povilas Milosz was born 21 July 1892. He was baptized by Fr. Zebrowski on July 26. Godparents were Motiejus Simikewicz and Marijona, wife of Feliks Sobotas.

Tomas Milosz, the son of Jonas Milosz and Magdalena Asakewicz, was born on 8 January 1854. He was baptized January 17. His godparents were Petras Prokopawicz and Kotryna, wife of Andrius Rincewicz. The priest was Fr. Aleksandras Eiditawicz. Tomas was alive in 1882. No other information is available.

Marijona Milosz was born on 7 October 1857 and baptized on October 13. Her godparents were Mykolas Prokopawicz and Viktorija, wife of Mykolas Giruleckas. Marijona died in infancy on 6 August 1858. She was buried in Turgeliai Cemetery by Fr. Jeronimas Vertusinski on August 8.

Ursula Milosz, my great-grandmother, was born on 9 November 1859. She was baptized by Fr. Vertusinski on November 15. Her godparents were Steponas Valeika and Ona, the wife of Baltramiejus Markewicz. An individual named Steponas Valeika also stood as godfather to her husband—we're not sure of the significance of this. Ursula married Mykolas Bielawski on 15 February 1881. She died in Kalniskes while giving birth on 16 April 1889. She was 29 years of age. She was buried in Turgeliai Cemetery. Details of her life will be presented in Chapter 15.

Kristina Milosz was born on 2 March 1864 and baptized on March 3 by Fr. A. Mirinawicz. Her godparents were Mykolas Jankewicz and Ona, wife of Baltramiejus Markewicz. There is no other information on Kristina's life—perhaps she is the "Regina" mentioned in her father's death record.

Tekle Milosz was born 29 March 1869. She was baptized April 6 by Fr. Juozas Barkawski. Her godparents were Motiejus Karpawicz and Kotryna, the wife of Petras Petrusewicz. Tekle was born three months before her father died. She was a change of life baby—Magdalena was 44 years of age at this time. Tekle—the name is distinctly Russian—died in childhood "of throat inflammation" on 15 October 1875. She was buried by Fr. Dilkewicz in Turgeliai Cemetery on October 18.

Chapter Eight

Lietuva—Tomas Storta & Agota Karuzas

My great-great Polish grandparents on the maternal side are **Tomas Storta** and **Agota Karuzas** and **Motiejus Juchnewicz** and **Kristina Blazys**. Both couples resided in Girdziunai village, which lies around 40 miles south of Vilnius on the border of Lithuania in that little comma or tail that extends into the present-day country of Belarus. People of a scholarly temperament call the locale the "Dieveniskes Appendix" after the largest town in the region. People of a less scholarly temperament call it "little comma or tail". This chapter documents the extensive records the Vilnius Archive provided on the Storta line. The following chapter documents the less extensive records we have on the Juchnewicz aide.

Tomas Storta married Agota Karuzas in Subotniki church on 21 January 1851. Their witnesses were Tomas Grita, Petras Kildanowicz, and Franciszk Kliukaitis. Fr. Karol Rukuiza presided.

The baptisms, weddings, and funerals of our Girdziunai ancestors were in the Church of St. George in Subotniki, the Parish town. Subotniki is nine miles from Dieveniskes and approximately 60 miles from Vilnius. In the Middle Ages the region belonged to the Radziwill clan. The town had a railroad station, a mill, a brewery, and a church. In 1882 the population was 523 inhabitants. In the nineteenth century the entire region was a province of Russia. In our time Subotniki lies a few miles inside Belarus. This has caused consternation among the people in Girdziunai, as they have to get documents to cross the border to go to church.

Tomas Storta was the son of **Laurynas Storta** and **Elzbieta Herodzas**. Tomas was born 17 August 1822. He was baptized in Subotniki Parish on

August 20. Fr. Juozas Laskowski presided. His godparents were Jokubas Scikna and Elzbieta Uliawicz. Tomas's death record has not been located.

Laurynas Storta and Elzbieta Herodzas married in Subotniki on 2 February 1814. Their witnesses were Laurynas Klukoye, Jokubas Hieroda, and Jurgis Hrytowicz. Fr. Laskowski presided. It is possible that Laurynas Storta was the son of **Laurynas Storta** and **Magdalena**—unfortunately, the family name was not indicated in the Parish record. The Vilnius Archive located a baptism record for their son **Gabriel Storta**. Gabriel was born on 18 September 1801 and baptized on September 22. His godparents were Jonas Beinoras and Ona Juchnewicz.

The Archive located records for three additional children of Laurynas Storta and Elzbieta Herodzas—they are Tomas's sisters.

Marijona Storta was born 22 November 1817 and baptized on November 23. Her godparents were Laurynas Klukoye and Marijona Stankewicz. The priest was Fr. Juozas Iwanowski.

Marcele Storta was born 20 November 1820 and baptized on November 23. Her godparents were Motiejus Jurasas and Elzbieta Janawicz. The priest was Fr. Jurgis Zukowski. (Marcele is a version of Marcella.)

Agota Storta was born 4 September 1825 and baptized on September 6. Her godparents were Motiejus Uliawicz and Kotryna Storta. The priest was Fr. A. Dziadekonski. We know nothing of the lives of Tomas's sisters. Agota may have served as godmother to one of her brother's sons in 1863.

Agota Karuzas (or Karuza) was the daughter of **Franciszk Karuzas** and **Ona Sarulis**. Agota was born 26 March 1831 in Pavydonys village, which is located a few miles north of Girdziunai. She was baptized on March 28 in Dieveniskes Parish by Fr. Juozas Petrawicz. Her godparents were Juozas Baidanas and Regina, nee Ustinawicz. Agota's death record has not been located. Both she and Tomas Storta were listed in the 1859 Census of Girdziunai. Both were alive in 1874.

The marriage record of Franciszk Karuzas and Ona Sarulis has not been located. The Vilnius Archive located the baptism record of Agota's bother. **Mykolas Karuzas** was born in Pavadonys on 17 September 1833. He was baptized September 18 by Fr. Petrawicz. His godparents were Kristupas Sarulis and Antanina Janawicz. We have no other information on his life.

The Vilnius Archive found the death record of Franciszk Karuzas. He died "of fever" on 8 May 1838 in Pavydonys village. His age was given as

40 years. He left the widow Ona and the children Agota and Mykolas. He was buried in Dieveniskes Parish Cemetery.

Ona Karuzas remarried after the death of Franciszk. This was to the happily named Jonas Plusta. The date was 25 June 1839. Jonas was described as a widower and as the son of Tomas Plusta and Kotryna Karuzas—Kotryna was likely related to Franciszk in some manner. Their witnesses were Jonas Artiomas (?) and Andrius Karuzas. The priest was Fr. Petrawicz. Ona's age was given as 30, her village as Chamuciai in Dieveniskes Parish. Chamuciai is located a few miles to the east of Dieveniskes. The name of Jonas's village was Miedzionys, which is located to the northwest of Dieveniskes. We have no other information on the Plusta family or whether Ona had additional children.

Ona's marriage record supplied the names of her parents—**Mykolas Sarulis** and **Agota Baidanas**. As with the Asakewicz and Vaiculewicz families, this is nine generations from the births of my great nephews.

As in Ireland, parties to a wedding in Lithuania stayed within religious and socioeconomic classes. There were professional matchmakers, but they were used only for hapless individuals. Generally, couples met in the same way couples meet nowadays—through mutual friends and family contacts.

In the early period the wedding was held in the home of the bride. There was an informal gathering of the families before the wedding. Unlike in America or Ireland, in Lithuania the bride's family played less of a role in hosting the wedding feast. This role was assumed by a "host" and "hostess" who usually were older people of means. The bride wore a wedding dress to the service. She carried a piece of salted bread in her undergarments to ensure a good marriage. She also carried a coin to ensure wealth. After the ceremony the couple was showered with flowers or with grain. Rice was not known in nineteenth century Lithuania. Gifts tended to be practical—the newlyweds would not be disappointed if farm implements and livestock were given as gifts.

Polish surnames can be daunting. There's no "Forde" or "Hunt" in these church registers. The surname *Storta* looks simple enough, but deriving its origin is not easy. It is not Polish or Lithuanian, unless it is a corruption of the surnames *Storasta* or *Storista*. (Storta is more commonly an Italian surname.) A village elder told Danislav Storta—see Chapter 13—that the original Storta in Girdziunai was either French or American. It doesn't appear likely the latter is correct, but the name may be French.

Russia employed French mercenaries in their eighteenth century wars with Sweden (a large one ending around 1720, a smaller one in the 1790s). There is a French word "*storto*" meaning "one-eyed" and pronounced "Stor-ta". My grandmother's brother Stanley had an eye turned white. There is no other related occurrence of this condition, so it might be a stretch to think a French mercenary stayed behind or was left behind.

It could be a Swede mercenary stayed behind. There is a Swedish word "*storta*" with the accent on the "o" that means "crush or overthrow". There is also a Swedish word "*storta*" with the accent over the "a" that means "big toe". I tend to think I like it better when the accent falls over the "o".

The surname Storta is quite infrequent in Lithuania and in Poland. It's localized between Dieveniskes and Subotniki and in the Jelena Gora region of southwestern Poland. Probably, people from Lithuania resettled— or were resettled—after the World War in Jelena Gora. There was an immigration of Stortas from Girdziunai and from the Subotniki vicinity in the early 1900s. People from the former vicinity settled in Jersey City, the people from the latter in Bayonne [27].

We do not know the origin of the *Herodzas* surname or where it is localized. The name was also spelled as "Herodas" and as "Hieroda". (The name may also appear as "Arodas".) After the outlawing of Polish (and Lithuanian) as official languages the name was spelled in the church records using Russian as "Gorodzas" or "Gorodas"—the letter "H" does not appear in the Russian language.

As with Herodzas we do not know the origin or distribution of the surnames *Karuzas*, *Sarulis*, or *Baidanas*. Karuzas was written inconsistently in the church registers as "Karuza" and as "Choruzis", which is how it may have sounded. Sarulis and Baidanas do not sound distinctively Slavic. Girdziunai lies in a heavily Polish region of Lithuania, but the area was an ethnic melting pot. The area had seen the tramp of armies—French, Swedish, German, and Russian. Certainly the tendency to end names with "—as" and "—is" looks quite different than what we saw in the Turgeliai region 20 or 30 miles to the north.

We have a number of records for the children of Tomas Storta and Agota Karuzas. Their known children were: Elzbieta; Kazimier; Franciszk; Juozas; and Marijona. It's likely not a complete list, as there was a long interval between the first and second child.

Elzbieta Storta was born 1 January 1852 and baptized January 6 by Fr. Rukuiza. Her godparents were Ignotis Kliokaitis and Marijona, the wife of Jonas Gorodis.

Kazimier Storta was born 1 March 1858 and baptized on March 2. His godparents were Vincentas Bikis (or Bilis) and Anna Satkovska. The priest was Fr. B. Sarosieska (?). We have no other information on the lives of Elzbieta or Kazimier.

Franciszk Storta, my great-grandfather, was born on 22 March 1860. He was baptized on March 25 by Fr. A. Znoma. His godparents were Vincentas Bikis and Marijona Arodzas. Franciszk married Rozalia Juchnewicz on 25 April 1882. He died 28 January 1911 in Girdziunai at age 50. He was buried in Subotniki. His son erected a stone that stands to this day. Franciszk's life will be described in Chapter 13.

Juozas Storta was born 10 March 1863 and baptized by Fr. Znosko on March 17. His godparents were Juozas Arodas and Agota Storta. No other information is available.

The Vilnius Archive found the death record of **Marijona Storta**. Marijona died at nine months of age on 15 December 1874. She was buried in Subotniki cemetery. If the date is correct Marijona was a change of life baby. Her mother was 43 years of age.

Chapter Nine

~

Lietuva—Motiejus Juchnewicz & Kristina Blazys

My second maternal great-great-grandparents are **Motiejus Juchnewicz** and **Kristina Blazys**. They married on 11 July 1843 in Dieveniskes Parish. Their witnesses were Petras Pruskawicz, Tomas Juchnewicz, and Simon Wasilewski. The priest was Petras Jakawicz. Motiejus was from Girdziunai. Kristina was from Vaisutkiai village, which is located to the northeast of Girdziunai.

Motiejus was 39 years old at the time of the wedding, which is fairly late for a peasant to marry. We don't know why he married at this age. There is no indication in the record, but a possibility is that he served in the Russian army. A number of peasants from each estate were required to join the Tsar's army. Service could last as long as eighteen years.

Motiejus was the son of **Jonas Juchnewicz** and **Kristina Milksys**. (In Lithuanian the name is "Miksyte". It also appears as "Miksza" and as "Mikszan".) He was born in Girdziunai on 12 February 1804 and baptized on February 13. His godparents were Motiejus Jursu and Marija Horonas (Heroniowa). Motiejus died 5 April 1862 and was buried on April 7 in Subotniki. He left the widow Kristina. The names of no children were recorded. Neither was the cause of death. His age was given as 70, which was off by 12 years. Perhaps the priest meant to write 60 years.

The Vilnius Archive did not locate a marriage record for Jonas and Kristina—they were born in the eighteenth century. The Archive found a record for the brother of Motiejus. This was **Baltramiejus Juchnewicz**. Baltramiejus was born 23 August 1802 and baptized on August 24. His godparents were Jurgis Juchnewicz and Rozalia Juruszewa.

Motiejus was described as 55 on the 1859 Census of Girdziunai. Kristina was described as 41. In the Census an individual named Agota Juchnewicz, aged 51, resided with them, as did Anna, aged 31, and described as "the sister". Agota was likely the widow (or wife) of Baltramiejus and Kristina was her sister.

Kristina Blazys was the daughter of **Antanas Blazys** and **Franciska Juchnewicz**. She was born in Vaisutkiai village on 16 March 1821. She was baptized in Dieveniskes Parish on April 3. Her godparents were Jonas Tomelaitis and Marcele Kropais. The priest was Fr. Kazimier Valickis. We do not know when she died—it was after 1859.

Antanas Blazys died on 28 May 1824 in Vaisutkiai village. His age was given as 49, which places his birth in the 1770s. He was buried May 29 in Dieveniskes Parish Cemetery. No cause of death was listed. The marriage record of Antanas and Franciska has not been located.

The Vilnius Archive provided records for a number of Kristina's siblings: Matausas; Adomas; Ona; Agota; Jonas Antanas; Franciska; Andrius; and Marijona. All births occurred in Vaisutkiai village. Baptisms and burials were in Dieveniskes. We do not know anything about their lives.

Matausas (Matthew) Blazys was born 14 September 1806. He was baptized on September 16 by Fr. Kazimier Chrapovickis. His godparents were Adomas Scerba and Kotryna Blazys. (Adomas would not be related to Kotryna Scerba, wife of Petras Asakewicz.)

Adomas Blazys was born 14 August 1808. Fr. Chrapovickis baptized him on August 16. Godparents were Adomas Scerba and Kotryna Blazys.

Ona Blazys was born on 14 June 1810 and baptized by Fr. Valickis on June 20. Her godparents were Matausas Blazewicz and Marijona Scerba.

Agota Blazys was born on 13 July 1812 and baptized by Fr. Valickis on July 14. Her godparents were Jonas Tomelaitis and Ursula Blazys.

Jonas Antanas Blazys was born on 5 June 1814 and baptized by Fr. Valickis on June 7. His godparents were Franciszk Ulickis and Franciska Kropais.

Franciska Blazys was born 11 June 1816 and baptized by Fr. Valickis on June 18. Her godparents were Stanislav Juchnewicz and Marcele Kropais. Franciska died on 8 February 1826 at the age of nine. No cause of death was indicated. She was buried on February 9 in Dieveniskes Cemetery.

Andrius Blazys was born 18 November 1818 and baptized by Fr. Valickis on November 24. His godparents were Stanislav Juchnewicz and Marcele Kropais.

Marijona Blazys was born 18 January 1824. She was baptized by Fr. Juozas Petrawicz on January 20. Her godparents were Tomas Maluzis and Marijona Kropais. Marijona died "of the fever" on 11 May 1832. She was eight years old. She was buried on May 13 in Dieveniskes Cemetery. Marijona's birth places an upper limit on Kristina Blazys age—Kristina would have been born in the 1780s.

The surname *Juchnewicz* also appears in the Parish records as "Juchniewicz". There were five families—possibly more—with the Juchnewicz surname in Girdziunai in the 1810s. There were three families in the 1859 Census: Motiejus and Kristina; Tomas Juchnewicz, aged 46, and his wife Anna; and Gabriel Juchnewicz, aged 57, and his wife Ona. We don't know how these families were related.

The surname *Blazys* was also spelled "Blazuk" and "Blazewicz" by the archivists, but it is not clear whether that was a quirk of the researcher— or of the priest. Names ending in "uk" are distinctly Russian. We're not certain what the name Blazys means, but the suggestion has been made that it relates to St. Blaise, patron of sore throats.

We have a few records for the children of Motiejus Juchnewicz and Kristina Blazys. All births took place in Girdizunai. Baptisms and burials were in Subotniki church.

Jonas Jurgis Juchnewicz was born in Girdziunai on 29 November 1845. His godparents were Tomas Juchnewicz and Magdalena Wasilewska. The priest was Fr. Mykolis Jurewicz. Jonas died in infancy on 7 February 1846. He was buried in Subotniki on February 9. Fr. Franciszk Zavisa presided.

Motiejus Juchnewicz was born 18 September 1847. He was baptized September 21 by Fr. Zavisa. His godparents were Tomas Juchnewicz and Anna Jurutis [28].

Tomas Juchnewicz was born 11 May 1850 and baptized by Fr. Rukuiza on May 14. His godparents were Laurynas Mackewicz and Ona Videicis.

Kristina Juchnewicz was born 22 December 1851. She was baptized by Fr. Rukuiza on December 30. Her godparents were Mykolis Wasilewski and Agota, the wife of Laurynas Mackewicz.

Marijona Juchnewicz died 4 February 1856. She was buried in Subotniki by Fr. B. Soroska. Her age was given as two years. No baptism record has been located.

Rozalia Juchnewicz was my great-grandmother and the daughter of Motiejus Juchnewicz and Kristina Blazys. Her baptism record has not been found—she is my single Polish great-grandparent for whom we lack a baptism record. This deficit may be due to a mistake of the priest. There are two records that may qualify as her baptism record. In both cases the priest indicated the surname was Juchnewicz in the index of the register but wrote different information in the text. The older record was for Rozalia Mickewicz, born on 31 December 1854 in Lintupe village. Her parents were Kazimier Mickewicz and Marijona Juralewicz. The second, and more likely record, was for the baptism of Rozalia Juchnewicz dated 24 September 1859. The priest wrote the parents' names as Tomas Korvackis and Karolina Kacinska. Godparents were Laurynas Bilis and Marijona Pucka. No village was indicated.

Rozalia Juchnewicz married Franciszk Storta on 25 April 1882. She died 4 February 1920. She was buried in Subotniki Cemetery. Her age was given as 62, which places her birth in 1858. It can't be any earlier than this, since her last child was born in 1901, when she would have been in her early 40s. And it can't be later than 1862 when her father died.

Girdziunai is a small village of around thirty homesteads located along a single lane. We visited our Storta home in 1997 and in 2000. On both occasions we were lavishly dined by Danislav Storta, my mother's first cousin, and his family. The village is located deep in the woods. Access to it is along deeply rutted and nearly inaccessible dirt roads. There's a steep rise on the southern side of the village. The farms lie in that direction. So does the Belarus border. The river Gauja runs in the woods to the immediate north. The word "river" is a little misleading—the river's span was no more than a few feet wide. There are telephone wires and automobiles, but there is no in-door plumbing. Privies stand amid the barns and woodpiles. Wood is used for fuel. I'm sure there's a great need for fuel. The winters must be very harsh.

Tomas Storta and his descendents resided at the entrance of the village. The home of Motiejus Juchnewicz was at the opposite side. Interestingly, the road simply comes to a stop in the woods past where the Juchnewicz family lived, so the village is literally at the end of the road—this makes sense given the location of Girdziunai at the very basement of Lithuania. The layout of the roads can be seen on Google maps.

The word "Girdziunai" is pronounced "Yur-shem-me". It means "the forest listens". We like to think to good things.

Chapter Ten

~

Erin—Thomas Forde and Mary Hunt

My Irish great-grandparents are **Thomas Forde** and **Mary Hunt** of Derrynacong, County Mayo, and **Denis Griffin** and **Ellen Allen** of Trippul West, County Kerry. This chapter examines the lives of Thomas Forde and Mary Hunt. The following chapter examines the lives and family of Denis Griffin and Ellen Allen.

Thomas Forde and Mary Hunt married in St. Patrick's Chapel at Garranlahan in Kiltullagh Parish in County Roscommon on 7 May 1884. (He obtained a certificate of release from the Annagh Parish priest on May 6.) Their witnesses were Michael Tully and Kate Fitzmaurice. The priest was Fr. P. (or R.) Molloy. Tom resided in Derrynacong at the time of the wedding, Mary in Laughil. Both were literate. Their fathers were deceased. The occupation of their fathers was given as "laborers".

Tom Forde was the son of Patrick Forde and Bridget Freeman. He was born in Derrynacong on 4 July 1856 and was baptized by Fr. William Scully on July 7. His godparents were Henry and Anne Hamrock of Leow townland. There are three records of Tom's baptism in the Parish books. One is a barely readable scrawl in the Annagh register. One is a carefully written record in the Bekan Parish book. The third is an 1870 copy in the Bekan Parish book—at some point a priest rewrote baptisms using a ledger style format.

According to the civil record Tom Forde died, aged 82, on 30 May 1939. The cause of death was "senility". The informant was his daughter Delia. On the civil record he is described as a "widower and pensioner". He was buried in the New Cemetery. He has no stone. The specific location has been lost.

Tom probably died a few days after May 30. His death notice appeared in the *Connaught Telegraph* on 17 June 1939. "Death took place on Tuesday last of Mr. Thomas Forde (85) … Remains were removed to St. Patrick's Church on Tuesday evening and funeral took place in New Cemetery after High Mass." If the *Telegraph* is accurate Tom died on June 13.

Tom Forde was the only one of our great-grandparents to have filed a will with the County. It was dated 15 July 1938. His will states:

> "I, Thomas Forde of Derrynacong, Ballyhaunis, County of Mayo, Farmer, make this my last will and testament hereby revoking all former wills and testamentary dispositions henceforth made by me. I will devise and bequeath all my property both real and personal of which I may die possessed to my daughter Bridget Forde absolutely and I appoint her sole executrice and residuary legatee of this my last will."

"Bridget Forde" was his daughter Delia. The witnesses were Charles W. Raynor and Kathleen Cribbin of Ballyhaunis. They noted on the document:

> "Signed by the testator as and for his final will and testament, same having been first read over to him when he appeared to understand the contents thereof clearly and affixed his mark thereto in our presence of each other, both of us being present at the same time, he being unable to write through failure of eyesight."

It's not clear what "failure of eyesight" meant. It could mean eye diseases such as glaucoma or macular degeneration. Or it could mean something as simple as not having glasses. The fact that Tom lost his sight by July 1938 and died nearly a year later indicates he did not have an easy time in his old age.

The value of his estate was 42 English pounds.

Tom Forde was by far the longest lived of our great-grandparents. There is a story about him that I heard many times growing up. Sometime near the start of the Second World War a seaman from the Ballyhaunis vicinity met Pat Ford, my grandfather, on the Hoboken docks and told him that Tom was still alive. This was not correct as it turned out, but it led to the supposition that Tom had reached some extraordinary length of life. Eighty two is pretty good considering the lack of medical care, but it is not the hundred years or greater he reached in the story.

The fact that Tom's body was taken to the church on the same day he died hints at how the church and civil authorities tried to avoid scandals arising over the "Irish wake". Before the rise of funeral parlors, the body was waked in the home. Local people prepared the body and constructed the coffin. The family was expected to provide meals, tobacco, and liquor to the visitors. Wakes were social occasions in which news and gossip were exchanged. The rosary was said and testaments to the deceased were offered. Keening or wailing over the body could take place—specific local people had the reputation of being especially good at keening and might even be paid a small fee to carry on. While this was going on, considerable *poteen* might have been consumed and the wake could turn rowdy. (This was especially true for the wakes of older people who had reached their proper life span—the deaths of young people were filled with deeper grief and were more decorous.) Stories could be told by the local story-teller—in Derrynacong this was John Deasy, who had served in the British army and had visited India. Songs and dancing could take place. Games could be played, including versions of "Simon says" and "Pin-the-tail on the donkey."

Authorities put the kill-bosh on this by having the body brought to the church the night before the funeral. This sounds like the typical suppression of genuine emotion by the uptight clergy, but it may not have been a bad thing. Wakes could devolve into drunken brawls as the games turned rough and buried resentments bubbled to the surface. My father said that it was a great thing the wake took place in a funeral parlor. He had lived through a few where grief turned into gamboling—he recalled the wake of his brother Dennis as particularly boisterous.

Mary Hunt was the daughter of Pat Hunt and Bridget Fitzmaurice. She was baptized in Kiltullagh Parish on 20 August 1854. Her godparents were Pat Flynn and Bridget Hunt. The priest was either Fr. William Feeney or Fr. Pat MacLaughlin.

Mary's death was reported to the civil authorities as occurring on 12 April 1897. She was 42 years old. The cause of death was "phthisis", an obsolete term for tuberculosis. She had been under doctor's care for a year. The informant was Tom Forde. The date he notified the authorities was May 27. We don't know where Mary was buried. It would be either the New Cemetery or the Parish cemetery in Garranlahan. We were told by Mrs. Josie Eaton of Main St., Ballyhaunis, that Tom worked as a handyman in the convent and that he was at work there when Mary died.

We don't have any photographs of Tom Forde or Mary Hunt. Mrs. Keigher remembered that her father Michael told her that Mary was tall and had black hair. Tom must have resembled his son Patrick, as Mrs. Keigher mistook a photograph of Pat for Tom. Mrs. Keigher remembered that Tom was a "nice man who never said much." Mrs. Fitzharris, who knew Tom when she was a child, remembered that he was an active man who did a lot of work even in his old age.

We can surmise that Tom and Mary were religious in a fundamental way. Tom worked as a handyman in St. Joseph's Convent in Ballyhaunis. And the Annagh Parish register noted that "Tom Forde's wife" was "churched" on 16 January 1894. This "pious and praiseworthy" practice (*Catholic Encyclopedia*) involved the "purification" of a woman who had recently given birth. In the rite the woman enters the church and asks God's blessing on herself and on the baby. The woman kneels in the vestibule, holding a lighted candle. She recites Psalm 23 and is escorted into the church by the priest. The priest prays, "Enter thou into the temple of God. Adore the Son of the Blessed Virgin Mary who has given thee fruitfulness." The priest then sprinkles the woman with holy water and blesses her.

The churching of women was not a common custom. It appeared infrequently in the Annagh and Bekan Parish registers. We can conclude that Mary was especially devout because she had to make a special request to be churched.

Tom and Mary were tied to the church in another way. They were young adults when the Knock Apparition occurred on 21 August 1879. I have no doubt they believed that Mary, Joseph, and John the Evangelist appeared to 14 people on the church wall that rainy Thursday evening. The appearance of supernatural beings may be related to the severe food shortages that occurred that year. After the horrendous events of the Famine, people would have beseeched heaven for help as soon as the harvest went bad.

Their lives also included a paganish folk side filled with vast numbers of strange superstitions. The nineteenth century Irish believed you could jinx a person by failing to say, "God Bless You" after giving the person a compliment. A mother could jinx her unborn child by cursing it or saying she didn't want it—this happened in Leeds Point to the creature that became the Jersey Devil. Travelers were sometimes *led astray* by the ever-present *good people*. They became confused and disoriented and sometimes found themselves wandering far from where they started. If a traveler became cognizant that he or she had been led astray, the solution was to turn the coat inside out. This simple deed would take the person back to familiar ground.

The world of ghosts and banshees and the *good people* involved considerable interest in divination. It was important to know the future or, at the least, to avoid coming to a bad end if that fate could be known ahead of time. In a bewitched world anything could mean anything. The flight of birds, the patterns on wet grass, the behavior of livestock—anything could turn portentous. Daily living involved favorable and unfavorable omens at every turn. Sometimes divination involved more elaborate social customs—these customs have continued in places to our own time. During Halloween a cake called "brambrack" was baked. Objects were placed inside the cake. The cake was randomly sliced and distributed. If a person's slice included a ring, marriage was foretold. If the slice included a rag, poverty was foretold. If the slice included a coin, wealth was foretold. Since this divination potentially involved biting physical objects, we can safety conclude dental problems were foretold.

Tom and Mary lived in much the same style as their parents. Their lives amounted to sustenance farming. The pig paid the rent when sold in the Ballyhaunis market. Like his father, Tom traveled to the Lancashire region as a migrant worker in the summer and early autumn. This was an important source of revenue. A thrifty *spalpeen* could earn as much as eight or ten pounds in the English fields. Mrs. Eaton told us that Tom met his second wife while working the harvest.

Their lives were like their parents in another manner. There were severe potato shortages in the West of Ireland in 1879 - 1880. Ballyhaunis was hit particularly hard. Fr. James Waldron, Parish priest in the period, wrote in January 1880 that over 1,000 people in the Parish of 12,800 needed public relief. Fr. Waldron wrote in March that more than 600 families were "destitute". In May he wrote that there was no employment in the area—"Unless by going to England as 'harvestmen' they cannot earn anything." Catastrophe was averted in this period, unlike in the 1840s, owing to the expeditious response of authorities. Catastrophe may also have been averted owing to the possibility of emigration as an option. The situation was so severe Lord Dillon gave a reduction in rent of six shillings on the pound.

Henry Doran, a commissioner for the Congested Districts Board, visited Ballyhaunis in April 1892. He reported that farming was done in a "primitive and slovenly manner." He attributed this to the absence of manure. Small farmers had only one or two cows. Bog mold—a mixture of manure and bog soil—was used as a substitute. So was lime when available. Doran reported that the typical small farm had an acre of potatoes, an acre of oats, and small plots of cabbage and turnip [29].

Doran also observed a cottage industry involving hens. This industry was run by housewives who kept the profits. He reported that 20 hens could produce 2,000 eggs a year. This could earn a woman three whole pounds. Interestingly, Doran noted tuberculosis outbreaks in hens in the 1880s. It's not known whether this could evolve into human tuberculosis or whether Mary Hunt caught tuberculosis from working in the henhouse.

Tom and Mary lived in a period of political agitation in their own backyard. Political self-determination and land ownership became interlocked concepts. The 1880s was a time when a movement arose with the express goal of having Irish farmers own the land they worked. "The land of Ireland belongs to the people of Ireland" became the cry. This concept was the intellectual breakthrough of Michael Davitt, one of the key "patriots" of the period. Aided by Charles Stewart Parnell and by John Devoy, Davitt founded the Land League with the explicit purpose of abolishing "landlordism".

Davitt and the others rejected the violence of the Fenians, a secret organization of the time, and recycled the concept of the mass rally made famous in earlier decades by Daniel O'Connell. A large rally was held in Castlebar, County Mayo, in June 1879. Archbishop MacHale, who could always be counted on to be on the side that kept his flock in cages, sponsored a counter rally in Ballyhaunis in July. This indicates that the people of Eastern Mayo were politically conservative to the point of opposing a progressive movement struggling on their behalf. Their conservative orientation may derive from a constitutional basis—they were fundamentalist in their religious views as well. Or it may derive from the amicable relationship they had with Lord Dillon. James Tuke, who visited the region in 1880, reported that the tenants of the region had "no ill feeling against their landlords [30]."

A second concept that advanced the cause of the Land League was the "boycott". Initially directed against Col. Charles Cunningham Boycott, this became a form of social ostracism toward any person abetting landlords. Local people were directed, in Stewart's words, "to shun as if he were a leper" any person who took the side of the landlord or who took advantage of a neighbor's plight—for example, by inhabiting the farm of a family evicted for not paying the rent.

The boycott was highly effective—mutually dependent, very few *townlanders* could afford to be ostracized. William Gladstone, the Prime Minister, authorized reforms in April 1881. Rents were fixed and legal mechanisms established to protect farmers who made improvements on the land. The Land League instigated a slow and inexorable movement toward private land ownership. Harold Arthur, the 17th Viscount Dillon, threw in the towel in May 1899 and sold his 87,669 Mayo acres to Ireland, which then loaned money at low interest to the farmers in order for them to buy their holdings. It was a towel rimmed with gold. The Viscount made 290,000 English pounds, the estimated rent for sixteen years.

The known children of Tom Forde and Mary Hunt were: Bridget; Mary Ellen; Patrick; Kate and Delia, fraternal twins; and John.

Bridget Forde was baptized 19 January 1888. Her godparents were Hugh Hunt and Maggie Tully. Civil registration listed the date of birth as January 7. Her grandmother Bridget Hunt was the informant. Mary Forde reported that Bridget died on 30 March 1889. She was one year of age. The cause of death was pertussis—perhaps *Dziadek* had reason to be concerned when I started whooping. We don't know where Bridget was buried, but it would likely be the New Cemetery.

Mary Ellen Forde was baptized 25 July 1889. Her godparents were James and Kate Waldron. Mary Ellen's birth was reported to the civil authorities as occurring on 10 October 1889. We do not know where Mary Ellen lived as an adult or when she died.

Mary Ellen presents the second great mystery in the Forde family. We have not been able to locate additional information on her life, which is regretful, since she may have shared the longevity of her siblings. Mrs. Fitzharris said that Mary Ellen lived in Longford, which we assumed meant County Longford, but there is no record of her there in the 1911

Census. It is possible she lived in Longford, England—there are several places by that name in Great Britain.

Mrs. Keigher remembered that Mary Ellen had a baby. She came to stay with Michael Hunt around 1919 - 1920. Mrs. Keigher remembered this because they stayed in her bed, dispossessing her—we have to be careful about the years, as memories are fragile and this event happened seventy five years before we heard it. Mrs. Keigher suggested Mary Ellen had been deserted by her husband. Perhaps it involved having a baby out of wedlock. The fact that she did not live near home suggests the possibility of a scandal. The Irish were known for sending their scandals to a distant part of Erin or to Great Britain. Unfortunately, none of our Irish informants knew Mary Ellen's fate or precisely what had happened.

Patrick Forde, my grandfather, was baptized 30 August 1892. His baptism name was "Patrick Austin". His godparents were Patrick and Bridget Fitzmaurice. The priest was Fr. Michael Burke. Civil registration listed his birth as occurring on August 26. Patrick immigrated to the United States on the White Star liner *Baltic*, arriving in New York harbor on 23 October 1910. He married Catherine Griffin in Our Lady of Grace Church in Hoboken on 20 April 1913. He became a citizen on 13 April 1937. Pat died in Jersey City at the age of 87 on 14 January 1980. He was buried in Holy Name Cemetery in Jersey City. Details about Pat and his family will be given in Chapter 14.

Kate Agnes and **Delia Forde,** fraternal twins, were baptized 27 December 1893. The civil record of their birth gives the same date. Their godparents were Michael Hunt and Mary Fitzmaurice and Pat Tully and Mary Waldron. It's not indicated who the priest was. The record was careful to note that Kate was born first at 8:32 AM, Delia second at 8:50 AM. The informant was their grandmother Bridget Hunt.

Kate died of heart disease on 14 June 1981 in the county hospital. Delia died 17 October 1981 in the hospital in Swineford. (Her stone lists the date as October 7.) Both ladies were 87 years of age. They are buried together in the New Cemetery.

We have a lot of information on their lives as we were fortunate to befriend Mrs. Fitzharris and Mrs. Eaton. We also spoke with Pat and Kathleen Hunt in Carrick and with their children, all of whom were close to their aunts. Mrs. Eaton's son was kind enough to forward a photograph of the sisters in old age. Delia is dressed in a blue dress. She resembles my grandfather, having a long lean face. Kate is dressed in a black smock. She resembles my father and my Aunt Mary, having decidedly squarish facial features.

Delia never married. She worked for a time as a dressmaker in Castlebar. While in Castlebar, she claimed to have been a member of a ladies auxiliary to a precursor organization to the IRA. She returned to Derrynacong after her stepmother died. Delia was close to her Hanlon—later Fitzharris—neighbors. The Hanlons would feed her dog if she came home late. Mrs. Fitzharris remembered that Delia was very active and outgoing. She was very good in math and had the personality of a school teacher. At the age of 70 Delia was godmother to Mrs. Fitzharris's son Patrick.

Delia lived in Ballyhaunis after she sold the farm in Derrynacong. She worked as a nanny to the children of Mrs. Eaton on Main Street. She appears to have been close to Mrs. Eaton's mother and to have done odd jobs for the Eaton family across the years. Mrs. Eaton recollected that Delia regretted not emigrating.

Neither Delia nor Kate lived in Derrynacong in April 1911. We haven't been able to locate Delia under that name or "Bridget"—Delia is a variant of Bridget. There is a 1911 record for Catherine Forde, aged 17, in Moneymore, a townland adjacent to Derrynacong. She resided with John Cribbin, aged 90, a widower, his son John and daughter-in-law Mary Anne, and their children.

Kate married John Flynn in St. Patrick's Chapel in Ballyhaunis on 8 August 1929. Their witnesses were John Walsh and Delia Forde. The priest was Fr. Patrick Moane. On the marriage record Kate started to write her name as "Kate", but stopped and changed it to "Catherine". Kate was 36 years at the time of marriage, John considerably older. They had no children. John was described as a widower. After their marriage they resided in the townland of Carrick in County Roscommon.

John Flynn was likely the son of John Flynn and Celia Flynn of Clooncrim townland in County Roscommon. He was baptized 23 November 1873. His godmother was Catherine Flynn. John's death was reported as occurring on 9 February 1950. His age was given as 80. Delia Forde of Derrynacong was the informant. He had been under doctor's care for two years with heart problems.

John's first marriage was to Delia Kedian of Derrynacong. This occurred on 7 January 1923. Their witnesses were Joseph Cullen and Mary Jane Dyer. Delia was the daughter of Michael Kedian. She died of cancer with the date given as 28 July 1928. She was 40 years of age.

John lived with his aunt and uncle James and Mary Lyons in Carrick. He subsequently inherited the house and property. Kate inherited the house from him and transferred the property in 1953 to Pat Hunt, her nephew and Dominick Hunt's son. As part of the terms of the sale it was stated that "no registration under any disposition for value by the registered owner affecting the bedroom on the north side of the house occupied by Kate Flynn in the dwelling house is to be made during the life of the said Kate Flynn except with her consent."

Kate did odd jobs after John's death. She was known locally as "Kate Hunt"—people were surprised to learn she was a Forde. Her nephews Kevin and Vincent remembered that Kate was a very religious and loving person. She prayed—out loud—on her knees every evening. She bought the children candy when she received her pension check. When she was old and sick she told the brothers that she was prepared to go to Jesus. It may be she had been exposed to alcoholism at some point in her life, as she had a saying, "The man will take the drink and the drink will take the man."

Kate and Delia were opposite types. Delia was a city woman and sophisticate. Kate was a country woman who was adept at doing farm work. Both were very short. Kate had ulcers and ate almost nothing but eggs, biscuits, and milk. And she smoked heavily. Mrs. Fitzharris remembered that both Kate and Delia "were an example to the Parish, ready to help anyone in need and so good-hearted, very good for the church. They didn't miss many Sunday Masses in their lives."

John Forde, the last son of Tom and Mary Forde, was born on 26 January 1896 according to the church register. He was baptized 2 February 1896. His godparents were John and Delia (or Celia) Waldron. The priest was Fr. Fallon. A notation in the Parish record appears—Friday 31, 1896.

John's death was listed in the civil record as occurring 23 August 1897. He was a year-and-a-half. Cause of death was "phthisis". He was under doctor's care for three months. It was possible John acquired tuberculosis from his mother, who died a few months before him of the same disease. He was likely buried in the New Cemetery [31].

Tom Forde married a second time. This was to **Bridget Lyons** of Larganboy townland, Bekan Parish. The ceremony took place on 11 November 1897 in Bekan Parish. Their witnesses were John Waldron and Anne Higgins. The priest was Fr. Greeley. Tom signed his name in the register. Bridget signed with an "X". The mark was witnessed by C.R. Crean, the registrar. They paid three pounds five shillings for the service.

Bridget Lyons was the daughter of Edward Lyons of Larganboy and Catherine Bones of Brackloon. Bridget was baptized in December 1866 in Bekan Parish. (The church record appears to be December 3 or 5. The civil record has the date as December 22.) Her godparents were William Lyons and Catherine Bones. Bridget's death was reported to civil authorities as occurring on 16 March 1920. The cause of death was "chronic constipation and exhaustion." She had been under a doctor's care for three months. Tom Forde was the informant [32].

Tom married again as he needed a woman to run the household. His choice of a wife may have been a poor one—or not. If he had married a pleasant peasant woman, I might have been writing this with a brogue. Bridget comes down through the years as the prototypical wicked stepmother. This was one of the few memories of Mayo my father heard from his father and passed down to us—Pat Ford's stepmother was a witch. She was described by all the Irish contacts we made who knew Kate and Delia as being mean to the Forde children and as advancing the cause of her own children. This is not unknown in stepfamilies—I once read that some Irish landlords refused to sanction second families to avoid this kind of problem.

According to Mrs. Keigher the situation in the home got so bad at one point the Forde children lived with Michael Hunt. It is instructive that when Mary Ellen Forde visited she stayed with Michael Hunt and did not stay in Derrynacong. Kevin Hunt remembered that Kate told him the Forde children got the potato peels and not the pulp—this may have backfired, as the peels are at least as nutritious as the pulp and maybe more so [33].

We can see the conflict in the pattern of who resided in the home. The Forde children are gone by 1911. The daughters are scattered in Ireland, perhaps in England. Pat Forde, the only son and rightful heir to the farm, has fled to America. When Bridget died in 1920 Delia returned to Derrynacong and the Forde and Lyons offspring commenced a chain migration to America.

This pattern if not of active discord than of dislike continued in America. My grandfather had little contact with his sisters. My father remembered that two of them came to his brother's wake in 1939. It may have been the only time he saw them. Until we did this research, my father did not know he had seven aunts.

The children of Tom Forde and Bridget Lyons were: Anne; Nora; Rose; and Agnes.

Anne Forde was baptized in Annagh Parish on 3 September 1898. (The civil record gave the date of birth as August 30.) Her godparents were James Waldron and Catherine Bones. Anne immigrated on the *Baltic*, arriving in New York City on 17 May 1920. Her destination was an aunt, Mrs. Foley, of Columbus Ave., New York City. Anne was described on the ship's log as 5'6 with dark hair, brown eyes, and a dark complexion. She paid for the trip herself and had $20 or $30 on her.

In April 1911 Anne resided with her grandparents in Larganboy. On the 1930 Federal Census she was listed with her sister Nora as residing at 436 W. 124th St. in Manhattan (roll 1564, p. 10B, ED 899). Both sisters were described as waitresses. The rent was $40 a month.

Anne married John McNamara on 29 May 1939 in the Church of the Annunciation in New York City. Her name in the record was "Anna". Their witnesses were Richard Walsh and Nora Ford. The priest was Fr. John Cunneen. She resided at the time of the wedding at 501 West 133rd St. in Manhattan. John was the son of John McNamara and Anne Healy. His date of birth was given on the marriage record as 14 September 1898. His profession was "porter". He was born in Ireland, but the place was not specified. It is unlikely they had children—Anne was 40 years of age when she married.

We have not been able to identify when Anne or John died or where they lived after their marriage.

Nora Forde was baptized on 16 January 1900. Her godparents were Edward Lyons and Mary Higgins. The civil record listed her birth as April 14. On the civil record she is called "Honny"—she's "Honoria" on the 1911 Irish Census. Nora immigrated on the *Baltic*, arriving in New York harbor on 28 May 1922. Her destination was her sister "Miss A. Forde" of Amsterdam Ave. Nora was described as 5'2, with fair complexion, blue eyes, and brown hair. Her occupation was "domestic". Nora had $27.00 on her. The log specifies that Nora's sister paid for the trip.

Nora married John O'Boyle in the Church of Corpus Christi in Manhattan on 28 June 1931. Their witnesses were Thomas York and Rose Ford. The priest was Fr. John Dooley. At the time of the wedding Nora resided at 1230 Amsterdam Ave in Manhattan. John was the son of William Boyle and Ellen Hickey. The marriage record gave his birth as 20 September 1898 in Bogualstown, County Carlow, Ireland.

Nora and John had two children: **Rose Mary Lynch**; and **Anna Teresa Crawford**.

Nora died, aged 73, in September 1973. She resided at the time of death in Stony Point, New York. John died 3 May 1966 in Park East Hospital, Manhattan. He was described as a "bus caretaker" for the Manhattan & Bronx Bus Co. He and Nora are buried in Gates of Heaven Cemetery in Hawthorne, New York. At the time of his death they resided at Broadway and 232rd St. in New York City.

Rose Forde, the daughter of Tom Forde and Bridget Lyons, was baptized on 26 December 1901. Her godparents were Michael Lyons and Mary Ellen Forde. Fr. Greeley officiated. The civil record gave the date of birth as 17 February 1902. The informant was Mary Ellen Forde.

Rose never married. She died 12 February 1974 at age 72 in the Arthur C. Logan Memorial Hospital in New York City. At the time of death she resided at 2720 Broadway. She was buried with her sister Agnes in St. Raymond's Cemetery in the Bronx (Our Savior section, range 54, grave 51, no headstone).

Rose immigrated on the Cunard steamship *Scythia*, arriving in New York harbor on 14 October 1924. Her destination was her sister Nora on Amsterdam Ave. She was described as 5'4, with a fresh complexion, brown hair, and blue eyes. He had $22.00 on her. Like Nora's, her occupation was given as "domestic". The log specifies her sister paid for the trip.

We do not know where Rose resided in 1930. The Federal Census listed two Rose Fords in New York City, both aged 21 and both working as maids.

Agnes Forde, the last child of Tom Forde and Bridget Lyons, was baptized 23 December 1903. Fr. E. Walsh officiated. Her godparents were Hubert Ford and Catherine Lyons. The civil record gave the date of birth as 4 February 1904.

Agnes never married. She died 18 July 1977 in the Hollis Wood Nursing Home in Queens, New York, at the age of 73. Her usual residence was given as 195 - 44 Woodhull Ave. in Queens. The informant was John O'Rourke, who may have been an employee of the nursing home. Agnes was buried with her sister Rose in St. Raymond's Cemetery in the Bronx.

Agnes immigrated on the White Star steamship *Republic*, arriving in the port of New York on 5 May 1927. Her destination was her sister Nora. Agnes was described as 5'3, with fair complexion, black hair, and gray eyes. Agnes had $25.00 on her. Her sister paid for the trip. A handwritten note on the ship's log reads "Med. Cert. Def. Vision." There's no way to relate this to the eye problems her father had.

We have not been able to locate Agnes in the 1930 Federal Census.

We can trace the Forde farm with a great degree of detail—Irish maps and land records are excellent. In the 1901 Census, taken on April 12, eight people resided on the farm. The walls of the two-room rectangular house were of stone, brick, or cement. The roof was of wood or thatch. There were two windows in the front. The house stood in the midst of three tall trees—the trees were standing when we visited in 1996 and they can be seen on the Google Earth map. Mrs. Fitzharris recollected that the house stood until the 1960s, when it "went under". There was a barn and stable on the property as well.

Tom could read Irish and English. His handwriting on the 1901 Census was exquisite and floral, as if he had studied penmanship. The same hand filled out the census forms for several neighbors.

The situation was different in the 1911 Census, taken on April 29. Tom and Bridget are listed, as are Nora, Rose, and Agnes. The property has built up since 1901. A cow house, piggery, barn, and shed are listed. Tom's handwriting has completely deteriorated. It is a nearly illegible scrawl thoroughly different from the elegant 1901 signature. Perhaps the scrawl reflected the family discord. Perhaps it merely reflected the aging process.

A lime kiln stood on the property halfway between the Forde and Fitzharris houses. Working the kiln was a complicated and dangerous process. Alternate layers of limestone and turf were heated in the kiln. Turf was used for fuel. The lime was used as fertilizer and as plaster in construction. The lime would be communally shared—its presence suggests the Forde house and the other houses in Derrynacong were well built. Patrick Fitzharris remembered the kiln was a horseshoe-shaped structure ringed with stones. He played in the kiln as a child and arrived home dirty because of the ash.

On 20 January 1902 a contract was signed with four local people who obtained the legal right to "cut, make, and take turf for fuel" for a fee from the Forde farm. They also obtained the right to take "bog-mould for manure". These individuals were John Quinn of Derrynacong, Patrick Lyons of Arderry, John Lyons of Spaddagh, and Anthony Morley of Clagnagh. John Quinn was Tom's next door neighbor. It is likely Patrick Lyons's farm bordered Tom's—Arderry is to the immediate south of Derrynacong. We don't know who the other two individuals were or whether they were related in some manner.

On 22 November 1901 the Irish Land Commission advanced Tom 32 pounds to purchase the farm. The interest rate amounted to four pounds a year. Tom Forde became the "full owner" of the farm "in fee" on 5 May 1902. This was a momentous occasion—they had been paying tenants on the site for fifty years. Delia Forde inherited the farm after Tom's death. She sold it to James McGarry on 13 August 1944—she appeared to have lived on the property for a number of years after the sale. We don't know whether James McGarry was a relative—people made attempts to keep the farm in the family as much as possible. At some point the Ronanye family purchased the farm. The farm is now a grassy field inhabited by a herd of cows.

Chapter Eleven

~

Erin—Denis Griffin & Ellen Allen

Our second Irish great-grandparents are **Denis Griffin** and **Ellen Allen**. They married in the Chapel at Ballydonohue, Galey Parish, on 26 April 1885. Their witnesses were Michael Hanrahan and John Allen. The priest was Fr. Mortimer O'Connor. Both signed the register with "X's". At the time of the marriage Denis resided in Ballyegan. After the marriage he resided with Ellen's family in Trippul West. This is another example of the "reverse dowry" in which the groom moved into the bride's house.

Denis Griffin was the son of Martin Griffin and Catherine Connell. He was baptized on 5 October 1859, according to the Ballybunion Parish book. His godparents were Robert Connell and Bridget Griffin. The priest was Fr. J. Walsh. The location given in the register was "Kilconly", which may refer to Martin's residence. Perhaps they were residing in a townland in Kilconly Parish at the time.

We haven't located the death record for Denis Griffin in Ireland, England, or America. The 1911 Irish Census reported that Ellen had been married for 18 years. If accurate, this would put Denis's death in 1903 or 1904. His children started chain immigrating in 1908, so it may be Denis died slightly later.

Ellen Allen was the daughter of John Allen and Johanna Linnane. She was baptized 14 January 1858. Her godmother was Ellen Linnane. The priest was Fr. J. Walsh. The Ballybunion register notes the location as "of Gale", which likely referred to the location of Johanna Linnane's family. Alternately, it may refer to where John Allen lived at that period.

Ellen died of heart disease in New York City on the morning of 15 September 1919. She was 61 years of age. She had been under doctor's care for nine months. Ellen died at 450 West 58th St. in the apartment of her daughter Mary McNamara. Ellen was buried in Holy Name Cemetery in Jersey City (plot E-5-93). The story is lost now, but my father remembered that there was some controversy over where Ellen would be buried. Pat Allen, her brother, wanted her buried in his family plot, but my grandmother overruled him and had Ellen interred in a new grave. This grave has filled with people over the years—five are buried there.

Ellen Griffin was our only great-grandparent to immigrate. She arrived in New York harbor with her daughters Hanna and "Ellie" on 1 June 1912 (National Archives roll 1873). The liner was the *Baltic*, a steamship that carried many of our relatives to America. She was described on the ship's log as a widow of 50 years, 5'7 in height, with fair hair and blue eyes. Her address in Ireland was that of her brother Timothy on Station Road in Ballybunion. Her destination was her brother Patrick. His address was 216 10th St. The city is not specified, but it was Hoboken. A brother paid for the trip. Ellen arrived without money.

Ellen and her daughters were detained overnight on arrival. The cause of detention was "L.P.C. 5.5"—they were considered to be "likely public charges". They received two meals in detention. They were released from the Island of Tears on 2 June 1912. The log doesn't specify who arrived to obtain their release.

Ellen altered her name to "Helen", a not uncommon change for immigrants, as it made them sound less Old World. There is a paper trail for Ellen in America. The 1915 New York City Directory listed Helen Griffin (widow of Dennis—a second "n" has been added) at 773 Columbus Ave. The 1917 and 1918 Directories listed Helen at 210 West 67th St.

The 1915 New York State Census listed Helen Griffin, aged 58, in residence at 773 Columbus Ave. Her son Jack Griffin, aged 28 and noted as "copper work, citizen", and daughter Helen, aged 13, lived with her.

Ellen Griffin is our only great-grandparent that we have a photograph of. In the photograph Ellen appears as a heavyset and imposing woman. She wears a long smock. Her face is full, her hair parted in the middle. She has a pleasant look that's not a smile. Nor is it a serious expression. Her hands look large and swollen—it's hard to tell. It's also hard to tell her age. The picture was likely taken after Denis died, perhaps as a memento for her children as they left for America. If that's the case, Ellen was in her forties. She looks younger than her age.

The 1901 Irish Census of Trippul West gave Denis's occupation as "general laborer" and Ellen's as "general servant". Denis cannot read. Ellen was described as being able to read and write. Denis, Ellen, and my grandmother Catherine spoke English and Irish. John Allen lived with them. John's age was given as 70. Denis signed the census form with an "X". Ellen was pregnant with her daughter Ellen.

The walls to their two-room home were wood or mud. The roof was thatch or wood. There were two windows in the front. There was a piggery on their property. Their immediate neighbors were Honoria Stack and Hanna Hannafin.

The situation has changed in ten years. The 1911 Census listed Ellen as a widow, aged 50. Her older children are in America. The youngest children reside with her. John Allen, described as 87 years of age, was listed as the property holder. The piggery was gone.

Denis Griffin and Ellen Allen had the following known children: Catherine; John; Mary; Nora; Hanna; and Ellen. The 1911 Census indicated that Ellen had an additional child who died, but we do not know the name or circumstance. There was no memory of this child among the people in America.

Catherine Griffin, my grandmother, was baptized 11 July 1886. Her godmother was Johanna Allen. The priest was Fr. Charles Godley. The civil record listed the date of birth as July 12. Catherine immigrated on the *Baltic*, arriving in New York harbor on 11 April 1908. She married Patrick Ford in Our Lady of Grace Church in Hoboken on 20 April 1913. She became a citizen on 13 April 1937. Catherine died at the age of 91 in Hoboken on 26 March 1978. She was buried in the Ford plot in Holy Name Cemetery in Jersey City. Details of Catherine's life and family will be described in Chapter 14.

John Griffin was baptized 14 April 1888. His sponsor was Johanna Allen. The priest was Fr. Godley. The civil record gave the date of birth as June 20. John never married. He died of influenza and pneumonia in Hartford Hospital in Hartford, CT, on 16 October 1918. He was brought back to New Jersey and was buried with his uncle Henry Allen in Holy Name Cemetery. He was 30 years of age.

John was, to my knowledge, our only ancestor who died in the Great Flu pandemic of 1918. Despite the fact that the flu kills thousands annually, "having the flu" means little to healthy young people today. Until recently we shared a collective amnesia about "The Spanish Lady" that devastated the world in 1918 – 1919 and that was the single greatest calamity ever to occur in America. Worldwide as many as 20 – 50 million people died of influenza in 1918. In one year 25 million Americans caught the flu. More than 650,000 died. This is virtually the same number as died in the horrendous Civil War and more than died in World Wars One and Two combined. In October 1918, 195,000 Americans died of flu. In the last week of October 2,700 American servicemen were killed in Europe and 21,000 people died of flu in the states. On the same day John died in Hartford 711 people died of flu in Philadelphia.

The pandemic nearly led to the undermining of American society. In many places public gatherings were forbidden, including funerals. In Philadelphia the dead were left on sidewalks and picked up by carts, a custom unheard of in the West since the Black Death. Face masks were advised and mandated in places and quarantines were enforced—both 1918-era face masks and quarantines were futile defenses against the spread of the virus. It sounds comical now, but it became a crime to spit, cough, or sneeze in public.

The course of the disease was unusually severe and rapidly fatal. Most of the victims were under 40 years of age. The pandemic occurred before the advent of modern medicine and it was misunderstood as a bacterial infection, as viruses had not been discovered. There were two unique events that may have contributed to the excessive mortality rates. It's believed that the virus was a mutation of bird virus that jumped directly into the human species. There was no immunity to the mutation. The First World War was in its fourth year—the first year for America—and people were moving worldwide in unprecedented numbers. The disease was believed to have evolved in army camps in the Midwest and then to have crossed the world on trains and troop ships.

We don't know why John Griffin was in Connecticut or who he stayed with. Martin Griffin and his family were in New Haven and there were Ballyegan people in Waterbury. My father claimed that his uncle fled to Connecticut to avoid being drafted. This is entirely to his credit given the pointlessness of the War to End Wars. But his story doesn't end happily. It's a kind of *Appointment in Sumatra* that leads to Hartford. John fled to avoid dying in battle and he succumbed to a disease incubated in barracks and trenches.

John arrived in the United States on the Cunard steamship *Carmania* on 21 April 1909 (Natl. Archives roll #1249). He last resided with Ellen

Griffin in Ballybunion. His destination was 217 Clinton St., Hoboken, where Kate Griffin lived. Kate paid for the trip. He had $10.00 on him. The ship's log noted that he wasn't able to read or write, which isn't accurate. He was described as a laborer, 5'10 in height, with a fair complexion, brown hair, and blue eyes. John was detained on Ellis Island until Kate Griffin arrived. He may have been detained because he didn't have sufficient funds. He received three meals in detention, so he waited more than a day.

John declared for citizenship on 21 July 1913. He was described as a longshoreman, 5'10 in height, 160 pounds, with blond hair and gray eyes. His date of birth was given as 12 April 1888, his address as 1915 Clinton St. in Hoboken—probably 915 Clinton is meant, as there is no 1915 address in Hoboken. John never completed the naturalization process.

The 1915 Census reported that John lived with his mother and sister at 773 Columbus Ave. He was described as employed in copper work—this is making baskets.

Whatever the motivation for his trip to Connecticut, John registered for the draft on 2 June 1917. His address was given as 210 West 67th St., the same as Ellen's. He was described as tall, slender, with light brown hair and blue eyes. He was listed as an employed laborer with the Dept. of Correction in "Workhouse B1". There is a notation "3172" on the bottom of the page.

Mary Griffin was born on 25 March 1891, according to the civil record. We have not been able to locate her baptism record. The date on her headstone gives her birth as 18 May 1890.

Mary sailed to America on the White Star liner *Oceanic*, arriving in New York City on 28 September 1910 (Natl. Archives roll #1565). Her last residence was with "Mrs. Griffin" in Tulla More, Ballybunion. Her destination was her uncle Pat Allen at 616 Park Ave. in Hoboken. Her uncle paid for the trip. Mary was described as 20 years old, a "servant", 5'6 in height with fair hair and blue eyes. She had $50 on her—this looks suspiciously high. Mary was detained on arrival until Kate Griffin of 616 Park Ave. arrived. They left Ellis Island at 5:14 PM on September 28.

Mary died approximately 65 years of age on 20 January 1957—this was one day after Pawel Bielawski (NYC cert. 1207). She was buried in Gates of Heaven Cemetery in Hawthorne, NY (Sect. 47, plot 376, grave 17). The headstone has a note: "Erected by County Clare Hurling Club of New York City."

Mary had the reputation of being kind-hearted. She may have resembled Ellen Allen as my father remembered that she was stocky in build.

Mary married Patrick James McNamara on 8 July 1917 at St. Matthew's Church in Manhattan (NYC cert. # 20664). Their witnesses were Patrick O'Brien and Helen Griffin. The priest was Fr. William Creedon. Mary resided at 924 West End Ave., Patrick at 51 Jane St.

Patrick McNamara was the son of Timothy McNamara and Margaret Lynch. His birth date was given as 17 March 1884—rather a special day—on naturalization papers and on his World War One registration. He was born in Cragboy townland, Quin Parish, County Clare. Patrick arrived in America on the *Baltic* on 16 September 1905. His destination was his sister Mary McNamara at Riverdale Ave. in Manhattan [34].

Patrick declared for citizenship on 1 April 1912 and was sworn as a citizen on 6 February 1918 (Vol. 270, p. 114, NYC Old Records). He was described as a butcher, 5'11 in height, 174 pounds, with gray hair and blue eyes. His witnesses were James O'Brien and John McNamara. He resided at 337 West 12th St., although a note dated September 1917 gave his address as 565 Amsterdam Ave.

Patrick registered for the draft on 12 September 1918. He resided at 450 W. 58th St. in New York City. He was employed as a butcher for a company named Milton Levy. He was described as tall with a medium build, blue eyes and gray hair.

Patrick died on 17 September 1949 at the age of 65. My father recollected that he died suddenly while in a park. He was buried with Mary in Gates of Heaven Cemetery.

We have not been able to locate Pat and Mary McNamara and their large family in either the 1920 or 1930 Federal Census.

Mary Griffin and Patrick McNamara had the following known children (the order is not certain): **Peg Boyle**; **Mary Ann McLoughlin**; **Helen Jones**; **Catherine Valente**; **Dennis McNamara**; and **Timothy McNamara**.

Peg Boyle was the only child I met. She was a tiny, thin lady in her 70s. She was an outgoing personality who worked as a waitress. Peg was born circa 1920 and died in February 1995. She generously provided information on her family.

Timothy McNamara was born 25 April 1925 in Misericordia Hospital in Manhattan (NYC cert. 16412). His family resided at 278 West 115th St. Timothy was killed in action in World War Two on 10 July 1943. He died in the amphibious landings at Licata, Sicily. Timothy joined the army on 31 October 1942, ID # 12-181-216. At the time of death he was in Company E, 7th Inf. Regiment, 3rd Infantry Division. He was buried in Long Island National Cemetery in Farmington, New York. My father claimed that Timothy drowned—in fact, nine men drowned when a landing craft overturned—but the funeral records indicated he died of a gunshot wound. He was seventeen years old.

Everyone has a final hour and Timothy's must have been terrifying. The last place a seventeen year old should inhabit is a landing craft plowing toward a beach in the black pre-dawn. He may not have known with certainty where he was. Licata, Sicily? He was from the Upper West Side—whoever heard of that place? There was nothing to see but the flashes of rifle fire and artillery from the coast. The flashes from the hills must have looked as if they came out of the sky. The water was black below him. He wouldn't see the surf except for the reflections of the incoming. If he didn't go on the water growing up, he sailed into the battle squeamish and seasick. Maybe he didn't know how to swim, so the thought of falling overboard would have deepened the terror. Even if he knew how to swim, he was heavy with combat gear. The choices were grim—the endless sea was below him and the bullet-ridden beach was ahead.

Honoria (Nora) Griffin was baptized 16 June 1892 according to church records. Her godmother was Honora Hannafin of Trippul. The priest was Fr. M. O'Connor. The civil record has her birth as July 7. Nora died 20 February 1971 at age 78. She was buried in Calvary Cemetery in Brooklyn.

Nora immigrated to America on the *Baltic*, arriving in New York City on 1 May 1911. She last resided with her mother, "Mrs. Griffin" of Tulla More. Her destination was her uncle Pat Allen, who paid for the trip. Nora was described as 19 and a "servant". She was 5'4, with fair hair and blue eyes. She had no money on the voyage. On arrival she was detained until her sister Kate Griffin arrived. She received lunch while in detention and left Ellis Island with Kate at 3:00 PM.

My parents described Nora as short and stocky. She had bad eyesight. She was very close to my grandmother.

Nora married Michael Connor on 19 June 1921 in St. Joseph's Church in New York City (NYC cert. # 1642). The witnesses were James Lennon and Helen Griffin. The priest was Fr. John Grogan. Nora's address was 123 W. 11th St., Michael's 329 E. 52nd St.

Michael Connor was the son of Michael Connor and Alice Campbell. He was born in Doagha townland, Magheracloone Parish, County Monaghan. His birth date was given as 19 September 1888. According to my father Michael was short and stocky. He didn't get along with my grandfather. His children reported that their father Americanized his name, dropping the "O", which led to some controversy in his family. However Irish Census records indicate the "O" wasn't used in the Old Country [35].

Michael died after a short illness on 1 May 1944 at 55 years of age (NYC cert. #10330). His death record gave his trade as a "rigger". He was buried in Calvary Cemetery. The address at the time of death was 447 W. 28th St., which was where his children lived as adults.

Michael declared to be a citizen on 1 March 1920 (#100759, Vol. 406, P. 159, NYC Old Records). His witnesses were John J. Cunnigham and Michael Lennon. He arrived in New York City on the *Cedric* in November 1910. His trade was given as "roofer". His birth date was given as 26 December 1889.

Michael served in the Army from 26 July 1918 – 7 July 1919. He was a private (ID 4144049) with the 4th Detachment Demobilized Group, Camp Devens, MA. My father recollected that Michael had been gassed in battle, but there is no documentation of this. He received the WWI Victory Medal and the WWI Victory Button (bronze).

Michael registered for the World War Two draft on 26 April 1942. That document gave his date of birth as 2 January 1892. His height was 5'6, his weight 130 pounds. He had black hair and a light complexion. He worked for Tietzen & Lang in Hoboken.

According to the 1920 Federal Census Nora and Michael resided at 437 W. 8th St. in Manhattan. In the 1930 Census they resided at 907 West 28th St. Their rent was $23.00. Michael was listed as unemployed.

The known children of Nora and Michael were: **Dennis**; **Alice**; **Jack**; **Harold**; **George**; and **Helen**.

The Connors were the only cousins of my father that I knew. We would meet at weddings and at wakes. Dennis, Alice, and Jack never married. They were short and slim people who were very sociable and well-spoken. Dennis and Jack had keen senses of humor. Dennis wore thick glasses and was an avid New York *Rangers* hockey fan. Alice was a quiet lady who also wore glasses. At some point around 1998 the three traveled to Ireland where they met Tom Allen of Ballybunion. My father had a running joke about the Connors whenever he met them at wakes. "Don't you Connors ever die?" he would ask. It is true they outlived the Fords, but the Connors died, too. Their dates are: Dennis (1922 - 2006); Alice (1924 – 2004); Jack

(1925 – 2005); Harold (1928 – 2002). George died as an infant and Helen died young. May they and their cousins rest in peace.

Johanna (Hanna) Griffin was baptized in Ballybunion Parish on 22 August 1897. Her godmother was Bridget Callaghan. The civil record has her birth on November 10. Hanna died 24 July 1946 of alcoholism in University Hospital, Baltimore. She was 48 years of age. At the time of death she resided at 2519 Arbuton Ave. in Baltimore. She was buried in the Banda plot in Holy Cross Cemetery, Baltimore (section C, lots 55 - 57).

Hanna immigrated to America with her mother and sister Ellen on the *Baltic*. They arrived 1 June 1912. Hanna was 14 years old. She was described on the ship's log as 5'2, with fair hair and blue eyes.

Hanna had red hair. She was a heavy drinker who upset social standards by going into taverns. Dennis Connor remembered that the older women were offended when Hanna and her sister Helen came out of a bar at his father's wake.

Hanna married Charles Vasila Banda on 6 November 1932 in the Church of St. Gregory in Manhattan (NYC cert. 22623). Their witnesses were Frank Schippert and Daisy M. Conaghy. The priest was Fr. Gustav de Leon. Their address was given as 261 W. 93rd St. Charles was described as a "tile setter". His age was given as 30. Hanna signed the certificate as "Anna T. Griffin". They did not have children.

Charles Banda was the son of Alexander Banda and Anna Pelreal. He was born in Budapest, Hungary, on 15 May 1903. He immigrated to America circa 1908. Charles died in Maryland 3 July 1992. His age was given as 89 years [36].

Charles remarried after Hanna's death and had two children in the second marriage. He was remembered fondly by the Connors. He appears to have been a generous person and to have stayed in touch with the Connors over the years—they outlived the Bandas, too.

We have not been able to locate Hanna in either the 1920 or 1930 Federal Census.

Ellen (Helen) Griffin was the last child of Denis Griffin and Ellen Allen. The Ballybunion church register listed the date of birth as 20 October 1901. She was baptized on 21 October 1901. Her godparents were John Scanlan and Anne Scanlan. The priest was Fr. J. Molyneaux. The civil record listed her birth as 21 December 1901, so she is yet another person born after her baptism.

Helen died of alcoholism on 23 April 1948 in Los Angeles County General Hospital (CA cert. #22847). She was 47 years of age. She was described as a solicitor for the National Medical Group. She lived at 2644 Gleneden St. in Los Angeles and had been in that state for thirteen months. The informant was Tillie Allen of 140 Cabiri St., New York City. Helen was brought back to New Jersey for burial in Holy Cross Cemetery in North Arlington (block 11, D202).

There are two moving stories my father told about Helen, who was his favorite aunt. Helen went to California with the hope that her daughter, who was considered very beautiful, might get into movies. This hope never materialized—perhaps the chance was cut short by Helen's death. My father was with his mother at the train station in Newark when Helen's body came back to New Jersey. Catherine insisted they open the coffin. She placed rosary beads in Helen's hands.

Helen immigrated on the *Baltic*, arriving with her mother and sister on 1 June 1912. She was 11 years of age. She was called "Ellie" on the ship's log. She was described on the ship's log as 4'7 with brown hair and blue eyes. Once past the Island of Tears her name altered to Helen.

Helen married Jerome Lawrence Kleinicke in the Church of St. Gregory on 1 October 1931 (cert. # 22847). Their witnesses were Charles H. Allen and Tillie Barton—we don't know if Tillie Barton was Tillie Allen. The priest was Fr. Eugene Callahan. Their address was given as 205 W. 91st St. Helen's name on the certificate was given as "Helen M. Griffin". Jerome was described as 29 years of age. His occupation was given as "cutter"—he worked in the garment industry. After their marriage they resided in Old Tappan, New Jersey. My father recollected that Jerome was friends with Charles Banda.

Helen Griffin and Jerome Kleinicke had two children: **Helen**; and **Charles**.

Jerome Kleinicke was born in Baltimore on 1 June 1899 (cert #B-1551). His father was Carl Bruno Kleinicke, who was born in Leipzig, Germany, and Regina Bothe or Boothe of Baltimore. Jerome registered for the WWI draft in Baltimore. He was described as medium in height and build with brown hair and blue eyes. According to the 1920 Census Jerome resided with Louis and Ollia Kirby at 1740 Webster, Baltimore. In 1930 he resided as a "roomer" at 405 West 91st St. in Manhattan. We have not been able to locate Helen on either the 1920 or 1930 Federal Census.

Jerome died 15 December 1936 in Hackensack Hospital. He was 37 years old. He was buried with Helen in Holy Cross Cemetery [37].

Chapter Twelve

~

Lietuva—Mykolas Bielawski & Ursula Milosz

My great-grandparents on the Polish side are **Mykolas Bielawski** and **Ursula Milosz** of Kalniskes village and **Franciszk Storta** and **Rozalia Juchnewicz** of Girdziunai village. This chapter reviews the lives and family of Mykolas and Ursula. Chapter 13 examines the lives of Franciszk and Rozalia.

Mykolas Bielawski and Ursula Milosz married in Turgeliai Parish on 15 February 1881. Witnesses were Motiejus Dulkys, Jonas Dulkys, Jonas Kavaliauskas, and Jonas Jukewicz. The priest was Fr. Kiprijonas Zebrowski.

Mykolas was the son of Juozas Bielawski and Petronele Falkewicz. He was born 29 September 1856 in Kalniskes village. He was baptized October 14. His godparents were Steponas Valeika and Marijona Liniauskas. The priest was Fr. Mackewicz. Mykolas died in 1916, according to his daughter Juzufa. His burial place is unknown, but it was likely Turgeliai Cemetery.

We have no pictures of Mykolas or personal characteristics, but he appears to have been a serious person who raised his children properly. We were told by Michail Bielawski of Kalniskes that Mykolas worked very hard in order to have his children immigrate to America.

Ursula Milosz was the daughter of Jonas Milosz and Magdalena Asakewicz. She was born 9 November 1859 in Malakonys village. She was baptized November 15. Her godparents were Steponas Valeika and Ona Markewicz. The priest was Fr. Jeronimas Vertusinskis. Ursula died while giving birth on 16 April 1889. She was 29 years of age. She was likely buried in Turgeliai Cemetery.

Mykolas and Ursula had the following known children: Josef; Pawel; Jonas; and **Adomas**. We have no information on the life of Adomas. It is possible he was the child born when Ursula died, but the Vilnius Archive provided no baptism record. We have no information whether he survived.

Josef Bielawski was born 8 February 1882 in Kalniskes. He was baptized February 9 in Turgeliai Parish. His godparents were Tomas Milosz and Regina Milosz. The priest was Fr. Zebrowski.

Josef never married. He died of a heart attack on 19 September 1935, aged 53, in the rest room of a tavern at 476 Henderson St. in Jersey City. He was buried in a pauper's grave in Holy Cross Cemetery in North Arlington (block 3, section H, tier Q, grave 90) [38].

Josef was known to be an alcoholic. In the newspaper article about his death he was described as "homeless"—he may have lived in a back room of the tavern. All our immigrant ancestors must have had a difficult time adjusting. The language barrier would have been nearly insurmountable for Josef who was over 30 years of age when he immigrated. Some of our ancestors—Pat Allen—showed that they could prosper in America. Josef showed that not everyone could make it psychologically in the furnace of the New World. He went from being a farm laborer in a village of less than 100 people to a foreign-speaking loner in a metropolis of several hundred thousand. In a place like Kalniskes money means little—there is nothing to buy and work is not an issue. In Jersey City money was the means to a better life. Finding work was crucial to making it in the merciless big city. It's easy to see that, lacking an immediate family and lacking immediate prospects of bettering himself, Josef lost himself in alcohol.

Josef immigrated from Hamburg, Germany, on the Hamburg-American steamship *Antonina*. He arrived in New York harbor on 12 May 1913 (Nat. Archives roll 473022). He was described as able to read and write—this would be Polish. He was a citizen of Russia. It is difficult to decipher, but his last place of residence was Kalniskes. His destination was his brother Pawel at 161 Pavonia Ave. in Jersey City. He was described as 5'7 with brown hair and blue eyes. He was 31 years of age. It looks like he had $35.00 on him—the amount seems high.

Josef registered for the World War One draft on 12 September 1918. He was described as a laborer for Swift & Co., a large meat-processing plant near the Holland Tunnel. He had dark brown hair and gray eyes and was medium in height and build. He resided with his brother at 143 Pavonia Ave. He signed his name "Joseph Bielewski". His date of birth was given incorrectly as 8 December 1882 in "Wilenska, Russia". There was a note on the draft card stating that he was "injured in both legs three years ago in Pittsburg, PA, Black Dawn Steel Co." We have no information on this or whether Pawel accompanied him to Pennsylvania. Neither my mother nor my Aunt Helen Ost remembered Josef as being crippled.

Josef resided with Pawel and his family at 143 Pavonia Ave. according to the 1920 Federal Census. He was described in the Census as a laborer for the Pennsylvania Railroad. He has not been located in the 1930 Census. As the Irish might say, he may have had "no fixed address" by this time.

My mother remembered that Josef played the violin and that his violin was valuable. The violin was passed to his nephew Henry but was subsequently lost.

Pawel (Paul) Bielawski, my grandfather, was born on 3 January 1884 in Kalniskes village according to Turgeliai Parish records. He was baptized on January 8. His godparents were Kazimier Milosz and Marijona Bielawska. The priest was Fr. Zebrowski. Pawel immigrated to the United States on 28 March 1909. He married Zofia Storta in the Church of St. Anthony in Jersey City on 29 April 1912. He became a citizen of the United States on 1 July 1930. He died in Secaucas, New Jersey, on 19 January 1957. He was 73 years of age. Pawel's life and family will be described in Chapter Fifteen.

Jonas Bielawski was the third child of Mykolas Bielawski and Ursula Milosz. He was born 7 June 1886 in Kalniskes. He was baptized by Fr. Zebrowski on July 6. His godparents were Motiejus Milosz and Ona Jankawicz. Jonas died in 1946 and was buried in Turgeliai Cemetery. The specific day and site are not known.

Jonas married Kotryna Kavaliauskas in Tabariskes Church on 8 February 1937. He was 50 years of age. We were told Jonas married late because he had to raise and marry off his stepsisters. Military service may have been another reason. Kotryna died in 1982 at the age of 83. If this age is correct, she also married late.

Jonas and Kotryna had two children: **Marijona**; and **Michail**.

We had the pleasure of meeting Michail and his energetic wife Helene, as well as their sons Mecislav and Viktor on our visits to Lithuania. We subsequently got the opportunity to meet Marijona and her husband. Michail and Helene demonstrated the ancient virtue of hospitality on our first visit in 1997. Our letter notifying them of our arrival went astray. Despite our dropping in unexpectedly from a distance of four thousand miles, they scrambled to put together an elaborate meal and a deeply satisfying visit.

Michail related that the original intention was for Jonas to immigrate to America, but he became too sick to travel and couldn't make the trip.

Like Tom Forde, Mykolas Bielawski married a second time. This was to **Rozalia Bagdziulis** on 24 February 1891. Their witnesses were Aleksandras Bizunowicz, Martynas Misiuta (?), Martynas Vilkinis, and Kazimier Satkewicz. Fr. Zebrowski officiated. Rozalia was from Beciuneliai village, which is located just to the south of Kalniskes. She was described as 20 years of age. Her parents were Jurgis Bagdziulis and Ona Matulewicz. According to her daughter Juzufa, Rozalia died in 1927.

Like Tom Forde, Mykolas discovered that a second bride can be more trouble than a first bride. Rozalia may not be in the same league as Bridget Lyons, but she comes through the years as a wicked stepmother. Pawel told his children that Rozalia was cruel to him and his brother Josef and that she always put her children before them.

The known children of Mykolas Bielawski and Rozalia Bagdziulis were: Feliks; Michalina; Malvina; Viktor; Paulina; Viktor again; and Juzufa. All births were in Kalniskes, all baptisms were in Turgeliai Parish.

Feliks Bielawski was born 13 June 1893. He was baptized by Fr. Zebrowski on June 20. His godparents were Petras Bizunowicz and Marijona, wife of Vincentas Blazewicz. Feliks died in 1978. He was buried in Turgeliai Cemetery. Feliks married a lady named Zofia—her surname is not known. Zofia died in 1972. They had two daughters. We met their daughter **Bronislawa** when we visited Kalniskes in 2000.

Michalina Bielawska was born 2 January 1897. She was baptized by Fr. P. Shepeckis on January 29. Her godparents were Vincentas Blazewicz and Paulina Bagdziulis. Michalina married a man named Kazimier Makewicz. They immigrated to Poland in 1948 or were resettled there and had five children.

Malvina Bielawska was born 17 August 1900. She was baptized by Fr. Shepeckis on September 3. Her godparents were Martynas Milosz and Marijona Bagdziulis. Malvina died in childhood "of paralysis" on 2 April 1908. She was buried in Turgeliai by Fr. P. Petkewicz.

Viktor Bielawski was born 2 April 1903. He was baptized by Fr. Zvierzewicz on April 13. His godparents were Kazimier Milosz and Paulina Bagdziulis. We have no other information on Viktor's life. It is likely he died young, since the name was used a second time, but we do not have the date.

Paulina Bielawska was born 3 July 1905. She was baptized July 13 by Fr. Shepeckis. Her godparents were Antanas Budzinski and Marijona Bagdziulis. Paulina died 13 March 1988, aged 82. She was buried in the city of Salcininki, where her family moved at some point. We saw her stone when we visited Lithuania in 2000 [39].

Paulina married Josef Wasilewski in Turgeliai Church on 3 February 1932. Josef was born in 1906. He died 25 October 1992. They had three children.

The second **Viktor Bielawski** was born 2 March 1908. He was baptized by Fr. Shepeckis on March 4. His godparents were Jonas Jukewicz and Kotryna Bagdziulis. This Viktor died as a baby on 16 July 1908 "of inflammation". He was buried in Turgeliai Cemetery on July 17.

Juzufa Bielawska was born 16 February 1911. She was baptized by Fr. J. Jankowski on February 22. Her godparents were Adomas Zila and Kotryna Bagdziulis. Juzufa died in Salcininki on 24 April 2002 at 91 years of age.

Juzufa married Bronislaw Kozlowski (1907 – 1973). They had four children. We had the pleasure of meeting Juzufa's daughter **Marijona Pupalaigis** and her children on our visits to Salcininki. Marijona's family is professional—she was a teacher and her son is an executive in the Customs Bureau. Like Michail Bielawski, Marijona was quite helpful in relating our Bielawski ancestors. And we had the privilege of meeting Juzufa in 2000. Juzufa was a frail lady who showed us pictures of her relatives and received us in kindly fashion. It was one of the highlights of our genealogical jaunts to meet a lady who was living history in addition to being living family history. Juzufa, after all, was born when Tsars ruled Russia. She survived the calamities of two World Wars and died in a freedom-loving Lithuania. Given the events of the twentieth century, that is something of a miraculous accomplishment.

Chapter Thirteen

Lietuva—Franciszk Storta & Rozalia Juchnewicz

Our second Polish great-grandparents are **Franciszk Storta** and **Rozalia Juchnewicz**. They married in Subotniki Parish on 25 April 1882, according to a record furnished by the government of Belarus. Franciszk was described as 22 years of age and Rozalia as 18, which cannot be the case, since she would have been born after her father died. Both were from Girdziunai.

The Vilnius Archive does not hold records for Subotniki Parish beyond the 1870s. The Belarus government was generous in providing this marriage record and a number of baptism records, but the names of witnesses, godparents, and priests were not included. This is the only family line where such information is lacking.

Franciszk Storta was the son of Tomas Storta and Agota Karuzas. He was born in Girdziunai village on 22 March 1860 and baptized in Subotniki on March 25 by Fr. A. Znoma. His godparents were Vincentas Bikis (or Bilis) and Marijona Arodzas. Franciszk died, aged 50, on 28 January 1911. He was buried in Subotniki Parish cemetery. His stone remains standing.

Rozalia Juchnewicz was the daughter of Motiejus Juchnewicz and Kristina Blazys. To the best of our knowledge she was born in the late 1850s (see Chapter Nine). She died in Girdziunai on 7 February 1920. Her age was given as 62. She was buried in Subotniki Parish cemetery.

The known children of Franciszk Storta and Rozalia Juchnewicz were: Tadeus; Maciej; Stefanie; Zofia; Stanley; Marija; Juzufa; and Jan.

Tadeusz Storta was born 22 July 1883 according to the Belarus government. We have no other information. Tadeusz may or may not be the same person as Maciej.

Maciej (Matthew) Storta was born in the period 1882 – 1886—no record was provided by Belarus. His headstone gives 1882 as the year of his birth. Maciej died 8 March 1934. His age was given by Belarus as 55, but this cannot be correct. Maciej's son Danislav indicated his age was 52. He was buried in Subotniki.

Maciej married Paulina Tuchovcha in 1922—the record has not been provided. According to their son Danislav, Paulina lived 1901 – 1990, which makes her nearly two decades younger than Maciej. If the year of her birth was correct she survived Maciej by 56 years.

Maciej immigrated to the United States on the Hamburg-American liner *President Grant*. The ship left Hamburg on 9 April 1910 and arrived in Hoboken on April 21. His age was given on the ship's log as 26, which indicates he was born in 1884. He was listed as a citizen of Russia and of the Polish race. He sailed under the name "Matweg", which is an old Russian version of Maciej. His last place of residence was "Gergowi". His destination appeared to be "Ignac Storta", described as a "brother", at 195 Newark Ave., Jersey City. We have no information of anyone by this name and there is no record at the National Archives. Maciej was described as 5'9, with brown hair and brown eyes. He paid for the trip himself [40].

Maciej returned to Lithuania sometime in 1914. Now there are small mistakes in life and there are large mistakes and this is a large mistake, considering the disparate histories of Jersey City and of Girdziunai in the twentieth century. Maciej returned to World War One—Danislav told us his father served in the Russian army and spent several years as a prisoner of war. His descendents experienced World War Two and the horrors of the Nazi and Soviet regimes. Lithuania lost one third its population to death and exile in the Second World War. Another 20,000 died in the savage partisan wars of the 1950s and 1960s—the area around Salcininki saw heavy fighting. The grungy over-populated wards of Jersey City look like heaven on earth in comparison to the bloodbath in Europe [41].

Danislav told us that his father worked on a barge in Jersey City. This is quite possible. His sister Zofia indicated his address was Provost St. when she arrived in America. This street is gone now—it is part of the Newport mall complex—but it bordered directly on the Hudson. Danislav told us that Maciej was an expert carpenter—he built the house we visited in

1997. He was also described as an expert fisherman, a vocation he put to profitable use in the Gauja River.

Maciej was unknown to us until we discovered him on the ship's log and made the acquaintance of his children. He played an important role in our family history—he worked with Pawel Bielawski and may have introduced him to my grandmother.

Maciej and Paulina Storta had five children: **Stanislawa** (born 1923); **Wladyslaw** (deceased); **Danislav** (1928 – 2004); **Anna** (died 2001); and **Adele** (dates unknown).

Danislav was very helpful with our family history. He was a heavyset man around six feet with thick glasses and thick white hair. He had three children, one of whom is a doctor in Salcininki. His son Josef died in 2009. The ancestral home in Girdziunai has been sold. For the first time in two centuries there is no Storta in residence there.

We met Adele and Anna only briefly on our jaunts to Lietuva. Adele was a tall thin woman. Anna was short and slight—she bore a strong facial resemblance to *Cocci* Blanche. We did not meet Stanislawa but we had the pleasure of meeting her daughter Wladyslawa Kucynska, who extended an extraordinary hospitality when we visited Dieveniskes in 2000 and who, like Danislav, was very helpful in narrating our Polish side.

Stephanie Storta was born 9 December 1885 in Girdziunai, according to records supplied by Belarus. No other information is available on her life.

Zofia Storta, my grandmother, was born 3 January 1890 in Girdziunai—this is the same day as my grandfather. She was baptized on January 6, but Belarus did not provide the names of her godparents. Zofia immigrated to the United States on the Hamburg-American steamship *Kaiserin Auguste Victoria*, arriving in Hoboken on 28 November 1910. She married Pawel Bielawski in St. Anthony's Church on 29 April 1912. Zofia died of a heart attack in Jersey City on 19 March 1936 at the age of 46. Her life and family will be described in Chapter 15.

Stanislaw (Stanley) Storta was born 1 November 1893 in Girdziunai. He was baptized Nov. 7 (Belarus record). Stanley never married. He died of a heart attack on 8 October 1951 in Jersey City. He was 57 years of age. He resided at 210 Pavonia Ave. at the time of death. He was described as a laborer for the Armstrong Trucking Co. He was buried in Holy Cross Cemetery in North Arlington (Block 70, section A, tier D, grave 42—or 72, no stone). We have a full paper trail for my mother's "Uncle Stanley".

The informant on his death record was his "niece" Antonia Stabkiewicz—in fact, she was his girlfriend. My mother related that Antonia planned an elaborate wake for Stanley and then absconded with the insurance money. Pawel Bielawski, certainly no wealthy man, had to foot the bill for the funeral.

Stanley immigrated to the United States on the Cunard Liner *Ivernia* from Trieste, Italy, arriving at the port of New York on 5 December 1913. His name on the ship's log was given as "Stord". His age was 20, his race "Ruthenian"—this is an obsolete term for Russian. He was able to read and write. No occupation was listed. His destination was Pawel Bielawski at 161 Pavonia Ave. in Jersey City. Stanley was described as 5'7, with brown hair and brown eyes. He had no money on arrival. Stanley was detained overnight until December 6, when Mrs. Zofia Bielawska of 139 8th St. arrived at 10:30 AM to escort him from the Island of Tears [42].

Stanley registered for the World War One draft on 2 June 1917. He resided at 143 Pavonia Ave. His occupation was given as bartender for John Valwenty at 143 Provost St. He was described as tall and stout with brown eyes. Stanley's place of birth was Girdzery, Wilenska, Poland—this location proved very helpful to the Vilnius Archive in finding Parish records.

According to the 1920 Federal Census Stanley resided with Pawel and Zofia at 143 Pavonia Ave. He was described as a laborer for the Pennsylvania Railroad. In the 1930 Census Stanley resided in a rooming house run by Stanley Urban at 147 9th St. His name was spelled "Sztorta". His occupation was given as blacksmith and wagon builder (roll 1350, P. 20A, ED 12).

Stanley applied for Social Security on 28 November 1936. His address was 1712 Jersey Ave. His employer was Burns Bros. No occupation was listed. His mother's name was given as "Rose Uckneva".

Stanley declared his intention to become a citizen on 6 December 1939 (#2-645932). He resided at 478 Henderson St. His occupation was "blacksmith". His age was given as 46 and his birth date as 30 October 1893. He was described as 5'7, 175 lbs., with fair complexion, black hair, and brown eyes. He signed his name "Storto" on the document.

On 23 June 1943 Stanley petitioned for citizenship. He resided at 189 8th St. His occupation was "utility man". He was described as 5'7, 165 lbs., with hair mixed gray and the "left eye turned white." His witnesses were Hilary Stanczyk, a tavern owner, and Bronislaw Ewadowicz, a carpenter [43].

On 27 September 1940 Stanley filed an Alien Registration Form (#2289883). This little known genealogical resource was required of all immigrants who had not become citizens. On the form Stanley's middle name was listed as "Franciszk". His address was 478 Henderson St. He was described as an unemployed blacksmith. He had no military service and had never been arrested. He was a member of the Association of the Sons of Poland.

On 27 April 1942 Stanley registered for the World War Two draft. He resided at 478 Henderson St. His height was 5'7, his weight 162 pounds. His eyes and hair were brown. His employer was given as Hilary Stanczyk, also of 478 Henderson St. Stanley listed a telephone number.

My mother remembered that Stanley broke his leg while working for the railroad and that he had insurance money because of the accident. It was this money that Antonia stole. My mother also remembered that he had been injured on a ride at Coney Island and that he had some type of infection involving the gums. My cousin Josephine remembered that Stanley played the accordion and told a lot of jokes. He gave his nieces a few dollars when they visited.

Stanley liked to drink—hard, apparently. My mother recollected that he had been in detox in Medical Center in Jersey City sometime in the 1930s. When she and *Dziadek* visited the hospital they found Stanley immersed to the chin in some kind of tank. This must have been a primitive medical treatment for alcohol abuse.

One photograph of Stanley survives. It is the photograph required for citizenship. Stanley has squarish facial features and prominent cheeks. His hair is cut short. He looks to be on the heavy side.

Marija Storta, the child of Franciszk Storta and Rozalia Juchnewicz, was born on 23 September 1898 in Girdziunai. She was baptized in Subotniki September 27. According to Wladyslawa, Marija died young. She married, however, and had at least one child.

Jan (John) Storta was born on 10 August 1901 in Girdziunai. He was baptized on August 18. John died in Jelena Gora in Southwest Poland in 1981. John's birth date sets an upper limit on the age of Rozalia Juchnewicz. (We always referred to Jan as "John".)

We corresponded with John's granddaughter, **Margaret Nalepa**, who supplied the following details. John married a lady named Helena Juchnewicz of Girdziunai. Helena died at an advanced age in 1997. They had three children: **Wladyslawa** (1929 – 1992); **Sigmund** (b. 1935); and **Franciszk**. John was in the Russian army before World War Two. He worked in metals and jewelry. He made a ring for my uncle Roman Rog, who visited Poland in the 1970s.

John and his family were in Girdziunai until the mid-1930s. They lived in Vilnius at one point and then immigrated to Poland, first to Silesia and then to Jelena Gora in 1970. The circumstances of their immigration are not clear. Russia and Poland were police states throughout the twentieth century and people did not just get up and move without sanction.

Uncle Roman showed us a picture of John Storta. The picture showed a thin old man with flat squarish features. He looked quite elderly, but had a fine head of white hair. My mother did not think he resembled Stanley.

Margaret Nalepa listed an additional child of Franciszk Storta and Rozalia Juchnewicz for whom Belarus did not provide any records. This was **Juzufa Storta**. She must have been born before John. Margaret indicated that Juzufa never married and that she worked for priests in some capacity, perhaps as a housekeeper. We have no other information on Juzufa.

Our Polish ancestors were deeply religious people. Religion ruled their lives in a way that is difficult for us to understand. Their lives—as, indeed, the lives of our Irish ancestors—were tied to the liturgical calendar. It was a calendar marked with strange customs and superstitions. On the morning of January 1 the devout folk of the past climbed hills to catch the first sunrise of the New Year. They brought pails of water to see the reflection of light shimmer. The devout folk also treated January 1 as a day of portents and omens. Girls placed the names of suitors under their pillows on scraps of paper. On awakening they selected one paper without looking—this was the man they would marry. The selection was random, we like to think, but the choice was fated by the matchmaker in the sky.

A game was played on New Year's Day that foretold the future. Objects were hidden under bowls that people chose at random. If a ring was picked the person would marry. If a goblet was picked the person would marry a souse. If a key was picked the person would move into a new house. If a coin was picked the person would come into wealth. I don't know how accurate the game was, but it was easier on the teeth than the brambrack the Irish chewed on.

As in many places Shrove Tuesday was a day of revelry. In preparation for the Lenten fast our ancestors ate and drank copiously on this day. In Lithuania there was a custom of adorning masks made of tree bark and twine. The usual costumes represented animals, witches, and devils. We don't know if our Polish ancestors shared this custom—the children probably did, as it was a kind of Halloween. The tradition of weaving masks continues. Masks were featured in the flea markets we browsed on Pilies St. in the Old Town in Vilnius.

Lent was a time of solemnity. Meat was not eaten. Parties were not held. No one married. The celebration of Easter was much like our own—High Mass followed by a huge meal and an egg hunt. There were the usual auguries—Easter weather foretold the weather for the rest of the year. An accident on Easter predicted calamities later in the year.

The eve of the feast of St. John on June 24 amounted to a summer exercise one short step removed from paganism. The Parish priest had to be discreet about the doings in the woods—the Pope would not be amused if he found out what the parishioners were up to. Bonfires were lit to protect the crops from witches. People hunted throughout the night to find ferns in bloom. If one was found it bestowed magical powers.

All Soul's Day was a solemn day. No merrymaking was allowed, as it would be disrespectful to the deceased. People had to pray for their dear departed on this day and visit their graves. Lighted candles were placed at the headstones. We don't visit cemeteries on November 2, but we keep up the tradition by having Masses said for our loved ones. For years I've watched my mother mail contributions to missionary fathers to remember our loved ones in their Masses.

Our ancestors fasted on Christmas Eve. After Midnight Mass a large meal was consumed. This meal did not include alcohol or meat. The Christmas wafer—*oplatek*—was exchanged among family members and guests. (*Oplatek* was a rectangular communion host blessed by the priest.) There was a tradition of caroling in the Old Country. The Christmas tree existed, but it was not decorated to excess and there was no gift giving as we engage in today. Children were expected to perform songs or recitations to get trinkets. As did the other holidays, Christmas had its share of superstitions. It was considered good form to break off a larger piece of *oplatek* than the person who offered it—this ensured more luck than the other person got. And there was a rather morbid superstition that the first person to leave the dining table would be the first person to die. This was the reason Christmas dinners tended to go on interminably.

Joseph and Sophia Ford

Kathleen, Sophia, Felicia, and Dennis Ford

Patrick and Catherine Ford

Pawel and Zofia Bielawski

Ellen Griffin

Dennis Ford and Thomas Ford

Bielawski siblings – Anne, Blanche, Helen, Henry, Sophia, and Carol

Delia Forde and Kate Flynn

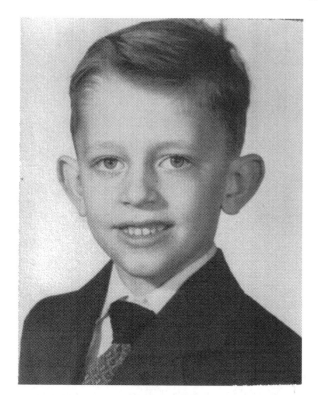

Tommie Grogan

Fred Ost, Jr.

Chapter Fourteen

~

America—Patrick Ford & Catherine Griffin

My paternal grandparents are **Patrick Ford** and **Catherine Griffin**. They married in the Church of Our Lady of Grace in Hoboken on 20 April 1913. Their witnesses were Thomas Brennan and Mary Griffin. The priest was Fr. Joseph Kelly. Patrick was described as 25, a "freight handler" in residence at 514 Park Ave. in Hoboken. The "e" in the name Forde got sliced off on his arrival in America. Catherine was described as 25 and in residence at 809 Park Ave. This was the address of her cousin John William Leonard. Their ages were incorrect, as were the dates of their baptisms. Patrick's was given as 24 August 1889 in St. Peter's Church in Bally—the writing is indecipherable. It took a long time and a lot of luck to identify the place as Ballyhaunis. Catherine's baptism was given as 10 July 1887 in St. Mary's Church in "Ballybonan".

Mary Griffin was Catherine's sister. We don't know who Thomas Brennan was. There were a number of Brennans in Hoboken in my youth. The surname occurs frequently in East Mayo.

The Annagh Parish register we viewed at the Family History Library indicated that Patrick was baptized 30 August 1892. His full name was "Patrick Austin". His godparents were Patrick and Bridget Fitzmaurice. They may have been his relatives in Laughil, but we can't say for certain. The priest was likely Fr. Michael Burke. The baptism cost two shillings, six pence. Patrick was baptized in St. Mary's Chapel in the townland of Logboy—St. Patrick's is the church in Ballyhaunis, but he was not baptized there. The civil record of his baptism, entered by Mary Forde on September 2, stated that Patrick was born on 26 August 1892.

Patrick—*Grandpa*—died in the Pollak Hospital (nursing home) of the Medical Center complex in Jersey City on 14 January 1980. He was 87 years of age. Cause of death was congestive heart failure and arteriosclerosis. He was buried on January 17 in the Ford plot in Holy Name Cemetery (plot E-5-93) after a 10:15 AM funeral Mass in Our Lady of Grace Church.

Grandpa immigrated on the White Star steamship *Baltic*, sailing from Queenstown and arriving in the port of New York on 23 October 1910. His ticket number or personal identifier was 12888. He was described as a "British citizen" and of the "Irish race". His age was given as 20, his occupation as "laborer". The trip was paid by "self". He had $15.00 on him. His father was Tom Forde of "Dernacong"—this led to an important genealogical breakthrough (see Chapter Twenty One). Patrick was described as 5'7, with a fair complexion, black hair, and blue eyes. His destination was his "cousin" Patrick Waldron at 2182 8th Ave., New York City. We were told by Mrs. Fitzharris that Patrick Waldron was the son of James Waldron and Catherine Fitzmaurice of Derrynacong and that he died young, but we have not confirmed this.

Patrick declared his intention to become a citizen for the first time on 28 April 1911 in the Southern District Court of New York. His address was given as 2182 8th Ave. His birth date was listed as 24 August 1889. His arrival in New York was given erroneously as 24 October 1909. His occupation was "fireman". He was described as 5'9, 150 pounds, with a fair complexion, brown hair, blue eyes, and no distinctive marks. As part of the naturalization process Patrick swore that "I am not an anarchist, I am not a polygamist nor a believer in the practice of polygamy; and it is my intention in good faith to become a citizen of the United States of America."

Patrick registered for the World War One draft on 5 June 1917. At the time he resided at 615 Willow Ave. He gave his birth date as 28 August 1889, the place as Ballyhaunis. He was a longshoreman for the Scandinavian Steamship Line located at 16th St. at the northern end of Hoboken.

The 1915 Hoboken City Directory listed Pat Ford, a "bartender", in residence at 915 Clinton St. The 1918 City Directory listed Pat Ford, a "laborer", in residence at 1011 Park Ave.

Grandpa declared his intention to become a citizen for the second time on 23 August 1934 in the U.S. District Court at Newark. The certificate number was 2-344776. His address was given as 815 Park Ave. in Hoboken. His date of birth was given as 24 August 1889. He was described as 5'9, 155 pounds, with a fair complexion, black hair, and blue eyes. A "portion of a finger is missing on his right hand"—this is a detail I recollected only when I read the Declaration.

Patrick petitioned for naturalization on 7 January 1937 in the Common Pleas Court in Jersey City. He signed the oath that declared, "It is my intention to become a citizen of the United States and to renounce absolutely all allegiance and fidelity to any foreign prince … particularly to George VI of Great Britain and Ireland." His witnesses were James O'Connell and James Mulhearn. Patrick took the oath of allegiance and became a citizen on 13 April 1937.

Patrick applied for Social Security on 2 December 1936. He resided at 815 Park Ave. His employer was given as Jules S. Sattral Co. at 17 Battery Place in Manhattan. The application revealed his mother's maiden name to us for the first time—Mary Hunt.

Patrick registered in the "old man's draft" in World War Two on 27 April 1942. His address was 931 Willow Ave. No phone number was listed. His date of birth was given as 24 August 1891. He worked for the Ryan Stevedore Co. at Pier 4 in Hoboken. He had a ruddy complexion, blue eyes, and gray hair. It was specified that the top joints were missing off the second and third fingers of his right hand.

My grandmother Catherine Griffin—*Nana*—was baptized on 11 July 1886 by Fr. Charles Godley. Her godmother was Johanna Allen—we can't be sure this was Timothy Allen's wife. She was baptized in St. Mary's Chapel, which was also known as the Doon Church. We visited the Doon Church in June 1996. It stands on the cliffs on the Ballybunion Road a few miles from the center of town. At the time of our visit the church was an empty shell under repair. It hadn't been used in decades. There was no altar nor any religious icons. The floor consisted of broken up tiles pale red in color. One tile sits on the shelf above my computer. It serves as a pedestal for the marriage photograph of Pat and Catherine Ford.

The civil record of Catherine's birth was reported by John Allen on 23 August 1886. He gave her name as "Kate" and the date of her birth as July 12.

Catherine Griffin died in her apartment at 320 Marshall Dr. in Hoboken on 26 March 1978. She was 91 years of age. She was buried with Pat in Holy Name Cemetery on March 29 after a 9:15 AM funeral Mass in Our Lady of Grace.

For many years Nana had been under doctor's care for a heart condition. X-rays taken later in life revealed that she had unknowingly broken a bone in her back. This may have occurred while swimming in the ocean in the Atlantic Highlands in New Jersey. My father recalled that Nana told him that she severely cut her foot as a child on Knockanore Mountain.

Catherine immigrated to America on the *Baltic*. The ship left Queenstown on 3 April 1908 and arrived in New York harbor on April 11. Her ticket number was 3361. Like Grandpa, she was a British citizen and of the Irish race. Her age was given as 22, her occupation as "servant". She had $10.00 on her. Her uncle paid for the voyage. Her last address in Ireland was with her mother Ellen Griffin in Trippul. Her destination was her uncle John Allen at 221 Clinton St. in Hoboken. Catherine was described as 5'4, with brown hair and brown eyes. This does not describe her—the agent must have been color blind. She was detained until 4:30 PM on April 11 when her uncle Patrick Allen of 202 Monroe St. arrived to escort her to her new home.

Catherine declared her intention to become a citizen in the Common Pleas Court in Jersey City on 15 August 1934. The certificate was 2-34429. At the time she resided at 815 Park Ave. Her occupation was "housewife". She was erroneously described as born in Ballybunion on 10 July 1887. Her appearance was given accurately as 5'7, 155 pounds, with a fair complexion, red hair, and blue eyes.

Nana petitioned for naturalization on 30 December 1936. Like Patrick, she renounced her allegiance to George VI. Her witnesses were Loretta Kammerer and Eileen Shields. Nana took the oath of allegiance and became a citizen on 13 April 1937.

Nana and Grandpa resided at 1011 Park Ave. according to the Federal Census taken on 7 January 1920. Pat's occupation was given as longshoreman. The 1930 Census, taken on April 2, listed them in residence at 803 Willow Ave—I lived in the same building as a child. The rent was $28.00. They had no radio. Pat was again described as a longshoreman. Their place of birth was given as "Free State Ireland." The 1920 Census gave their place of birth as "Ireland"—the difference represents the partition of Ireland in 1922. Their son Dennis, aged 16, was described on the 1930 Census as what appears to be a "waiter". My father appeared on that census. He was four years of age.

I had the pleasure of growing up with Nana and Grandpa owing to their excessive longevity. They lived for a time next to the parking lot of the Safeway supermarket on 8th and Willow Ave. They moved to 320 Marshall Drive at the western end of Hoboken. We visited there regularly, usually after Sunday Mass. My father was the "baby" in his family and the only child to live in Hoboken, so he kept in close touch with his parents. They moved to Marshall Drive when the "projects" were new. Located alongside the train tracks below the Palisades, Marshall Drive rapidly descended into a slum. By the end of their lives the vicinity was occupied by unsocialized minorities. It was not a safe place.

Nana had thick white hair and deep-set blue eyes—these derived from the Griffin side, as did her longevity. She was thin in old age, but photographs taken in the 1950s show a stocky lady. She always prepared instant coffee and cookies when we visited. She slipped us a dollar or two when we left. She always did this out of Grandpa's view.

Pat Ford was wire thin. He didn't have an ounce of fat on him. Like his father, he was a "nice man who didn't say much." This silence was probably a good thing, since he had a heavy brogue and a gargly voice, so he was sometimes difficult to understand. My father said that Pat was "tight as a clam" when it came to money and that "he wouldn't give you the right time of day."

Grandpa was never harsh with us, but he must have been difficult to handle in earlier decades. He was known to be a tough man and a heavy drinker. At one point my father nearly arrested him for disorderly conduct (See Chapter Sixteen.). Pat drank and smoked heavily throughout his long life, although the rowdiness had receded in his old age.

Pat worked as a "chenango" on the Hoboken docks. This was a laborer who "shaped up" on a daily basis for work. It is a life style that no longer exists in America. Today freight is shipped in containers that are placed on trucks and unloaded by forklifts. In Pat's time laborers descended into the holds of cargo ships and manually placed the freight box by box on pallets cranes hoisted up. The work was backbreaking and dangerous—the movie *On the Waterfront* portrays the physical conditions and political harassment the longshoremen endured. The average pay in the 1920s for this kind of labor was $10.00 a week. Pat must have been a good worker—he stayed employed throughout the Great Depression. Unlike many freight handlers who squandered their retirement fund, Pat had a steady source of income in his old age—this may have been due more to Nana than to him. My mother remembered that Catherine Griffin personally collected his checks.

Grandpa was known to be scrupulously honest. At one point he was told to steal something from the cargo so that he would appear to be "honest". His fellow workers became suspicious that he didn't take anything. They thought he was a detective.

Nana and Grandpa never spoke against their family or criticized their children. Nana seemed to have a fatalistic viewpoint, saying that a person makes the bed he lies on and that no one forces a person to drink. She would have been well acquainted with the effects of alcohol in her husband and children.

Like 40% of the ancestors of our fellow citizens, our grandparents on both the Irish and Polish sides arrived in America through Ellis Island, "the Island of Hope, the Island of Tears." Between 1892 and 1954 more than 15 million people entered the United States through Ellis Island. In the peak years as many as 5,000 people a day underwent the inspection process.

In 1892 Ellis Island was selected to replace Castle Garden in Lower Manhattan as the point of entrance. This was at a time when the Bureau of Immigration was established to bar "idiots, insane persons, paupers or persons likely to become public charges, persons suffering from a loathsome or dangerous contagious disease, persons who have been convicted of a felony or other infamous crime or misdemeanor involving moral turpitude" from entering the country. I think they needed to add "polygamists" to the list to round it off.

We don't know how much our grandparents paid for their voyages. The average fare from Ireland in the early twentieth century was six or eight pounds. It cost nine pounds to travel steerage class on the *Titanic*—this didn't turn out to be as good a deal as advertised. Both Nana and Grandpa traveled on the White Star liner *Baltic*. The *Baltic* was built at a cost of four million pounds in 1904 in Belfast by Harland & Wolff. It was 709 feet long. Tonnage was 23,884 pounds. For a time it was the largest liner built. It was a two-stacker. The stacks were the same as the *Titanic's*—gold and tipped black. It carried 425 passengers in first class, 450 in second, and 2,000 in steerage. The maiden voyage of the *Baltic* was from Liverpool to New York on 29 June 1904. It was broken up in Japan in 1933.

White Star steamships docked in Manhattan at 16th – 22nd Sts. Traveling on the Hamburg-American line, our Polish ancestors docked at 1st – 4th Sts. in Hoboken. First and second class passengers were able to disembark at the terminals. Steerage passengers were taken by barge to Ellis Island for processing. They would have seen the Statue of Liberty, but the Manhattan skyline was completely different from what we see. It was different from what the photographs of the mid-twentieth century show—the Woolworth Building wasn't built until 1913.

Passengers wore manifest cards taped to their clothing—this number matched the identifier on the ship's log. Passengers deposited their luggage—all they brought with them to the New World—and proceeded to undergo a cursory medical inspection on the second floor of the reception building. Part of the medical inspection included checking for eye infections by "buttonhook men" who used small tongs to lift the upper eyelid. Any person suspected of having a disease or of being disabled or mentally ill was marked with chalk and detained. Twenty percent of arrivals were detained, but only two percent were denied entry. These low figures derived from a selection process that started in the ports in Europe. The steamship companies inspected outbound passengers—this may have been what kept Jonas Bielawski from embarking. They were responsible for paying the return fare, so there was some hesitation in letting sick people cross the sea.

After the medical inspection our grandparents proceeded to the Registry Room—to the Great Hall as we know it. The Hall is devoid of furniture now, but in those years it was crowded with small benches arranged in tight aisles. Arrivals waited for their turns at windows where they were asked a series of questions about their families, marital status, and prospects for employment. Until 1914 arrivals had to have $25.00 to be released. Those who didn't had to wait for a sponsor to produce the money or for a charity organization to vouch for the cash.

The Great Hall is 200 feet long by 100 feet wide and 56 feet tall. The famous vaulted ceiling was added in 1916, so we see a detail of the building none of our grandparents saw. I'm not cursed with psychic talents, but the emotional impact of the Great Hall is devastating. If anyplace contains the ghosts of memory, it is this empty room. The Hall is filled with the thoughts and emotions of millions of people. These thoughts and emotions have become palpable. Fear, hope, anticipation, excitement, sorrow, and impatience drown our minds as if the atmosphere were water and the vacant air a vitreous glue that binds our identities across the decades. It's not easy to stay in the Great Hall for more than a few minutes. There is too much empathy in it. You don't entertain it, you don't think it, you don't imagine it, you *feel* what these people went though.

After registration the arrivals passed to the "stairs of separation" and to their entrance to America. They could reclaim their luggage, exchange currency, and purchase rail tickets if they were heading west. Male immigrants could leave unescorted, but female arrivals without husbands or brothers had to be accompanied by their sponsor. If they had to wait for their sponsors, arrivals stayed in rooms on the mezzanine level. They were fed meals while in "detention", bread and butter and coffee for breakfast and beef stew or herring for lunch.

These are the children of Patrick Ford and Catherine Griffin: Dennis; Thomas; John; Mary; Edward; Francis; and Joseph. They are my aunt and uncles.

Dennis Ford was born 26 May 1914 in Hoboken. Dennis was baptized in Our Lady of Grace Church on June 7 by Fr. Joseph Kelly. His godparents were Thomas Brennan and Mary Griffin. His full name at baptism was "Dennis Joseph"—this is my name as well.

Dennis never married. He died in St. Mary's Hospital of pneumonia on 19 October 1939. He was 25 years of age. He resided at 931 Willow Ave. He worked as a foreman on the shipping piers. The funeral mass was at 9:00 AM in Our Lady of Grace. Dennis was buried in the Ford plot in Holy Name Cemetery.

Dennis's death was unexpected. Rita Nelson and Kitty Fleming recollected that Dennis fell when he came to their mother's wake the week before he died. The people who saw him fall thought it unusual, since there was no rug and he was not under the influence of alcohol. Nana took his death very hard and may have become seriously depressed afterward. Dad mentioned that the young children had to stay with the Leonard family for a time. Because of Dennis's death, Nana had a lifelong aversion to the smell of flowers and would never allow fresh flowers in her home.

My father remembered Dennis was tall and resembled his brothers Jack and Francis more than him or Edward—this means he was bald. Kitty Fleming remembered Dennis was thin and that he was called "The Black Diamond". (This was the name of a steamship line, but we don't know if there was a connection.)

My father and Uncle Jack remembered there was considerable conflict between Dennis and his father. And both expressed the same sentiment that Dennis's death was a disaster for the Ford family. I recall sitting in Uncle Jack's office in the early 1990s and hearing him say that Dennis's death changed everything for their family and that things would have turned out differently if he had lived.

At one point things got so bad Dennis left home and didn't tell anyone where he went. Nana and one of the Keane sisters went to a psychic to learn where Dennis was. The psychic said he was near water and rocks. Nana interpreted this as meaning that he had drowned. My father believed he had been in New York City the entire time. When he returned home Nana never asked where he had been.

Thomas Ford was born 6 April 1916. Thomas was baptized on April 23 in Our Lady of Grace. His godparents were John Allen and Nora Griffin. The priest was Fr. Edward Kirk.

Thomas died of peritonitis in St. Mary's Hospital the morning of 3 June 1928. He was 12 years of age. He resided at 803 Willow Ave. at the time of death. He had been under a doctor's care for five days. His funeral mass was at 9:30 AM on June 5 in Our Lady of Grace. Thomas was buried in the Ford plot in Holy Name Cemetery.

Peritonitis is a bacterial infection of the lining of the abdominal cavity. Symptoms include pain, fever, and shock. It is a major medical emergency. Today antibiotics are used to treat the infection. In those days, of course, there were no antibiotics. I recall that my father said that Thomas cut himself on a spike while climbing a fence in the park at 10th and Hudson Sts. in Hoboken. The injury occurred on May 28—the death certificate notes an operation was performed on that day.

We have a photograph of Dennis and Thomas Ford—my father said the picture was of his brothers. Dennis looks assured and self-confident. His facial features are round like his brothers Jack and Francis. Thomas most definitely resembles my father in having facial features that are more horizontal than vertical. Poor Thomas looks frightened, as if he knows the grim fate that waits in a city park. If you look closely at his clothing, you can see that he wears hand-me-downs. The buttons on his jacket are of different sizes.

John Francis Ford was born in Hoboken on 1 August 1918. He was baptized in Our Lady of Grace Church on August 18. His godparents were Raymond Allen and Hanna Griffin. The priest was Fr. Edward Begley. They resided at 1011 Park Ave. at the time of his birth. Uncle Jack died of cancer on 19 September 1994 in New York City. He was 76 years of age. He was buried in St. Joseph's Cemetery in Hackensack.

Jack married Bertha Spence in Our Lady of Grace Church on 21 July 1940. Their witnesses were Joseph Peluso and Cora Southwick. Fr. Ignatius

J. McCarthy, OSB, officiated. Bertha was described on the parish register as a "doubtfully lapsed Presbyterian."

Bertha—Aunt Betty—was the daughter of Christopher Spence and Elizabeth Hartje. She was born 2 March 1918 and died 2 January 1992. At the time of her marriage Betty resided at 84 Bostwick Dr. in Jersey City.

Jack and Betty Ford had two children. **John Ford, Jr.** was a schoolteacher. **Nancy Bertini** was an accountant in her father's business. Nancy died suddenly in December 2004 at the age of 62. The Ford cousins and relatives were not close, but Nancy was an exception. She was the only Ford niece who stayed in contact with my parents throughout the years.

Uncle Jack worked as a bursar for the Moore McCormick steamship line. Afterward, he ran a successful tax and accountancy business on Queen Anne Road in Teaneck, NJ. Uncle Jack was short, round-faced, and bald. He had an engaging upbeat personality and was very affable. The Irish would say he had the "blarney" and the "gift of gab". He was by far the most successful of his siblings.

Jack and my father became close in the last decade of their lives. We drove to Teaneck every few months to pay a visit and chat. Dad took Jack's death very hard. At one point in Jack's wake someone remarked that Dad was the "last of the Mohicans", a phrase that moved him deeply.

Mary Ford was born 29 June 1920. She was baptized in Our Lady of Grace Church on July 11. Her godparents were Patrick McNamara and Mary McNamara. The priest was Fr. Edward Murphy. Aunt Mary died of congestive heart failure in her apartment in Hoboken on 3 September 1986. She was 66 years of age. She was buried in the Ford plot in Holy Name Cemetery. She was the last person in the grave, which means she has her hands full. There is an Irish folk belief that the last person in a grave must wait on and become the servant of the other people buried. I hate to think of the mayhem going on.

Aunt Mary was twice married. Her first husband was Anthony Unucozyuski. They married on 11 September 1943 in Our Lady of Grace. Their witnesses were Charles Witczak and Helen McNamara.

Anthony Unucozyuski was baptized 14 May 1916 in Our Lady of Czestochowa Church in Jersey City. He was the son of Constantine Unucozyuski and Cepolonia Miller. At the time of the wedding he lived at 515 Jersey Ave. in Jersey City. Anthony was called "Joe Palooka" because of his resemblance to the comic book character. My father described him as a rough person who had spent time in jail and who worked as a strong arm for waterfront mobsters. My father heard that he lived into the 1980s and may have gone blind at the end of his life.

Mary and Anthony had a stormy marriage. Both drank heavily. It's likely he beat her. In one incident my father had to hit and physically restrain Anthony from getting to Mary.

Mary's second marriage was to Tom Grogan. The parish record has "Frank", but my mother remembered him as "Tom"—perhaps Frank was a mistake of the priest. Tom was the brother of John Grogan, who was mayor of Hoboken in the 1960s and a prominent labor leader in the longshoreman's local. At one point Tom and Mary ran a liquor store on 9th St. in Hoboken. This was not the ideal profession for either, since both liked to party and to carouse.

Aunt Mary was tall with black hair and square features. She most definitely resembled my father and Kate Flynn. Near the end of her life Mary fell on a sidewalk in Hoboken. Ptl. Harry Coppinger, a friend of my father's, wrote the report in such a way that Mary got a healthy settlement from the city. My mother remembered that "people had to like Mary." She was full of fun and dressed smartly. She worked as a waitress and was known to be good with figures. For some reason she disliked the color green and never wore it.

Every family has a tragic character and ours is Tommie Grogan. **Thomas Grogan** was the son of Mary Grogan and Anthony Unucozyuski. He was born in Hoboken on 9 December 1944 and baptized on December 24. His godparents were Edward Ford and Wanda Brosseau. The priest was Fr. William Brennan. Tommie was legally adopted by Tom Grogan on 21 June 1950. Tommie was shot to death in New York City in November 1984. He was 39 years of age. He was buried in Potter's Field on Hart's Island in New York City.

Tommie married Rosemary O'Shea on 9 December 1967 in Sts. Peter and Paul Church in Hoboken. Rosemary was the daughter of Joseph O'Shea and Margaret McNally. Both parents were deaf. Tommie and Rosemary had one son.

There must have been a lot of conflict in Tommie's life. Nana did a lot of the child-rearing owing to Mary's erratic life style. He use to stay with my father and mother—we lived for a time in the same building. My mother has vivid memories of Tommie sitting in our red recliner at 803 Willow Ave. Certainly, the school record provides evidence that Tommie was living an undisciplined life. (We have his school records.) He repeated the second grade. His final grade average in grade four was 84 with 10 days absent. In grade eight his final grade had declined to 73 with an astounding 32 days absent. His IQ was assessed as 114 in October 1950. His IQ declined to 96 when he was tested four years later.

Tommie wanted to go in the Navy, but his mother refused, believing he would get killed in combat—this was the Vietnam era. The road not taken proved to be an unwise choice. At some point Tommie became addicted to heroin and descended to life on the streets. This was a shame, because he was a good-looking person with a lot of connections on the Grogan side. Tommie had blond hair and stood well over six feet.

An unsupervised person, Tommie got little guidance from adults, all of whom were preoccupied with their own addictions. He came to a bad end—to an end as mixed up as his life. My father got a call from the New York City police department that Tommie had been killed. I drove Dad and Uncle Francey to the morgue in Manhattan. The body was not Tommie's. The relief was short-lived, since the morgue had made a mix up. We drove to Manhattan a second time and Francey identified the body.

This book is filled with the varieties of death—death from tuberculosis, death from cancer, death from pertussis. I suppose there is a police trail, but I never wanted to travel it. I have happy memories of horsing around and roughhousing with Tommie when I was a kid—he was nine years older than me and might have played the role of an older brother. But that's another road not taken.

Edward Patrick Ford was born 3 July 1922. He was baptized in Our Lady of Grace Church on July 16. His godparents were Michael Connor and Nora Connor. The priest was Fr. William Ferury. Uncle Ed died suddenly of a heart attack on 16 January 1978. He was 55 years of age. He was buried in the Schoanhooen plot in Holy Name Cemetery. There was a major snowstorm the day of Uncle Ed's wake, but somehow my father and mother made it to the cemetery.

Uncle Ed married Natalie Schoanhooen on 7 October 1945 in St. Aedan's Church in Jersey City. Their witnesses were Edward McLaughlin and Agnes Foley. The priest was Fr. J. Van Wie. They lived in Jersey City after their marriage.

Aunt Natalie was the daughter of Francis Schoanhooen and Ann Lane. She was born in Manchester, NH. Natalie worked for many years as an aide in Medical Center in Jersey City. She died 11 November 2002. Her age was given as 78. She was buried in Holy Name Cemetery.

Uncle Ed was a tall thin man—like my father and unlike his brothers, he had a full head of hair. He worked odd jobs, including retail and truck driving. He suffered from emphysema for a number of years. He served in the Army from 12 December 1941 – 5 September 1945 (ID 12038086)—the date of enlistment indicates considerable patriotism. I believe he served in the quartermaster corps, but we have no specific information.

Ed and Natalie had four sons: **Edward, Jr.**; **Kevin**; **Jeffrey**; and **Lawrence**. Our families were not close and we visited infrequently, so we don't have many details of their lives.

Francis Patrick Ford was born 14 March 1924. He was baptized in Our Lady of Grace Church on March 30. His godparents were John Lynch and Helen Griffin. The priest was Fr. John Donnelly. His baptismal name was "Patrick Francis", but he never used "Patrick". He went by the name "Francey". He died of cancer on 6 June 1989 in Christ Hospital in Jersey City. He was 65 years of age. He was cremated.

Uncle Francey married Marie Fugazzi on 28 September 1943 in Our Lady of Grace. Their witnesses were my father Joseph Ford and Leorandine Frasente. Fr. William Brennan officiated.

Marie Fugazzi was the daughter of Charles Fugazzi and Catherine Schneider. She was born in Hoboken on 25 November 1924 and baptized on December 7 in Our Lady of Grace by Fr. Lestor Quinn. She and Francey had one daughter, **Denise Frances**.

My mother remembered their marriage as stormy. They separated at some point. It's possible Marie married a second time to a man with the surname "Izzo" or "Zggo".

Every family has a "black sheep" and Francey is ours. He seems to have been a criminal type throughout much of his life. According to the *Jersey Journal* he was arrested in a "stick up" try at the Grand Hotel at 3rd and Hudson Sts. in Hoboken on 11 June 1950. He spent a number of years in Sing Sing prison for check fraud. When he got out, he ran with a dangerous crowd and "kept the books" for a known killer. This man—I don't know his name—visited my grandmother, who never knew his occupation and thought he was a decent fellow. Francey was stabbed at one point by a jilted girlfriend. Only the quick thinking of a Hoboken policeman saved his life by taking him to the hospital in the squad car rather than waiting for the ambulance.

Francey calmed down or burnt out the last decade of his life. He lived with his parents and took care of them in their extreme old age. He later moved to the Heights section of Jersey City. He took up with Virginia Bello of Jersey City. Virginia was a divorced mother of six children. She was a steadying influence on him.

I knew Francey only when he moved to Jersey City. He was a slight bald man with a red face and nasal voice. I found him knowledgeable and a good conversationist. He was a roughhewn version of his brother Jack. He had the sunk-in eyes of the Griffins and was, like his siblings, a hard-drinking man. He worked for the city of Hoboken for a while and in a liquor store run by his nephew Kevin—this was asking for trouble. Francey became ill at the same time as my father—the summer of the bad year 1989. Francey's decline was rapid. His doctor made inquiries whether Francey had been exposed to asbestos or to some other carcinogen in his life. This was quite possible, given the contaminated conditions of factories in the twentieth century.

Joseph Thomas Ford, my father and the last child of Pat and Catherine Ford, was born 24 July 1926. He was baptized August 8 in Our Lady of Grace Church. His godparents were Thomas Keane and Margaret Keane. The priest was Fr. Edward Begley. He married Sophia Bielawska married in a civil ceremony sometime in 1951 or 1952. We have marriage records going back to the early 1800s on several sides of our family, but we have not located the marriage record of my parents. The full story will be told in Chapter Sixteen. Dad died of lung cancer on 14 June 1999. He was buried in Holy Cross Cemetery in North Arlington.

The church of our Irish ancestors—it's my family's church, too—was Our Lady of Grace in Hoboken. This was the church where the Fords were baptized, married, and buried. It was the church where we took the sacraments of confession and communion. It was the church where I served as a Knight of the Altar. I served at innumerable funeral Masses—although I may not be around to see it, I expect to have my funeral there.

Archbishop Hughes of New York directed Fr. Anthony Cauvin of Nice, France, to take charge of the "mission of Hoboken" in 1851. The original church stood on the site of the school on the west corner of 5th St. and Willow Ave. This church served from 1854 – 1878. The church that now exists was constructed at 4th St. from 1875 – 1878. The architect was F.G. Himpler. The building is 200 feet long and 130 feet wide. It takes up the entire block. It is on the National Register of Historical Buildings.

I've seen many churches, but none as beautiful as Our Lady of Grace. Several stories tall, the exterior is a beautiful red brick. The effect is not ponderous, but delicate and distinguished owing to the long stained glass panels that run nearly the entire length of the walls. The church was meant at one point to be the cathedral of the archdiocese of Newark, so the pulpit is raised and to the left side of the altar facing the congregation. There are three altars. The main altar is elevated five or more steps. The back wall of the altar is shaped in the outline of a church. There is a bas-relief of the Last Supper under the altar. After Vatican Two a simple table-style altar was built near the communion rail. To the chagrin of the old-time laity, this altar faced the people.

There are five aisles in the church. Large bas-reliefs of the Stations of the Cross run along the walls. The organ and choir occupy the loft over the main entrance. The baptism font stood in a separate room at the right entrance. At one point a large crucifix hung over the altar. The interior was always well lit owing to the windows on every wall. A beautiful round stained-glass window shone a rose light over the choir loft.

Fr. Cauvin was pastor from 1851 – 1872. Fr. William Masterson was pastor in my father's time. He was reputed to be a very tough man. The pastor in my time was Fr. Daniel Meehan. He was no slouch in the tough department. Fr. Meehan had been a chaplain in the World War and was said to have served in some rough places. He was a short man, bald and stocky with puffy eyes. He was very much a priest of the old school who demanded obedience and perfection. He gave the white glove treatment to the janitorial staff—he gave the same treatment to the non-janitorial staff. He was a hard-drinking man who said Mass at the side altar late in the morning. I was frequently called out of school to serve as the altar boy. They were nerve-wracking experiences. I lived in fear of missing a step or saying the Latin wrong. I think I must have clipped off a few decades in Purgatory serving at Fr. Meehan's Masses.

I've lived outside Hoboken for more than half my life and our family is widely scattered, but Hoboken will always be our ancestral Irish home in America. It's the place where generations of immigrants came. Many stayed. They married and raised families in Hoboken. They died in Hoboken and had their funeral Masses said in Our Lady of Grace. The ones who left remembered Hoboken fondly. It's the place where I was a child and where I became a teenager.

The "Mile Square" city is located across the Hudson River from Midtown Manhattan. Our bedroom window at 1208 Hudson St. faced the Empire State Building. It was a view people would die for—given the fires that accompanied gentrification in the 1980s, that quite possibly happened. Hoboken goes back to the very founding of America. Henry Hudson and the crew of the *Half Moon* noted a greenish outgrowth of rock on the western shore. The last exposed portion of this rock, formally called "serpentine", is in Hudson Square Park at 4ᵗʰ and Hudson Sts.

Hoboken has undergone major transformations in its history. In the nineteenth century the northern end of town was called the "Elysian Fields". It was an idyllic garden of woods and grassy trails bordering the Hudson. The first baseball game was played there in June 1846. The site remained rural until the 1860s, when the city slowly converted into an overcrowded industrial cauldron.

Hoboken has the distinction of housing the first tavern in America. This was opened in the 1640s. Business must have been brisk. Business hasn't slowed since. There were more than 200 taverns in Hoboken in 1917. I doubt that the number declined after the war. Located near the waterfront, River St. was a row of taverns from 1ˢᵗ to 4ᵗʰ St. The waterfront held no monopoly on taverns. There was literally a tavern at the corner of nearly every block. Sometimes, there was more than one. In my youth there were two taverns on the corner of 8ᵗʰ St—The Suwannee and The Blue Point. There was a tavern in the middle of 8ᵗʰ and Willow Ave—I don't recall the name. There was The Dixie on 9ᵗʰ St.—this was my father's hangout. There was a tavern on the corner of 10ᵗʰ and Willow. And so staggeringly on from block to bleary block.

Hoboken was the point of embarkation for the troops in World War One. More than 600,000 soldiers left for Europe from Hoboken in 1917 and 1918—the *Spanish Lady* traveled as a viral stowaway on board the troopships. Pathetically, the only remembrance of this monumental effort was a nondescript knee-high rock and barely readable plaque at the entrance to the shipyards on 2ⁿᵈ St.

The war years must have been a difficult time for the residents of Hoboken. The population boomed to 60,000. Severe food and coal shortages occurred. People voluntarily went without heat on Mondays to conserve fuel. The Army requisitioned as many beds as they could as the troops prepared to march "to hell or Hoboken". They marched to other places as well. Newspapers complained about public drunkenness and about "actions unfit for publication" occurring between soldiers and local girls.

Hoboken was a gritty industrial city for most of the twentieth century. There were shipyards and industries from one end of town to the other. In my youth there were Lipton Tea, Todd Shipyards, and Bethlehem Steel at the northern waterfront. Maxwell House and American Can were at 11ᵗʰ St. The Holland-American line occupied the piers on 5ᵗʰ and

6th Sts. The American Export Line occupied the piers on 1st – 4th Sts. These piers formerly belonged to the Hamburg-American line. Our Polish grandparents disembarked there when they arrived in America. One pier extended 900 feet into the river—this pier lasted until 1988 when it went under. A long red depot ran nearly the same length as the shipyard. The northern side of the depot was the site of the climactic fight scene in *On the Waterfront*. The barge where Terry Molloy called out the corrupt labor leader Johnny Friendly survived into the 1970s. Inland from the docks were Hostess Bakery, Tootsie Roll, The Ferguson Propeller Co., and the Keuffel & Essar plant, which specialized in fine lenses and instruments.

All of this is gone. The piers are gone. The waterfront factories are gone. The docks are gone. The steamships and container vessels put in other ports. There is no industry in town—or none that occurs outside of taverns. Small things are gone, too, like the call boxes attached to street poles. Today, police use cell phones. Police on the street beat in the 1960s called headquarters from those boxes. One time I struck my head on a call box when I wasn't watching where I was walking. That was a different age—pedestrians can no longer knock themselves out on a police phone. Gone, too, are the sounds of the factory whistles—these are sounds that will never be heard by the people of this generation. Factories announced the start and conclusion of the workday with a whistle. The lunch breaks started and ended with whistles. Different factories used differently pitched whistles. I was able to time the return walk to school using the Maxwell House whistle. If I left our house at 1208 Hudson St. when it blew I could get to Hoboken High before the school bell rang.

The waterfront is a mixture of high rises and parks. The factories left standing are condominiums. The tenements are lofts and luxury apartments. The brownstones are refurbished and rented at exorbitant rates. Hoboken has become a bedroom community for New York City. It is a version of Greenwich Village in New Jersey. The population has declined from 60,000 in 1917 to 38,000 in 2000. The only connection the Hoboken of today has with the Hoboken of the past is the number of taverns that dot the street corners. The fact that visitors can have a drink on nearly every block remains a wobbly bond with the past. There are rumors that before visitors can do that they have to prove they have enough cash or credit to traipse from tap to tap. I don't know the rumors to be true, but given the upscale reputation of the Hoboken of today, that may well be the case.

Chapter Fifteen

~

America—Pawel Bielawski & Zofia Storta

My grandparents on the Polish side are **Pawel Bielawski** and **Zofia Storta**. They married in the Church of St. Anthony in Jersey City on 29 April 1912. Their witnesses were Felix Macanka and Mary Bogdzuil. The priest was Fr. Boleslaw Kwiatowski. Pawel's residence was 180 7th St. Zofia's residence was 145 Provost St., which was likely where her brother Maciej lived.

Felix Macanka (1883 – 1963) came over on the same boat as Pawel. We don't know where he lived in Lithuania—the village name appears on the ship's log to be Miksenle. He married Ludwika Waskiewicz and had seven children. He worked as a butcher and grocer. Mary Bogdzuil was likely related to Rozalia Bogdzuil, but we have no information about her. There was some confusion over her name. The civil record listed it as "Mary", but the name on the church register looked to be "Martha".

Cocci Helen remembered that Pawel met his wife through Maciej Storta. Helen added that Pawel met Zofia at Ellis Island and that he was surprised how tiny she was.

Pawel was the son of Mykolis Bielawski and Ursula Milosz. He was born in Kalniskes village on 3 January 1884. He was baptized by Fr. Kiprijonas Zebrowski on January 8. His godparents were his uncle and aunt Kazimier Milosz and Marijona Bielawska. We're not sure why, but Pawel celebrated his birthday on December 24. The Parish register indicated he was nearly a year older.

Pawel—*Dziadek*—died on the morning of 19 January 1957 in the Hudson County Hospital for Mental Diseases on County Road in Secaucus,

NJ. The cause of death was cerebral thrombosis due to arteriosclerosis. He was 73 years of age. He was in the hospital for nine days. He resided at the time of death with his daughter Blanche at 255 8th St. in Jersey City. Pawel was buried in Holy Cross Cemetery in North Arlington (block 8-section E-B-80) after a solemn high funeral Mass.

Pawel arrived on the Hamburg-American steamship *Patricia*, which sailed from Hamburg on 13 March 1909 and arrived in the port of New York on 28 March 1909. The Hamburg-American Line used a different format for personal identifiers, listing immigrants by page and line number. Pawel's was page 190, line 30. On the ship's log Pawel was described as 25 years of age and able to read and write. He was of the Polish race and Russian nationality. His last address in Europe was Kalniskes—we know this now, but there was a serious stutter in our research because the village listed on the log appeared to be *Skalmierz*, which is a place in south-central Poland. His destination in America was to a "friend" Kazimier Rakiewicz at 145 Pavonia Ave. Pawel had $2.00 on him. He was described as 5'9 with brown hair and gray eyes.

Pawel's surname was spelled "Bulawski" on the ship's log, suggesting it sounded like "Bu-lawski" rather than "Biel-lawski". I pronounce it "Be-lop-ski", but I have a notorious Jersey accent.

The *Patricia* was built in Stettin, Germany, by the Vulcan Co. It was 560 feet long with a tonnage of 13,424 pounds. It had four masts and one stack—the color of the stack was dark gold. It carried 162 first class passengers, 184 second class, and 2,100 in steerage. The *Patricia* was impounded by the United States and used as a troop ship in World War One. It was sold to a British line and broken up in 1922.

Pawel registered for the World War One draft on 12 September 1918. He resided with his family at 143 Pavonia Ave. He was described as a cook for Swift & Co. and as having a medium build and height with dark brown hair and gray eyes.

Dziadek declared his intention to become a citizen on 8 May 1928 (vol. 165, #87821) in the Court of Common Pleas in Hudson County. My mother believed that Jersey City Mayor Frank "I am the law" Hague was the instigator of this—the mayor liked to get immigrants to become citizens so they would vote for him. Pawel was described as a laborer, 5'8, 166 pounds with brown hair and grey eyes. He stated he was born in Wilno—this is Polish for Vilnius. He lived with his family at 471 Henderson St. in Jersey City.

Dziadek petitioned for citizenship on 1 July 1930 (vol. 206, #577534). He was again described as a laborer and in residence at 471 Henderson St. His witnesses were Michael Grabowski and Edward Scale. He swore the oath of allegiance on 18 November 1930.

Pawel applied for Social Security on 3 February 1937. He resided at 712 Jersey Ave. and gave his occupation as a trucker. As he didn't drive, he would have been a laborer on the truck or on the receiving platform. No employer was listed. The Social Security number was in the category of a railroad worker.

Pawel registered for the "old man's draft" in World War Two on 27 April 1942. He was described as 5'6 and 136 pounds, which is on the light side. The form noted that he worked for the WPA. The Works Progress (later Project) Administration was a Federal work program established by President Roosevelt to provide part-time employment during the Great Depression. The WPA employed as many as eight million people. Started in 1935, it ran to 1943. Among its many projects the WPA employed professional people to record the indexes of the ships' logs available at the National Archives. Pawel had a less cushy job than writing names on index cards—the location of his employment was "Paterson Plank Road".

Pawel worked as an unskilled laborer for a number of companies. We know a few—Swift & Company, the Pennsylvania Railroad, and the WPA. My mother remembered that he worked at the Tootsie Roll plant in Hoboken and as a watchman in Mosquito Park at Manhattan Ave. in the Jersey City Heights. *Cocci* Helen recollected that Pawel told her that he once worked in a coal mine. (This may connect to Josef Bielawski's WWI draft report that he had been injured in Pennsylvania.) Pawel was injured at one of his jobs, but was denied settlement money when a co-worker refused to testify on his behalf. My mother recalled that Pawel had a slogan that it was important to have steady work because the most important things are "Having a roof over your head and food on the table."

According to the 1920 Federal Census taken on January 3 Pawel and Zofia resided at 143 Pavonia Ave (T625, #1043, ED 119). Only their daughters Blanche and Anne were born. Zofia was pregnant with Helen. Their siblings Josef Bielawski and Stanley Storta resided with them. Pawel's occupation was given as laborer for the Pennsylvania Railroad. His name was spelled "Powell Bielawski". This is how the census-taker heard "Pawel".

The 1930 Federal Census taken on April 7 found my grandparents at 471 Henderson St. (T626, #1350, P. 14B, ED 23). Their rent was $21 a month. They did not own a radio. The brothers-in-law are gone and replaced by a burgeoning family. My mother was listed. She was four years old. Only Carol was absent. Blanche was described as 17 and a worker in a furniture store. Pawel worked for the railroad. Zofia was described as being able to speak English.

The life of Pawel Bielawski parallels that of Patrick Ford. Both lost their mothers at early ages. Both experienced cruel stepmothers. We heard about the notorious Bridget Lyons. My mother remembered that Pawel said his stepmother—Rozalia Bogdruzil—preferred her own children over him and his brother Josef. My mother remembered him saying that he and Josef ran away from home on one occasion. Both Pawel and Patrick had stepfamilies that were rather large. Both immigrated at roughly the same time. Both worked as laborers. Like Patrick, Pawel said next to nothing about his life in the native land.

Cocci Helen thought Pawel or Josef (or both) were in the Russian-Japanese War of 1905. My mother didn't remember anything about a war, but she remembered Pawel saying that he was in Siberia and that it was so cold saliva froze before it hit the ground. He said they wrapped newspaper around their feet to keep warm and that they could hear wolves howling.

Dziadek was a religious man who attended Mass faithfully. My mother remembered that a lady in the church was interested in him, but that he had no interest in marrying a second time—he had experience with second families and may have wanted to spare everyone the aggravation. On one occasion in church his hat was stolen. He said the rosary aloud while sitting on his bed. This practice, which we met previously with John Keane and with Kate Flynn, is a beautiful custom no longer practiced. Few people in our family pray the rosary silently.

Pawel had the reputation of being very neat—he cleaned the house after my mother. And he was somewhat old-fashioned in comparison to his wife, or so my mother thought. He used to roll cigarettes. He enjoyed a beer in his old age, but would never buy one. On one occasion he got intoxicated at a wedding.

Pawel liked to sit in West Hamilton Park with his friends. He was always well-dressed when he went outside—in those days men wore suits and ties on every occasion. As his friends died or moved away, Pawel became lonely in his old age. Helen remembered that he said he wanted to return to Europe.

Polish was the language in their home—this was true into the 1950s. Everyone in their section of Jersey City spoke Polish. Most of the retail shops conducted business in Polish. Pawel spoke broken English. He made it a point to speak English when friends of his children visited so as not to embarrass them. He tried to learn to write English, but no one helped him. My mother regretted this—of course, she was a teenager and he was a middle-aged man.

He liked to watch professional wrestling on television. Like many people, he believed it was real. And he liked to watch the Jack Benny show. My mother recollected that he went to see the movie *The Song of Bernadette*. She thought it was the first movie he ever saw.

My father remembered that Pawel was bothered by the hot sand at the beach in Keansburg, NJ, when they went swimming.

Pawel told my mother that an explosion blew the windows of their home out. This was the "Black Tom" explosion on the Jersey City waterfront at 2:00 AM on Sunday morning, 16 July 1916. Theirs weren't the only windows blown out. Glass blew out of windows for 25 miles when German saboteurs ignited 2,000 tons of explosives stored near what is now Liberty State Park. The blast measured 5.5 on the Richter Scale. There were seven casualties, including a baby thrown from a crib.

Pawel disciplined his children by tapping them on the head with a spoon. My mother recollected that one time she ran around the table to avoid getting tapped. Regardless of the discipline, he must have been proud of his children. My mother remembered that she felt his pride in her appearance when she wore a uniform during a May Day ceremony. And he raised his children very well for being a single parent. All his children grew up to be decent, God-fearing people who obeyed the law and who raised decent children in their turn. He must have been a fine man to set an example that continues through four generations.

Pawel cooked for the family. My mother recollected that he always cooked fish on Fridays—they never ate meat on Fridays. He made a lot of soups—cabbage soup, chicken soup, spinach soup, cold beet soup with cucumbers and sour cream on the side. *Cocci* Carol remembered that he would have hot chocolate and a baked potato for her when she returned home from school in the evenings.

Pawel seems to have been somewhat sickly, perhaps in later life. He wore glasses as an adult and had asthma. Strangely, he lost the sense of smell for a period of time. He had differently colored eyes, one brown, one blue-gray. My mother thought this had something to do with being burned when he was young. (He had no scars, however.) Pawel had minor surgery of some sort that he recommended to a friend who had the same malady. Tragically, the friend died during the surgery. Toward the end of his life Pawel became confused at times. He accused my father of stealing a suit and, one time, he jumped over the banister of a stoop. As his dementia worsened, he was committed to the hospital in Secaucus. While there he fell, bruising himself badly.

Zofia Storta was the daughter of Franciszk Storta and Rozalia Juchnewicz. She was born in Girdziunai village on 3 January 1890 and baptized in Subotninki church on January 6. We do not have information on her godparents.

Zofia died of a heart attack in Margaret Hague Maternity Hospital on 19 March 1936. She was 46 years of age. At the time she lived at 471 Henderson St. She was buried in Holy Cross Cemetery in North Arlington. The headstone gives her dates incorrectly as 1893 – 1936.

Zofia was described as tiny and thin with brown hair. We don't know her medical situation before March 19. It's likely she had undiagnosed high blood pressure. It appears that Zofia panicked when she heard that her daughter Blanche was in labor and that it was a difficult labor. She and her daughter Anne rushed to the hospital in a cab and Zofia collapsed when they arrived. My mother recollected that Anne felt badly, believing she traveled too slowly. That night, Anne had a dream that her mother was at her bedside, telling her not to blame herself.

My mother was ten years old when Zofia died. She doesn't have many memories of the event. She recollected that a nun tried to comfort her. Blanche, who was 22 at the time, married and starting a family of her own, ran the household. A few ladies of the neighborhood visited sporadically to help. They included Mrs. Wasilewska and Mrs. Macanka. Also, ladies named Mrs. Kudzin and Mrs. Lewandowska, who ran a variety store in the neighborhood. And Mrs. Wisniewska, who was a widow and who owned a butcher's shop.

Zofia sailed to America on the Hamburg-American steamship *Kaiserin Auguste Victoria*. The ship left Hamburg on 18 November 1910 and arrived in New York harbor on November 28. Her identifier was page 191, line 28. Zofia was described as 19 years of age. Her occupation was "maid". Her nationality was Russian and her race was Hebrew. This was a mistake and probably derived from the names ahead of her on the log, which appear to be Jewish. Her father was listed as "Grawik Storta" and her last permanent address as "Girzing". Her destination was to her brother Maciej Storta. She paid for the trip herself. She had $12.00 on her. Zofia was described on the log as 5'2 with brown hair and blue eyes. We don't know what Zofia paid to sail on the *Kaiserin*. In American currency steerage class cost $38.00 in 1907.

She was detained overnight on arrival, receiving supper and breakfast on Ellis Island. Maciej Storta arrived at 10:50 AM on November 29. His address was given as "145 Powat". If family rumor has it correctly, Pawel may have accompanied him to Ellis Island.

The *Kaiserin* was built in Stettin in 1905 by the Vulcan Co. It was 677 feet long with a tonnage of 24,581 pounds. It had two masts and two gold-colored stacks. It carried 472 first-class passengers, 174 second-class, and 1,820 in steerage. The ship was built by the architect Charles Mewes and was considered a particularly beautiful ship in the interior with ornate ceilings, parquet floors, and Oriental carpets. The ship had a number of expensive restaurants including one—the Ritz Carlton—that cost as much as a steerage ticket to dine in.

The *Kaiserin* remained dockside in Hamburg during the World War. She was ceded to England as a war reparation. She sailed in the Cunard Line for 12 years as the *Empress of Scotland*. She was broken up in 1931.

Sea travel in our time involves luxurious accommodations aboard *cruise* ships. The voyage is a thrilling and romantic ride—it's a comfortable ride, too. The gray Atlantic is below us. A picture perfect sky floats above. Life is a continuous carnival on every deck. Sea travel wasn't like that for Zofia and our other grandparents. They left their homes and traveled to a very different world. They didn't know what they were going to find in America—despite what they heard, they must have known the streets weren't paved with gold. Our Polish ancestors didn't know the language— how were they going to get around? Unlike the first-class passengers, they didn't have the run of the ship. Accommodations were adequate in the period they traveled, but steerage was a short step above barracks life and the swanky state rooms we see in the books and postcards were strictly off limit. The sea may have been gray, the sky blue, but our grandparents weren't filled with awe and excitement. They were filled with a potent mix of hope, regret, and fear. They may have tried to stay focused on the better life that summoned them, but midway on the great sea they must have been terrified they wouldn't find that life.

We don't have a lot of information on Zofia's personality and there is little in the way of a paper trail. She never applied for Social Security and we have found no application for citizenship. We have only two photographs, her wedding photograph and a picture taken with my mother at a religious shrine. Zofia resembles my sister Felicia in the wedding photograph and my mother in the second photograph. She has a thin round face and a definite Slavic appearance. My mother remembered that Zofia was more "modern" than Pawel. They had the first phonograph in the neighborhood. One time Zofia yelled because she wanted modern things. But *Cocci* Helen, who was six years older, remembered that she thought Zofia was old-fashioned, since she wore an Old World style hat or headdress. Helen walked behind her mother so as not to be embarrassed.

It must have been difficult for Pawel and Zofia. Like many Polish immigrants, they may have found it difficult to blend into American society. Josef never made the transition and Maciej returned to Europe. They lived in a provincial section and found it difficult to learn English. Born in America, their daughters wanted to fit in. Helen was embarrassed by how her foreign-looking mother dressed and my mother recollected that she was embarrassed during a school ceremony when she saw Pawel carrying coal he found on the train tracks that ran along 6th St.

Pawel and Zofia lived in a historic site. "Lower Jersey City" is one of the oldest localities in the United States. It was "Pavonia", the first permanent settlement in New Jersey. Founded by Michael Pauw of Amsterdam in November 1630 the settlement included farms extending from what is now Communipaw Ave. to 4th and Henderson Sts.

Early twentieth century Lower Jersey City was an industrial stretch of docks and factories that started at the Emerson Radio plant at 16th St. and continued southward a few miles to the huge Colgate-Palmolive plant. Lower Jersey City was an overpopulated section where waves of immigrants—Irish, Polish, Italian—gained a toehold on the American continent. The immigrant experience resembles the evolutionary process of colonization. The first generation arrives like a foreign species in a new niche. They're like the creatures that float across the sea on logs and come ashore in a strange environment. They hold on, living day-by-day and barely eking out an existence. The second generation moves inland and away from the waterfront. The third generation surrenders the coast altogether and heads for a place called "the suburbs". The fourth generation returns to the waterfront—it's now a fashionable section of condominiums and luxury apartments.

Like Hoboken, Jersey City managed to revitalize itself in the 1990s. The residential section around Pavonia Ave. converted from slums to an exclusive district that serves as a bedroom community for Manhattan. Skyscrapers and a shopping mall were built on the waterfront. The section is so upscale it refuses to use the name "Jersey City" and calls itself "Newport" instead.

Pawel and Zofia, as did Pat and Catherine Ford, lived through one of the twentieth century's most calamitous events—the Great Depression. We had heard that Pat Ford worked regularly. We don't know how steadily Pawel worked, but my mother recalled that they always had food on the table. Probably the lives of my grandparents changed little in the Depression. The 1930s were hard years, but so were the 1920s. So were the 1910s. Work was sporadic. Coal was found along train tracks. Food was basic. Gardens were kept on rooftops. Clothing was handed down. Extended families pulled together and shared apartments. Amenities did not exist. We live in a plush and cozy world of endless amenities, many of them electronic—the economists claim these amenities depend on "disposable income". (My interest in genealogy depended on having disposable income.) This world of superfluous material goods and goodies was inconceivable to our immigrant grandparents. There was nothing superfluous in their world.

Regardless of their status, our grandparents were exposed to the bleak conditions of the Depression. Families evicted from their flats lived in rickety built huts in shantytowns called "Hoovervilles" after the do-nothing president. Our grandparents observed the "bread lines" that wound their way in front of government buildings and charity organizations. The bread line was the American version of "outdoor relief" in the Irish Famine. We like to think the meals were more nutritious than "Soyer's Soup". Certainly, the scale was vaster. The lines started forming at the break of dawn. People lined up regardless of the weather. Children in hand-me-downs. The elderly in frayed sweaters and snoods. Unemployed fathers in tattered clothing with the empty pants pockets turned inside out. Unemployed vagrants who deserted their families in shame and desperation. We often consider the physical effects of hunger and neglect the humiliation of begging and of homelessness.

President Herbert Hoover was, like Lord Russell of the 1840s, a staunch believer in laissez-faire. The government would help the people, but only to a point. The main relief efforts in his administration were run by private groups. Prototypical of these efforts were the "soup kitchens" run by charities. In these places men were required to hear a short homily before receiving a bowl of soup supplemented by bread, cheese, and coffee. After a short period they were required to leave to make way for the next round of recipients. It wasn't until Franklin Roosevelt assumed the presidency that the government aggressively intervened. Programs such as the WPA were only partially successful in reversing conditions. America fully emerged from the Depression only when World War Two broke out.

In the 1930s the unemployed were desperate to face the future. The employed were terrified that they would become unemployed. Work was so unpredictable that people started to stand on street corners peddling household wares and articles of clothing. Neckties were a favorite. So were apples. The apple hawker became a stock figure of the period. My father recalled seeing them in Hoboken.

The children of Pawel Bielawski and Zofia Storta are: Blanche; Anne; Helen; Henry; Sophia; and Carol. We have a lot of detail on their children, as the sisters were close and the brothers-in-law sociable. I grew up with my Bielawski aunts, uncles, and cousins.

Blanche Bielawska was born 6 February 1914 in Jersey City. She was baptized "Bronislawa" in the Church of St. Anthony on February 15. Her godparents were Maciej Storta and Stephanie Wieckiel. The priest was Fr. Kwiatkowski. *Cocci* Blanchie died of cancer on 28 October 1976. She was 62 years of age. She was buried in Holy Cross Cemetery in North Arlington.

Blanche married John Szustek on 13 August 1932 in St. Anthony's. Their witnesses were Jan Zdanowicz and Anne Bielawska. The priest was the ubiquitous Fr. Kwiatowksi. At the time of the wedding Blanche resided at 471 Henderson St. John resided at 158 7th St. After their marriage they resided in the same house as *Dziadek* on Monmouth and 8th Sts. Later in life Blanche resided in Cliffside Park and in Wallington, NJ.

John Szustek was the son of John Szustek and Stanislawa Chmielewska. He was born in Jersey City on 21 February 1911. Godparents were Antanas Ajdul and Aleksandra Chmielewska. John died of a heart attack in the summer of 1954—we do not have the specific day. He was 43 years of age. He and Blanche returned from Coney Island when he took ill. In her excitement Blanche called my father in the Hoboken Police Dept. rather than the Jersey City police. John had likely been sick for a while, as my father remembered that his legs were swollen. He is buried with Blanche in North Arlington.

Blanche and John Szustek had three daughters: **Josephine Reehill**; **Mary Anne Volkman**; and **Antoinette Briggs**.

My mother recollected that Blanche took John's death hard. She had to raise three daughters as a single mother. She worked as a cleaning lady in office buildings. In one of these buildings she made the acquaintance of Jeanne Lowe who was a supervisor in the proxy department of Merrill Lynch, Pierce, Fenner & Smith. Jeanne allowed Blanche to practice typing after-hours. Later, Jeanne hired Blanche. Around 1971 Blanche transferred to the preliminary prospectus unit that Jeanne founded and in which I worked part-time. Blanche worked there until she took ill. Sadly, I recall that Blanche returned to the office crying with the bad news that her cancer, which had been in remission, had returned.

Blanche had it easy the last few years of employment. There wasn't a lot of work in the unit and she and Jeanne took long lunches at the South St. Seaport. To avoid discovery Blanche walked one flight down to the 24th floor where she could take the elevator without being seen by managers [44].

John Szustek was called "Mack" on account of his stocky build. Photographs show a solidly built man with a round face and receding hairline. He liked sweets and Bock beer. John worked as a laborer for Swift & Co. His father remarried after his first wife died. He had a stepbrother named Benjamin. Mack kept pigeons in coops on the roof. At his funeral a feather fell on the coffin as it was carried from church.

Anna (Anne) Bielawska was born on 15 October 1916 according to the baptism certificate. The New Jersey state record lists October 16 as the day of birth. To confuse matters Anne celebrated her birthday on October 10. She was baptized in the Church of St. Anthony on October 22. Her godparents were Boleslaw Macanka and Teresa Rusakiewicz. The priest was Fr. Kwiatkowski. Anne died unexpectedly on 28 April 1989. A thief broke into her home in Elizabeth, NJ, surprising her and causing a heart attack. (Anne had heart problems previously.) She was 72 years of age. She was buried in Holy Cross Cemetery.

Cocci Anny was twice married. Her first husband was Henry Kuminski. They married in the Church of St. Anthony on 28 October 1939. The witnesses were Joseph Zalucki and Jean Just. The priest was Msgr. Ignatius Szudrowicz. At the time of the wedding she resided at 712 Jersey Ave.

Henry Kuminski was the son of Joseph Kuminski and Mary Kuc. The marriage record described him as 22 years of age. Henry's reputation is not very good. He comes across the years as a womanizer and two-timer. His grandfather warned Anne against the marriage, as did an army officer in Florida, where Henry was stationed. (He may have made a career of the military.) He had an extra-marital affair and stole money from Anne shortly after World War Two. She and Henry had no children.

Anne's second marriage was to Roman Rog in a civil ceremony. Roman Rog was born in Krakow, Poland, on 24 March 1915. Roman was the longest-lived of our relatives. He died at the age of 95 on 9 June 2010 while this book was in progress. He didn't reach 100 as he wanted, but he outlived his five brothers-in-law, which gratified him. We don't have information on Roman's family. He had a number of sisters and brothers, several of whom reached great ages. He was the only one in his family who immigrated.

Anne met Roman at the Polish House at St. Mark's Place in New York City. Roman first asked my mother to dance, but she declined because he asked in Polish—if he asked in English, I might be typing this in Polish. He then asked Anne. They married in a civil ceremony when they couldn't afford the annulment money. Their married friends, Viktor and Olga (last names unknown), were witnesses.

Anne and Roman had one child, **Michelle LaVenia**.

They lived on 52 East 7th St. in New York City. They had a grocery store on 7th St. between First and Second Aves. Later, Roman had his own business as a general contractor. In the 1960s Anne worked near Battery Place in Lower Manhattan. They bought Henry Bielawski's house in Elizabeth. At one point they wanted to move to Mansonville, Canada, where they had friends. Anne couldn't get permission to move, as there was something wrong with her lungs.

Cocci Annie had a pleasant and generous personality. She had a good singing voice. She used to smoke using a cigarette holder like President Roosevelt. She had thick hair that she dyed. My mother remembered that the dye ran one time in Coney Island and that Anne would be late for work because she stayed up all hours of the night fixing her hair.

Anne and her sisters met on Friday evenings to play bingo at St. Paul of the Cross Church in Jersey City. Afterward they met in *Cocci* Carol's house on Bleecker St. She called her sisters, "The girls."

Uncle Roman lived in a senior citizen complex in Manhattan after Anne's death. He drove until he was ninety and, exhibiting exemplary interest in family, regularly visited my parents and Carol Castrovinci, as well as the graves in Holy Cross Cemetery. I visited Roman several times in New York City. We would walk to a Polish restaurant on First Ave. where Roman repeated his joke that he was on a "seafood diet"—when he saw food, he pushed it away.

Uncle Roman had an European style of kissing hands and calling women "darling" in a thick Polish accent. He was a world traveler. He fled across Europe in World War Two. He encountered KGB recruiters and traitorous comrades, among other adventures. He served in the Polish and American armies in the World War. After the war he became a merchant marine and visited Africa and Madagascar. He told a number of stock stories about his travels, including one about a "Mrs. Piano" he met overseas and about visiting an opium den. He planned to write his memoir, but I don't believe he did, which is a shame.

Helen Bielawska was the third child of Pawel Bielawski and Zofia Storta. Her name on the parish register appeared as "Helen Veronica". According to St. Anthony Parish records Helen was born 14 May 1920. Helen celebrated her birthday on May 21. She was baptized on June 6. Her godparents were Stanley Storta and Julia Alencewicz. The priest was Fr. Szyman Nawrocki. *Cocci* Helen died of heart disease on 9 January 2001 in Holy Name Hospital in Teaneck, New Jersey. She was 80 years of age. She was buried in St. Raymond's Cemetery in the Bronx (sect. 17, range 112—this is the part of the cemetery near East Tremont Ave.)

Helen married Fred Ost on 27 June 1943 in St. Anthony's Church. Their witnesses were Henry Bielawski and my mother Sophia. The priest was Fr. Edward Majewski. At the time of the wedding Fred was in the army. His family lived at 1011 East 178th St. in the Bronx. They met at a small chemical company in New York City.

After their marriage they lived above a bar on Jersey Avenue in Jersey City. Later, they moved to Cliffside Park. Helen spent her last years there in a senior citizen complex.

Fred Ost was the son of Charles Ost and Anna Petz. He was born in Hoboken on 11 April 1920. He died suddenly of a heart attack on 21 October 1970 in their apartment in Cliffside Park. Fred worked as a milkman for Sealtest. He is buried with Helen in St. Raymond's Cemetery.

Helen and Fred had two sons: **Fred, Jr.**; and **Carl**.

Fred Ost, Jr. was born 6 July 1947 and died 28 September 1992. He was 45 years of age. Like Tommy Grogan, Cousin Fred was a tragic character. He was an immensely likeable and good-looking person who could not escape the addiction to alcohol that eventually claimed him. Great-aunt Kate had it right about drink "taking the man"—in Fred's case, much too early.

Uncle Fred was a large, red-faced, red-haired man. He wore glasses and was balding. He and Helen played cards with Blanche on Friday nights. Both he and Blanche had rough vocabularies. We use to go with Fred to a lake in North New Jersey called Green Valley Lake. This was a secluded spot where we could swim, fish, and hike.

My mother remembered that Uncle Fred owned an old-fashioned tripod camera with a hood. One time he fell asleep under the hood while taking pictures.

Fred's mother died in 1951. His father remarried, but died shortly afterward. Fred had a younger sister named Anna who married a sailor and lived on a farm in Iowa. Fred's older brother was Charles (1915 – 1971). "Charlie" was buried with a can of beer—if he wanted to impress the Ferryman, he should have brought stronger stuff and a few vials of tears.

After Fred died *Cocci* Helen worked for a chemical company in Weehawken near the Lincoln Tunnel and for a medical supply company in Union City. She learned to drive after the age of 50.

Helen had a saying that a person's hand would rise up and stay straight in the coffin if he talked back to his parents—if this is true, I'm going to have an odd looking coffin. Helen used the expression, "better than boopkey" to indicate that whatever a person had, however small and insignificant, was better than having nothing.

My mother and father visited Helen regularly in the senior complex where she lived. She and my mother took a bus to Atlantic City to lose money several times a year. In the early 1990s Helen accompanied us to a Kennedy assassination conference in Chicago. This was around the time that she started to experience heart problems. During a medical test she suffered a stroke and was confined to a wheel chair for the last year or so of her life.

One of *Cocci* Helen's desires was to see the turn of the millennium. I'm happy to say that she achieved that goal.

Henry Paul Bielawski was born 6 January 1924 in Jersey City. He was baptized January 20. His godparents were Francis Grynuk and Anna Wasilewska. The priest was Fr. Francis Nowak. Uncle Henry died 4 November 1992 at the age of 68. He died unexpectedly during a medical test for lung disease. He was cremated.

Henry married Sophie Mnich on 2 August 1947 at the Church of St. Stanislaus on East 7th St. in Manhattan. Their witnesses were her brother Ignacy Mnich and my mother Sophia Bielawska. The priest was Fr. Joseph Grono.

They met through Anne who lived in a building, possibly on East 12th St., in which Sophie's father served as the janitor. My mother recollected that Henry went out with Fred Ost's sister, Anna, for a time. My mother went out with Ignacy Mnich briefly. As with the first generation of immigrants, we are dealing with an interlocked group of people who resided in the same limited vicinity and who were acquainted with one another.

After their marriage Henry and Sophie resided in New York City. They later bought a house in Elizabeth. They sold this house to Roman and Anne Rog and moved a few doors down to a smaller place. Henry and Sophie separated late in their marriage. Henry spent his last years in a retirement community in Red Bank, NJ.

Sophie Mnich was the daughter of Stefan Mnich and Marianna Turon. The marriage record indicated she was born in Dutza, Poland on 16 November 1927, but she may have been born before that. *Cocci* Sophie immigrated with her father, brother Ignacy, and sister Jessica to the United States. She was a quiet person with a thick Polish accent. She worked as a cleaning lady. In later years she became a Jehovah Witness. She lived for a number of years in California. Sophie's sister Jessica died at a young age. As of this writing *Cocci* Sophie and Ignacy are alive.

Henry and Sophie had two children: **Paul**; and **Elizabeth Lauer**.

Uncle Henry graduated Ferris High, where he played football. My mother recollected that he became seriously ill in his youth after drinking a poisonous substance. He was hit one time and seriously injured by an irate man who wanted to use a pay phone he happened to be on.

Uncle Henry was a pleasant and likeable person. He always remembered people's birthdays with a card. His slogan was Fred Flintstone's "Ya-pa-dapper-do!" Henry worked for an import-export line for a number of years. He frequently socialized with other businessmen at parties. (At one of these parties, he introduced Josephine Szustek to her future husband—it's still a small world.) Unfortunately, Henry could not manage his drinking. He lost his family and his job. He had several bad experiences as a drinker, including having his clothes set on fire. Henry was a decent person who encountered the savagery of this world on a number of occasions.

Shortly before his death the family visited him in the retirement community in Red Bank. My father and mother were there, as was *Cocci* Carol. It was a very happy experience for everyone. Afterward Henry called to say that my father had left his hat behind. I don't think he got it back.

Sophia Bielawska, my mother, was the fifth child of Pawel Bielawski and Zofia Storta. Mom was born on 23 February 1926 in Jersey City. She was baptized April 11 in the Church of St. Anthony. Her godparents were Casimir Wasilewski and Stanislawa Lakiewska. The priest was Fr. A. Wisniewski. Mom and Dad married in a civil ceremony on 14 February 1951. The place of their wedding is unknown. It may have been in Maryland, but we have not been able to identify the location. Mom's life will be described in Chapter 17.

Carol Bielawska was the last child born to Pawel and Zofia. *Cocci* Carol was born 25 July 1934 in Jersey City. She was baptized on August 19 in the Church of St. Anthony. The name given on the baptism certificate was "Karolina Helena". Her godparents were Alexander Szczesny and Antonia Wisniewska. The priest was Fr. Wisniewski. Carol married Anthony Castrovinci in February 1954.

Uncle Tony Castrovinci was born circa 1933. He was the son of Anthony and Concetta "Connie" Castrovinci. We're uncertain whether Uncle Tony was named after his father—we have not been able to locate his parents in the 1930 Census. Uncle Tony worked as a foreman in a corrugated box plant. He died 11 September 1997 of heart disease. He was approximately 64 years of age.

Connie Castrovinci died at an advanced age in August 1995. Uncle Tony had three brothers: Lawrence (deceased); Basil (Bobby); and Ronald.

Uncle Tony and *Cocci* Carol were introduced to one another by my mother. They were together in biology class in Jersey City State College. After their marriage they lived for a time near Journal Square in Jersey City and then on Lake St. a few houses up from where my family moved many years later. They bought a house on Bleecker St. in the Jersey City Heights section. This house served as a center of our extended family activity for many years.

Cocci Carol was too busy with her large family to work steadily when young. After Uncle Tony's death she worked with autistic and severely handicapped children in the Jersey City school system.

Carol and Tony had the following children: **Anthony**; **Judy Rieling**; **Lawrence**; **Anne Marie**; **David**; **Amy Caspari**; **Carol Anne Connolly**; and **Stephen**.

I have many happy memories of Uncle Tony, who served as my confirmation sponsor, and of *Cocci* Carol. Our families are now scattered, but we were very close growing up. I played with cousin Anthony and my sisters played with cousin Judy. There was a swimming pool in their back yard that we often swam in. Uncle Tony was a fun-loving man who often jumped from a neighbor's shed into the pool Geronimo style. I can still see him leaping recklessly into the pool. Uncle Tony owned a motorcycle at some point and gave us rides along Jersey City streets. The rides were faster when we visited their summer home in the Poconos. My mother visited 20 Bleecker St. regularly for Friday night bingo. If they arrived early my father and Uncle Roman played cards with Tony and his brothers. If I picked Mom up and arrived early I was sure to hear Uncle Roman's narrative of his European adventures. There was always something going on in the Castrovinci house. Those were very good times.

I recall speaking with one of our Irish contacts. He said that the word "cousin" meant something when he was young, but that it no longer meant much. He said that in former years cousins knew one another and socialized and visited one another. Today cousins can go through life without knowing one another—even without meeting one another. His description matches our experience with the Castrovincis. It meant something back then to be cousins with Anthony and with Judy and, later, with Lawrence and with the rest of their family. We were fortunate to experience the "old world" custom of an extended family.

Chapter Sixteen

~

Joseph Thomas Ford

My father **Joseph Thomas Ford** was born in Hoboken on 24 July 1926. He was the son of Patrick Ford and Catherine Griffin. He was baptized August 8 in the Church of Our Lady of Grace. His godparents were Thomas Keane and Margaret Keane. The priest was Fr. Edward Begley. Kitty Fleming and Rita Nelson told us that Dad's name was supposed to be Patrick Joseph, but that Margaret purposely reversed it to Joseph Patrick. Dad died of lung cancer on 14 June 1999 in our home at 3247 Kennedy Blvd. in Jersey City. He was 72 years of age. He was buried in Holy Cross Cemetery in North Arlington (block 39, sect. B, tier K, grave 134).

We have marriage records dating to 1798, but we have not been able to document Dad and Mom's marriage. The date we have is 14 February 1951. The location is said to be in Maryland, but we haven't been able to find the specific place. Mom and Dad engaged in a whirlwind romance—they met six months previous to their marriage. Mom related that she and Dad had been partying with his friend Ray Weber and a lady named "Frankie"—her last name is not remembered. The four decided to elope and marry—this is what is called an "impulse". Mom and Dad carried out the marriage in a civil ceremony, but Frankie was a married woman at the time and couldn't go through with the ceremony. She and Ray Weber served as witnesses. Whatever certificates existed have been lost over the years and Maryland county archives have not been able to find the records.

We don't know Frankie's name or dates. Ray Weber (1921 – 1974) was a prominent Hoboken resident. He was a band leader and instructor. He was afflicted with skin cancer the last years of his life. He never married.

Joseph Ford and Sophia Bielawska had the following children. **Dennis Ford** was born in 1953. My life is documented in Chapter 18. **Felicia Ford** was born in 1954. Felicia's life is documented in Chapter 19. **Kathleen Ford** was born in 1955. Kathleen's life is documented in Chapter 20.

Dad stood slightly over six feet. Everyone said he was "six foot two", but that may have been a little too tall. He was a thin man in his youth—165 pounds—and gained weight only in the 1980s. He had blue eyes, black hair, and a cleft in his chin. He had the prominent brow and sunken eyes characteristic of the Griffin line. Probably, his height derived from the Griffins as well. Dad had a squarish look to his face. In this he resembled his sister Mary and Aunt Kate Flynn. As he aged, he came to resemble his father, gaining the somewhat owlish features we see in the Fords.

Dad had the reputation of being very strong. He told us that he was always called on when there was a brawl and the heavy-hitting cops were needed. Dad told a story about a Southern—"Rebel"—truck driver who was arrested in Hoboken. This man was gigantic—Dad called him "Man Mountain Dean". He started a fight in the precinct house. I'm not sure how the situation was resolved, but Dad said it took several cops to subdue the guy.

We know little about Dad's childhood. We don't know who he hung out with or what games he played. We have to assume they were the same people he hung out with as an adult and that the games were much the same games we played. Dad told me that growing up he slept in the same bed as his brothers Eddie and Francey. He said one of his earliest memories was falling asleep on the sidewalk as he and Nana waited for a bus. He was with a friend named Jerry Driscoll when Orson Welles's *War of the Worlds* broadcast came on the radio on 30 October 1938. Dad said he never ran home so fast once he heard the Martians had crossed the Pulaski Skyway.

Dad broke his leg as a child when he was hit by a car at 8th St. and Willow Ave. A traffic light was erected at the intersection because of the injury. Dad said he broke the leg a second time in St. Mary's Hospital when he stood before the break healed.

Dad attended Our Lady of Grace grammar school. If the system was the same then as now he attended ninth grade in Brandt Junior High. Demarest was the high school in Dad's time—Hoboken High wasn't built until the 1960s. Dad claimed he had an "11th grade education" and his Navy discharge papers credit him with one year of high school, so it is possible he never finished high school.

Dad had a lot of street smarts. He could tell who was "on the level" and who was not. He wasn't a book-learned person. I can't recall him reading a single book. His life was very different than mine in that regard. He had no connection with the topics I studied in college and little curiosity about them. I do not remember having a single conversation about psychology. He probably held many middle-class prejudices about the value of psychology. We spoke a few times about the Kennedy assassination. He was a lone-gunman advocate and thought conspiracy theories nonsense. He once stated he found it suspicious that Jack Ruby was able to kill Oswald so easily. He was worried that the FBI would make inquiries about me for associating with the sleuths. Ironically, many of the sleuths thought I was an agent.

Dad related that he was on duty when the assassination happened and that he saw the assassination on television. This is an interesting blended memory. The Zapruder film was never shown on television until the early 1970s, so Dad could not have seen it on 22 November 1963. He inserted the film into his memories of the events of that sad day.

I've tried to recall my first memory of Dad, but I'm not sure which would qualify.

I remember playing tap ball with a friend on Willow Ave. across the street from what was then the Safeway supermarket. This is the game where you tap the ball across a line on the pavement. Dad came along and was in his cups. He may even have been carrying a six pack. To my embarrassment he insisted on joining in and tapping the ball.

A happier early memory. There was an adult softball game in the Weehawken High field near the Lincoln Tunnel. It was likely a game sponsored by Our Lady of Grace. Some of the fathers couldn't hit the ball to save their sons' lives, but Dad blasted a shot that was either a triple or home run depending on how fast he ran. I remember feeling very proud that my father could hit, whereas the rest of the boys' fathers couldn't so much as lay down a bunt. Dad joked about that hit for a long time afterward. He use to say the ball still hasn't come down.

I'm not sure of the context, but a bunch of fathers and sons went to Yankee Stadium. Sonny Garrick, a rambunctious friend of Dad's, got into an argument with a fan. This fan warned Sonny that he was going to call a cop and Sonny started to yell that Dad was a cop if he wanted one.

Another early memory. We lived at 803 Willow Ave. Mom cut her foot badly on a milk bottle. It was a nasty cut that bled a lot. The scar is still visible on her shin. I'm not sure how we called the police—the neighbors may have—but Dad arrived in uniform. He picked Mom up and carried her down the stairs.

Another 803 Willow Ave. memory. It was very late when someone tried to get inside our apartment by using a key. The man who lived on the floor above us probably had too many to drink and had lost count of flights. He knocked on the door loudly when the key didn't work, frightening us. But Dad was home and he pushed against the door and protected us.

Another early memory. We were at Coney Island with Mom and *Cocci* Blanchie and her family. Suddenly, Dad was there. He had found us—by finding the "Polish section" he claimed. I'm not sure it's the same memory, but Dad once drove us home from Coney Island in an old beat-up car. The springs in the car broke after the trip. Dad said they broke because there were so many heavy people in the car.

Another early memory. We were walking in New York City near the bus terminal. I'm not sure where we were going. Dad was never interested in visiting New York City, which he disliked and avoided. Maybe we were coming from the Circle Line cruise of Manhattan Island. I was walking slightly ahead. A strange man approached. Dad immediately stepped forward and pulled me back to the family group.

Dad's parents lived at 923 Park Ave. when he was born. They lived at 931 Willow Ave. when he entered the Navy in 1944. Afterward, they lived at 832 Willow Ave. This is the house Dad considered his family home. Like every other building on the block it was a five-story tenement of railroad rooms.

Dad and Mom's first home after their marriage was 48 West Hamilton Place in Jersey City across the park from St. Francis Hospital. *Dziadek* lived with them for a time. The house was owned by a lawyer named McGovern. They had to move when civil service officers were required to live in the city where they worked.

They moved to 803 Willow Ave. in Hoboken This is where I lived as a child. Today, the neighborhood is upscale. When I was a child 8th and Willow was a solid row of five-story buildings from one side of the block to the other and across the street. It was one of the most congested sections of the city. The block is still congested, only the cold-water flats are now swanky condos.

Mom recalled that Dad and Francey painted the kitchen when they moved, but left it unfinished and went out for beer instead.

We lived on the fourth floor right. We entered into the kitchen. There was a black stove to the right. I think Mom hung a clothesline over the stove. One time the clothes caught fire. The cabinets were along the left wall near the window. They were glass on the top and wood on the bottom. There was a counter between cabinets. I played toy soldiers on this counter. On Sunday mornings we sat on the floor against the bottom cabinets. Mom read the comics to us. There was a red recliner between the cabinets and the refrigerator. The windows opened to the backyard. There was a clothesline in the backyard. When the line broke, some brave soul from the neighborhood earned a few bucks to climb the pole and reattach the line.

Our bedroom was next. Felicia and Kathy slept on a bunk bed. There was a window—a shelf—between the kitchen and bedroom. Mom sang us to sleep through this window as she worked in the kitchen.

Mom and Dad's bedroom came next. I don't remember much of it, except that there may have been a large mirror on a light-colored bureau. The living room was last. The windows looked out over Willow Ave. I was always scared when Mom sat on the sill and cleaned the outside windows. We put the Christmas tree between the windows.

We had wonderful family parties at 803 Willow Ave. They were birthday parties and a huge celebration on Christmas Eve. The Bielawski aunts and uncles came with all the cousins. Mom made a ton of food. Beer and liquor flowed generously and quite a few people finished in their cups. Dad always had his share. He would sit in the red recliner at the end of these parties and sing. He had a "bar voice", meaning he sang only when drink loosened the cords. But he had a good voice and was always asked to sing. The relatives insisted they couldn't leave until "Joe Ford sang." *Danny Boy, I'll Take You Home Again Kathleen, Because of You, Harbor Lights, Martha, Rambling Rose of the Wildwood.* These were the standards.

We moved to 1208 Hudson St. when I was around ten years of age—I became a teenager there. Five flights up, our apartment commanded a great view of the Empire State Building. It also commanded a view of the dry docks in Bethlehem Steel and the enormous derrick on the 12th St. pier. A great thing about living on the top floor was that we had access to the roof. We sat, read, studied, and sunbathed on the roof. And we walked our dog—"Big Sam", a black mongrel subject to too much discipline—on the roof.

The rooms ran off a long corridor. The largest room faced New York. This room had a pair of Chicago windows. The inside rooms opened to a courtyard between buildings. The kitchen was the last room. The stove was on the left, across from a functioning dumbwaiter. Snooze, the elderly caretaker who lived in the basement, rang the bell periodically and we placed the garbage inside.

We moved from 1208 Hudson when Applied Housing bought the block—and promptly ruined it. Our next apartment was 60 12th St., which was around the corner in the Yellow Flats. We lived on the second floor. The rooms were small, sunless, and cheaply constructed. The entrance was into the living room. A tiny windowless kitchen was to the left. My bedroom was first. There were two bedrooms along the right and a tiny room in the rear. There was no view whatsoever.

We moved to 137 Lake St., Jersey City, around 1980—we left Hoboken for good. It was a two-family house owned by a Polish lady named Stephanie. She sold the house to a lady who subsequently married a Jersey City policeman. We moved when she sold the house to a family from India.

The apartment at 137 Lake had once been occupied by a Hudson County elected official—this official later went to jail for corruption. The living room was two large rooms separated by wood paneling. Mom and Dad's bedroom was next. My room was to the side. I also had a tiny office at the head of the stairs. I was into physical fitness at the time and kept a set of weights in the office—I used a kitchen chair for the bench presses.

The years at 137 Lake were mixed in quality. There were good times with the kids. Jason York was in grade school. We picked him up at Mount Carmel grade school. One time the car overheated and I had to walk— at 35 mph—to be on time. Jason learned to play baseball in Mosquito Park on Manhattan Ave. I lobbed soft pitches to him in the handball court—they soon became harder pitches. Kathy and Joe Pecoraro married. Mom watched their daughter Jennie on Saturdays—Kathy worked in the Medical Center as a licensed practical nurse. I entered graduate school.

Dad settled into the pattern that occupied him for the next few years. He drove Mom to work and picked her up. He was still involved in Hoboken social activities, but slowly disengaged and settled on Brophy's Tavern on Kennedy Blvd. The slow walk into the sickness of drinking became a trot at 137 Lake St.

We moved around the corner to 3247 Kennedy Blvd. a year or so after Dad entered sobriety. This was a private house owned by an Italian couple. We lived on the ground floor. They lived one flight up. Dad was a good tenant and was careful not to rile the landlords, who he judged excitable types. Dad was a private individual and resisted their attempts to be friendly. He rarely made conversation and he tried to avoid them as much as possible.

We had good times at 3247 Kennedy Blvd. Felicia and Kathy and their children visited every Sunday. Mom cooked huge meals for the family. Afterward we walked to Pershing Field where the kids romped in the playground. Sometimes, they went on walks on Central Ave. and shopped in the five-and-dime stores. After dinner there were arguments over who would wash the dishes. Dad tried to wash them, which caused Mom grief, as she claimed he didn't wipe them properly. About the only time he got to do the dishes was when Mom walked with the kids. He had them properly washed and ready for desert that followed when everyone arrived home.

Dad preferred to eat alone, either sitting at the table ahead of the rest of us or at the blue recliner in the living room. He also took his plate into his bedroom and used the night stand as a table. During Christmas and family get-togethers he sat and chatted with Mom and the girls.

Dad had a routine on Kennedy Blvd. He woke up early and went for the morning papers and for the lotteries. He bought a lot of lottery tickets—I don't think he ever hit. His favorite numbers were 756, the number of the license plate of his Tempo, 2257, the last four digits of his Social Security number, and the ages of his grandchildren for the pick five and pick six. He insisted we play his numbers even when he grew ill and was in the hospital.

It wasn't uncommon for Dad to venture out four or five times a day. He put a lot of local miles on the car. He never left the house without buying something. He drove Mom to the stores in the morning. When the weather was nice they drove to Liberty State Park. Dad never liked to walk, so they would sit on a bench near the parking lot. By the late afternoon Dad dozed in bed or in the blue recliner, which he favored until he became ill. Seven PM was bedtime for him. He'd wake up around 11 PM, make coffee, have a smoke, and go back to bed. I worried about his making coffee so late, since he brewed only a cup or two and the pot got hot fast.

Things I'll miss now that Dad is gone—the smell of witch hazel, creamed onions, mashed potatoes, bottles of Tylenol, the most delicious jelly donuts after bingo on Thursdays, newspapers waiting at the breakfast table.

Dad served in the Navy in World War Two. His enlistment was from 29 April 1944 to 14 May 1946. He enlisted at the age of 17, a fact he pointed out many times over the years. He obtained the rank of Seaman First Class. His serial number was 713-07-22. His job was gunner's mate—he was responsible for the maintenance and supply of armaments [45].

Dad enlisted in New York City and was discharged from Lido Beach, Long Island. He was described on the enlistment papers as 6 ft., 1/4th inch in height, 162 pounds, with dark hair and blue eyes.

His mustering out pay was $100.00—he got $1.30 transportation money. He was awarded the Victory Medal, the American Theatre Medal, and the European Theatre Medal. He received the State of New Jersey Distinguished Service Award in March 2000.

Dad served from 1 July 1944 to 12 March 1946 on board the USS *MacLeisch* (DD-220), a destroyer, and from 22 March 1946 to 22 April 1946 on board the USS *Great Sitkin* (AE-17), a supply and fuel ship.

The *MacLeisch* was 314 feet long. She could sail as fast as 25 knots, but her usual speed was 14 knots. She was a four-stacker initially, but was converted to three stacks shortly before World War Two. Her weaponry included .50 caliber guns, a 20 mm. gun, and depth charges. She could hold 100,000 gallons of diesel fuel, so she was a buoyant powder keg. She was named for Lt. Kenneth MacLeisch of Glencoe, IL. He had been a flyer shot down in World War One. She was commissioned in August 1920. In the pre-war years she served in the Black Sea and in the Pacific. She was decommissioned in 1938 and returned to active duty when the United States entered the World War. Early in the war she served as a convoy escort ship, making runs from Norfolk to the Caribbean and from Norfolk to Casablanca. She was credited with one submarine kill off the Florida Coast. She was decommissioned in March 1946.

The *Great Sitkin* was named after a volcano in the Aleutian Islands. She was commissioned in January 1945. The *Sitkin* was 459 feet long with a crew of 267. In the 1950s she served in the Mediterranean Sea. In 1962 she served as an ammo ship in the blockade of Cuba in the Missile Crises. She served in the Vietnam War and was decommissioned in July 1973.

Dad said little about his service in the Navy. He told us that on shore leave in Costa Rica the crew took a trolley car up a steep hill. Their destination was a saloon. And he told us how the sailors swam in the sea protected by crewmen with rifles at the ready to fend off the sharks—I suppose every sailor tells this story. And he told a story about a theft on board the *MacLeisch*. The ensign announced there would be no questions asked if the items were returned. The items were returned and the ensign went back on his word, promptly pressing charges against the thief. Dad greatly respected this ensign, who suggested he make a career of the Navy.

Dad said little about his time in the Navy, but Mom and I reconstructed his service literally day-by-day. On 9 November 2005 we visited the National Archives in College Point, MD, and reviewed the original typed and handwritten deck logs preserved there. Here are the highlights of Dad's life aboard "DD-220" [46].

On Saturday 1 July 1944 the *MacLeisch* was moored at pier three in the South Boston Naval Annex. Seaman Second Class Joseph T. Ford reported for duty with sixteen other sailors. Lt. Commander Robert Winkel was in command. Six days later Winkel was replaced by J.W. Fitzpatrick. The *MacLeisch* left Boston for Brooklyn, arriving on July 16. On July 18 the ship left New York harbor as part of a task force sailing for Falmouth, England. It arrived in England on August 17 and then steamed for Cherbourg, France.

On August 21 general quarters sounded at midnight when radar made contact with three unidentified vessels. When the ships failed to respond to flashing lights and radio contact the *MacLeisch* opened fire, expending 29 rounds of ammunition until the targets identified themselves.

The convoy entered Cherbourg harbor at 9:30 AM (0930 military time). Their arrival did not run smoothly. Two barges went aground and two other barges had to be cut loose when the tow lines entangled.

The *MacLeisch* left Cherbourg at noon on August 22 and returned to Falmouth. It then sailed to Belfast, Northern Ireland, where it docked from August 24 - 30. Dad was not interested in accompanying us to Ireland on our genealogical jaunts in the 1990s. He claimed he "touched his feet in Ireland" and didn't need to go again—I'm not sure whether Northern Ireland counts as Ireland. After a stop at Milford Haven, Wales, the ship arrived on the East Coast of America on October 1.

On October 25 the *MacLeisch* docked at Norfolk. The next day it left for the Panama Canal Zone, which it reached on October 30. It proceeded through the Canal and moored at Taboga on the Pacific side and at Balboa, which is part of Panama City.

The *MacLeisch* spent December 7 – 13 in Punterienas, Costa Rica. The deck log noted that shore parties visited Costa Rica. The log didn't mention their destination.

On December 16 Donald S. Cramer replaced Lt. Fitzgerald as commanding officer. Three days later fires broke out on the *MacLeisch* while it was docked in Taboga. The fires were quickly extinguished, but two sailors were hurt and hospitalized and one—Logan J. Ferguson—was burned to death.

On December 28 the *MacLeisch* left the Canal Zone for Boston at a speed of 18 knots. It arrived on 22 January 1945. On January 27 she escorted the Italian submarine *Vortice* to Port Everglades, FL. She returned to the Bay of Panama where she remained until July 2, when she steamed for Narragansett Bay. The time in the Canal Zone was uneventful—the highlight was striking a periscope of a submarine on March 2.

From 7 July 1945 until 1 February 1946 the *MacLeisch* participated in maneuvers along the East Cost in the area of Block Island and Quonset Point, Rhode Island. At 2010 on 11 October 1945 a fighter aircraft crashed in the sea 1,500 yards to the starboard. The *MacLeisch* illuminated the site and lowered a boat, but neither the plane nor pilot were recovered. On 13 January 1946 Lt. Donald T. Burke replaced Lt. Cramer in command. On February 1 the *MacLeisch* steamed for dry dock in Boston.

On 8 March 1946 the *MacLeisch* was decommissioned from active duty. With the officers and crew on the quarterdeck the colors were sounded and the pennants removed. Seaman First Class Joseph T. Ford was detached to the Naval Receiving Station in Boston.

Seaman Ford reported for service on *The Great Sitkin* on 22 March 1946. The *Sitkin* was anchored in Hampton Roads, VA. Captain E.B. Perry was in command.

Dad's service on the *Sitkin* was brief and uneventful. The ship practiced supplying and fueling destroyers. March 26 was a typical day. At 0700 the *Sitkin* rendezvoused with the USS *Greene* (DD-711) and the USS *Gearing* (DD-710). At 0920 it fired a .40 mm. machine gun. At 1002 it practiced a man overboard drill. April 13 was also a typical day. At 0515 it left Hampton Roads at a speed of 14 knots. It rendezvoused with the USS *Renate* at 1028. At 1805 it returned to Hampton Roads.

On April 20 the *Sitkin* left Hampton Roads for the Naval Ammunition Depot in Earle, NJ. On March 21 *Barnegat* Lightship was sighted at 0412. The *Ambrose* Lightship was sighted at 0749. The *Sitkin* dropped anchor off Sandy Hook at 0934. The next day it docked at 0710 at pier two in Earle.

Dad disembarked in Earle, ending his life on the sea, and spent his last month in the service in the naval yard in Brooklyn.

More things I'll miss—ham and cabbage, Remy Martin at Christmas, the smell of fresh coffee at 11:00 PM, rides to the PATH Station, being handed the tokens on the Parkway on our trips to Wildwood miles ahead of the toll plaza.

Dad was appointed to the Hoboken Police Dept. for the first time on 29 October 1946. His badge was #148. He said that Catherine Lovett, his politically-connected cousin, had a lot of influence getting him into the department. He was granted a six-month leave of absence in November 1947 and resigned—or was terminated—on 4 December 1947. This leave of absence was related in some manner to civil service, which the administration opposed and which the younger cops desired.

Dad was reappointed to the police department on 23 September 1948 and commenced to serve on 1 October 1948. This second appointment was through civil service. Dad said he trained and physically worked out to meet the requirements. He retired on 1 February 1975 after 28 years of service. His badge was #78. His nickname was "Bosco".

Dad was part of the in-crowd when he started "on the force". He supported George Fitzpatrick, a "rebel cop", against the local boss Mayor Barney McFeeley. On one occasion Mayor McFeeley walked up to Dad and told him to "remember the party." Dad got punishment details, such as extensive traffic duties, for bucking Mayor McFeeley.

Dad always spoke highly of George Fitzpatrick. Dad recalled that Fitzpatrick's wife brought him lunch when he was on traffic duty. He ate lunch standing in the street. I believe Fitzpatrick got a lucrative position in New York City after leaving the force. Ironically, the manager in Bosworth's funeral home when we went to make arrangements for Dad's wake was a great-nephew of Barney McFeeley.

McFeeley was voted out of office and replaced by five commissioners, two of whom were Fitzpatrick and John Grogan. With Fitzpatrick in control of the force, Dad got to drive one of the few police cars in the city. The procedure was different then—the cars were driven home by the officers who used them. When Fitzpatrick lost control Dad reverted to foot patrol. Dad said he had sore feet—"barking dogs"—when he started as a cop. The shoes he owned were not meant for extensive walking, but they were all he could afford. Later, Dad was back in the driver's seat when John Grogan became mayor. By the time John Grogan died in 1965, there were enough police cars in the city to go around, so everyone got the chance to drive whether or not they were in the "in-crowd" or not.

Dad was a detective for a while. I don't know why he transferred to the detective bureau or back to uniform duty. Perhaps it was a patronage position. I dimly recall hearing that he disliked the hours. Dad was also involved early in his career with the Police Athletic Association and with Hoboken PBA local #2.

One of Dad's posts was River St., at that time a rough section across from the docks with taverns from one corner to the next. There must have been considerable violence and public drunkenness. The violence was likely on a small scale, since Dad said he never fired his gun in all his years on the force. The gun was a Smith & Wesson Victory model. It was issued to him on 21 August 1946 at a cost of twenty dollars.

Virginia Bello, Uncle Francey's lady friend, claimed that Dad had a slogan when he rousted drunks or trouble-makers. "Up, out, or in," he would say. This translated as, "Get up, get out, or go to jail."

Dad told the story of an accidental shooting that occurred many years ago. The police were called when a man was spotted on a fire escape. This man was either a burglar or an unfortunate who had locked himself out of his apartment. One of the responding officers accidentally shot the man, killing him. A superior produced a gun that they planted on the dead man and used to justify the shooting. This officer afterward quit the force. Dad claimed his life was ruined and that he didn't come to a good end.

Dad also told the story of a rabid dog that had to be put down. Patrolmen took shots at the dog, but the bullets either missed or had no effect. A canny old sergeant arrived, held his gun out, and let the dog bite the barrel as he pulled the trigger.

Hoboken experienced racial disharmony following Dr. King's murder in 1967. There was a riot in the western end of town around First or Second Sts. This part of town had been Irish at the turn of the century. By the 1960s it had become a slum and blighted section. Dad arrived in a phalanx of police that marched to the site to restore order. They wore riot gear of helmets and shields. When they arrived someone threw bags of garbage off the roof of one of the tenements, eliciting laughter and applause from the onlookers.

Dad often told a story about a fight in Maxwell's Tavern on 11th and Washington Sts.—this was long before Maxwell's became trendy in the 1980s. The bar was owned by a husband and wife. The husband had a drinking problem and the wife was a thrifty lady who controlled the cash register. One night a fight broke out. The police were called. The husband promised gratuities if the police broke the fight up without breaking any furniture. They succeeded. The next day the wife reneged on her husband's promise.

Dad also told a story about a fight that broke out in the Union Club on Hudson St.—this was the upscale restaurant and meeting place at the time. The fight was between Anthony Provenzano—"Tony Pro" of Mafia fame—and dissident members of the union. The police were called. They got Tony Pro out of the building safely. As a reward each cop, Dad included, got $20. This was no small gratuity when the weekly pay was $63.00.

Dad often told the story of riding with Harry Coppinger on a cold winter night. They turned onto Fifth St. and saw a huge fire on the Holland American piers. They were the first unit to respond to what Dad insisted was "Jewish lightning".

Dad told a story about testifying at a trial at the Brennan courthouse in Jersey City. The trial was so boring and the heat so intense, his partner fell asleep and started to snore. This cop didn't get into trouble, as the judge was also sleeping.

Dad told a story about guarding the Christmas collection at Our Lady of Grace Church. An officer stayed in the rectory overnight to guard the collection, which would have been a heavenly sum. He complained that a rich Parish like Our Lady of Grace didn't give the officer so much as dinner—or a drink—but that a poor Parish like St. Joseph's left the officer who stayed to guard their collection dinner and wine.

When we lived on Willow Ave. a child was killed in a factory near Columbus Park. Somehow the child got caught in an elevator shaft and must have suffered a broken neck. Dad was called to the scene. We asked how the child looked and whether there was blood. Dad said the child looked like he was sleeping.

I recall Dad marching in parades on Washington St. He wore his dress uniform with white gloves and cap and the long black jacket that buttoned in the front. He nodded and waved when we called.

Dad was commended a few times. He was commended as a detective on 5 October 1953 for arresting a fugitive charged with attempted murder. He was commended on 26 February 1962 for discovering a raging fire in the Copa tavern on 6th St. On 1 March 1966 he was commended for apprehending two individuals who forced an entry into a tavern. On 29 December 1970 he was commended for arresting three individuals.

Dad's last years on the force were not enjoyable. The climate of the times had changed—people showed little respect for police at that time period. He wasn't in the "in-crowd" and he was performing inside duties rather than being on the street. The assignment was called "doorman", meaning he sat at the front desk, handled walk-in complaints, and took care of prisoners. Maybe his superiors thought they were doing him a favor, but Dad was a street cop and not an administrator. After a quarter century he had served long enough. Twenty eight years is too long a time to be a cop.

There were distressful events early in his career. Dad often spoke of rousting his father and his friends when they had drunk too much and loitered in the parks. These friends included Red Ruane, the father of Joe Ruane, and the father of Mike McNamara. Dad spoke with bitterness of being cursed by the old men as he forced them to move on. It must have been very difficult for Dad to have to tell his father, "Up, out, or in." He may have resigned after one of Pat Ford's antics. It took the intervention of a lawyer named Gottschalk to get Dad reinstated without penalties.

Dad was scrupulously honest as a cop. Mom claimed that we stayed poor because Dad didn't rob the dead or help himself to valuables in an empty apartment. Dad insisted the cops who enriched themselves in these ways came to bad ends.

I'd like to enter the names of some of Dad's fellow officers—I knew some of them. Joe O'Riley was a tall red-haired man who died rather young. Dad was in the hospital at the time and couldn't attend the wake. Mickey Lynch also died young and unexpectedly—Dad got the call when the body was found. Charley Hetzel was a particularly close friend. Paul Costa was a tall and well-dressed cop who visited Dad regularly in the hospital. Duke McCord also visited Dad in the hospital. Walter Scologzio was a loud and funny man who was a pillar of Our Lady of Grace Church. Anthony "Rocky" Romano was a classmate of Mom's at Ferris High School. Dick Carroll entered the force at the same time as Dad and remained active until the 1990s. He was a professional police officer who set up departments overseas, possibly one in Vietnam. Steve Johnson was another cop who joined the force with Dad, but I don't remember anything about him or how he looked. Tom McDonagh also joined with Dad. Later, he became chief of the Hudson County police force. Tom Kennedy became a politician and city councilman. Harold Dewey and Walter Drew were older cops. A still older cop that Dad talked about and who might have broke him in was Bull Hanrahan. And there was a cop named Mike—last name unknown—who lived for a time on 8th and Willow and who afterward shot himself. The suicide was a shocking event that lingered in memory for many years in the neighborhood.

Dad's partner I remember best was Little Al Striancowski. Al was a short man with heavy eyes and deep jowls. Dad claimed Al's father owned the first pizza parlor in Hoboken.

In his retirement Dad stayed friendly with only two brother officers. Harry Coppinger was a heavyset man with reddish hair. Vic Lehbrink was an honest officer. Dad once related that a person died on the PATH train and was found to be carrying a hefty bankroll. Vic got the call and refused to help himself to the cash. He also refused any other responding officer the same opportunity. In later years Vic lived in the same senior citizen complex as Helen Ost.

Dad said he never fired his gun in all the years on the force, but he did fire his gun. This is one of the fundamental stories of Dad's life. It is a story he told dozens of times.

The Murphy brothers—their names were Michael, William, and Francis—were hiring bosses on the docks. Somehow, Dad was involved with them. Perhaps he refused to join their crew. Perhaps he crossed one or arrested one. (The likeliest candidate was "Willie", who Dad mentioned by name.) But he got them angry for some reason. Someone called our house one night. I answered the phone. The person who called said that my father was going to die. I must have become upset—I don't recall any of this—and passed the message to Dad, who went ballistic. He rushed to the Murphy brothers' bar on 2nd and Hudson Sts. and shot up the place. I vividly recall Dad yelling when in his cups, "I shot up the Murphys!"

This is the story as I wrote it. But it might have happened differently. Or maybe there were two threatening calls. Dad reported to his superiors on 15 September 1959 that Mom received a threatening phone call claiming she would shortly become a widow.

Whatever the story, the Murphy Brothers were dangerous men. They had been indicted, but not convicted, for murdering a longshoreman in the early 1950s.

One of Dad's best friends was Mike McNamara, who worked for the Murphys in some capacity. Dad said it was Mike McNamara who had to dig the bullets out of the walls. I don't know what happened to the Murphy brothers, but Dad regularly met Mike McNamara in the 1990s.

We can be sure that Dad drank from an early age—*Dziadek* was concerned about his drinking when they lived at West Hamilton Place. He came from a drinking family and from a drinking culture. Alcohol was a prominent feature of the milieu in which he traveled. Drinking was an occupational hazard for sailors. And drinking was an occupational hazard for policemen. Dad was not a happy individual at the end of his career. Alcohol would have deepened his depression and the depression would have deepened the need for drink.

When we lived at 803 Willow Ave. Dad's hangout was The Dixie tavern, which was next to Charley's candy store on 9th St. between Willow and Park Aves. The interior of The Dixie was the model for The Come On Inn in *Red Star*. The bar was on the left. A stairway on the right led to a balcony. There were seats and booths on the balcony, but I don't think they were ever used. There was a storage area underneath the balcony on the first level.

When we moved to Hudson St. Dad hung out at Harrigan's, a tiny "old man's" bar on 12th and Washington St. Dad also drank at the Fat Man's, a bar on 13th and Hudson. This was owned by—well, a very fat and friendly man who used to sit outside the bar. Despite the fact that the bar was across the street from the entrance to Bethlehem Steel, there never seemed to be any patrons inside.

When we moved to Jersey City Dad hung out in Brophy's, a tiny tavern on Kennedy Blvd. next to the Monto Insurance Agency and across the street from Basil Castrovinci's actuarial company. I have nothing but depressing thoughts about Brophy's, a hole-in-the-wall place with a bar and a few seats and nothing else. Dad was retired by this time—he was still a young man—and had lost control of his drinking. The physical and psychological toll of liquor caught up by the late 1980s. He was admitted to St. Mary's Hospital in 1989 with a diagnosis of liver disease.

This was a dark time for us, as Dad spent a long recuperation in the hospital. Dr. D'Alberti, the family physician, told us there was a 50/50 chance of survival. Dr. Lee, who became his regular physician, admitted he had no idea how Dad recovered. The only pills he took were vitamins and diuretics, but these are the only pills prescribed for liver disease. It would not have been a nice way to lose Dad.

This was a difficult period for our family. Dad was very sick. So was Uncle Tony. *Cocci* Annie died of a heart attack when her home was burglarized. Frank Ford died—at one period the brothers were a few doors from one another in the hospital. And Frank Pecoraro, Kathy's father-in-law and a very fine man, died during Dad's recovery.

Whether it was a spiritual awakening or the simple awareness of how he had hurt himself, no one can say. Dad said only that he "got smart."

He gave up drinking and remained sober for the last ten years of his life. Dad was a very lucky man in that he was given a decade of life with a clear head. He was able to make a contribution to the family. He saw the birth of three additional grandchildren and the birth of a great-grandson.

The Listowel writer Bryan McMahon has a poem about the "corner men" who stand at the crossroads and idle the time with gossip and talk of the grand 'ould days. Dad was definitely a corner man when we lived at 803 Willow Ave. He hung out at a clubhouse in the middle of the block between Willow and Clinton Sts. The clubhouse was next door to Garrick's Candy Store, a rather dilapidated and poorly stocked store used more for the Italian lottery than for newspapers, magazines, and milk. The clubhouse was no more than a long narrow space with a table and restroom inside.

This area was home to Dad. There was a butcher on the southwestern corner. Brody's was across from the butcher's. This was an amazingly cluttered department store—shoes in the rear—owned by Herman Brody. Seligman's Drug Store was on the northwestern corner. Seligman, the owner, was Jewish. He lived to a great age and was greatly beloved by the locals. Across from Seligman's was an auto parts store. Behind the auto parts store was Charley's candy store. The Dixie Tavern came next. Further up the block was the liquor store that Tom and Mary Grogan ran.

George and Mary Anderson lived above Brody's. Mrs. Anderson, George's mother, and her brother Gary Kiely lived above Seligman's. Across the street was Henry and Lena Minoli. Jerry and Kay Mahoney lived around the corner on Clinton St. Warren Nobile and his family lived on Willow and 8th. So did Harry Coppinger and his family. Across from us at 803 were Billy and Paula and their children Billy and Babsy.

There was a regular cast of characters involved with the clubhouse. Dad, Joe Ryan, and Joe Ruane were the "three Joes". I don't know what happened to Joe Ryan. He was a tall and slim-shouldered man. Joe Ruane stayed in touch with Dad to the end. He was a tall ruddy man with thick white hair. He was involved with the Italian lottery. Mike Steuben was a short stocky man who always sat the reverse way on a chair. I believe he lost a leg in the war. He owned the only car in the group. There were the Garricks, Sonny, who was crazily boisterous, and Frank, his stepfather. Frank had been Frank Sinatra's godfather and a regular at the eight o'clock Mass at Our Lady of Grace on Sundays. This was the same Mass I attended. Pat Ford was also a regular.

Dad smoked from a young age. He said that he stole cigarettes off his brother Dennis. Since Dennis died in 1939, this means Dad smoked for sixty years.

Dad started to lose weight in the early summer of 1998. Pictures we have of him in Wildwood Crest show a much slimmer man than from the year before. At the time we misread his weight loss as the effect of aging. There were no behavioral differences that summer. Dad did the same things he did the summer before.

The first indication I had that something was seriously wrong occurred in Keansburg. We sat on the beach for a while. Dad was always restless and wandered back-and-forth. After we left the beach we walked the "concrete boardwalk". Dad lagged behind and Mom rushed from one bally stand to another playing chances wildly. Some of the chances were for cartons of cigarettes. We stopped at a restaurant for sandwiches. I noticed Dad grimacing. I asked if anything was wrong. He said there wasn't.

Shortly after this trip I came home late from school and found a note on the table to wake Mom up. She said that Dad had to go in for tests, since there was a suspicion of a spot on his lungs. The next morning we shook hands—something we almost never did. I wished him well.

Dad's stay in St. Mary's Hospital was from mid-September to mid-October, 1998. It was a disaster by any estimation. He was diagnosed with cancer, but he walked into the hospital a relatively well man and became progressively sicker the longer he stayed. The decisive test for cancer is a painfully intrusive test in which a camera in a tube is swallowed and pushed into the lungs. Dad handled the test well physically, but psychologically the test bothered him greatly. He complained about it for weeks. The length of the stay was due to a low-grade infection caused by the tumor blocking the release of fluids.

Dad had a choice of treatments in October. His lung doctor, a surgeon named Kozel, recommended surgery. He called us at home and claimed that if Dad had the surgery he would "leave the hospital cured of cancer." Those were his exact words. Dr. Lee, however, downplayed the operation. He said that surgeons always wanted to operate and that he would rather have Dad make a peaceful exit from life.

This medical difference of opinion was moot, since Dad decided from the outset that there would be no operation. He had friends in similar conditions who died soon after the surgery. He believed the cancer would spread once he "was opened up." When he came home, we had fierce arguments over the surgery, which I believed was his only option.

Dad opted to refuse treatment of any kind. The only cure for lung cancer is surgery. Chemotherapy and radiation merely delay the inevitable. At the time we believed it was the right decision—everyone said it was a brave decision—but I am not so sure. Treatment came with serious consequences, but it staved off death and offered the possibility that he might be with us for a few more years.

Dad was "fortunate" in the course of his disease. He was able to maintain the quality of his life until the middle of April 1999. Even in his final deterioration he was blessed that the cancer never spread in ways that caused him to be bedridden or to lose his mind. He maintained the ability to think clearly and he was able to walk to the very last morning of his life.

Around midnight on Monday June 14 Dad wanted his medicine. I told him that he had taken it an hour or so previously. He said he was "All loused up" with his medicine. I had prepared a computer printout to keep track of his medications. I told Dad about the printout. He said he wanted to see it and that I should get his glasses. He put his glasses on and looked at the sheet, but I'm not sure he made sense of it.

At daybreak Dad came into the living room, sat for a while in his favorite black chair near the window, and got back up. Mom and I helped him to bed. (I was home from work that day, as I intended to go to the motor vehicle agency.) He said he wanted his shoes on. We put his slippers on instead. I tapped his foot as I left the room. Kathy came to the house about a half hour later. We chatted for a while over coffee. I went into the back room to get my wallet and house keys and that's when we found Dad. He passed away noiselessly and with no apparent discomfort. Death came quietly for him, "like a thief in the night." But that kind of thievery is very merciful.

Dad was courageous in his illness. It must have been difficult to slip away. Except for the arguments early on about the course of treatment—it was obligatory for me to make the attempt—he never lost his self-control. There were occasions when I could see he was becoming annoyed, but he always controlled his temper. In many ways Dad was a self-effacing person. It must have been hard for him to suffer the demands he made on other people. And it must have been terrible to endure this awful illness. He did the best he could under difficult conditions. He left this life with dignity and with his family caring for him. It was the way families cared for one another in the long ago in places like Derrynacong and Girdziunai.

Dad had a well-earned reputation as a cook. His specialties were steak, creamed onions, roast beef, and mashed potatoes. The mashed potatoes were legendary. He beat and stirred the potatoes until they were as soft and as swirly as clouds.

The situation may have been different when we were younger, as we often ate at Leo's Grandevous or at the Blue Point restaurant, but Dad disliked eating out as he got older. If he went out, he ate only half portions. He usually left the table and went outside and sat in the car and smoked and waited for us. Dad rarely ate take-out or fast foods. When we lived in Hoboken he bought fish cakes and pasta in Frank and Elsie's deli on Park Ave. He bought the same for us in the Podewitz deli on Central Ave. when we lived in Jersey City.

Dad had a habit of tipping his hat whenever he passed a church. If he didn't tip the hat, he touched his index finger to his forehead in a kind of salute. Dad was generous with beggars. He always gave a few quarters to the beggars at the Tonnelle Ave. traffic circle. "For luck" he would say.

Dad's language could often be rough—he never went lightly on the profanity—but he told clean jokes. Here's one I recollect. There was a man who had been in prison for many years. When he got released there happened to be a peddler outside the prison. The peddler sold a variety of fruits and vegetables, including peas. He had a horse named Garibaldi. When the prisoner saw the peas he exclaimed, "I haven't had a pea in years." The peddler quickly saddled up the horse when he heard this. "Gideap, Garibaldi," he said, "there's going to be a flood."

Dad had a slightly Irish way of clipping his words. "At all" became "a-tall". "Theater" was three syllables, "the-eh-tra". Dad had a number of stock expressions he used on a regular basis. "A mere bagatelle", he said when asked to do something he agreed with. "Hold the fort," he said whenever he disagreed with something. "Umbriago" was his term for being intoxicated. So was "feeling no pain." "Dumper" was his term for a heavy drinker. Beer was "ammunition". "How are you fixed for blades?" was his way of asking for a few bucks to get ammunition. "Getting your hat blocked" was his euphemism for sexual experience. "Zofftig" was his term for a beautiful woman. "Madame Lasanga" was an imaginary woman he referred to on many occasions—we don't know how zofftig she was or whether she looked like "the cat's meow". A "Mickey Mouse operation" was a shady or incompetent organization. "Bedbug" was a crazy person. "To boff" was to hit a person. "To scrimmage" was to have a fist fight. "On the arm" was to buy something on credit. "Fin" was Hoboken slang for a five dollar bill. "Dime" was a ten dollar bill. "Yard" was a hundred dollar bill.

I recall him using "ridiculous" on many occasions. He frequently repeated Jimmy Durante's slogan, "Good night, Mrs. Calabash, wherever you are" and he asked, "Who put the spider in Mrs. Murphy's chowder?"

I taught at Kean University—it was Kean College at the time—on the nights when Mom and *Cocci* Helen took their bus excursions to Atlantic City. (The bus left the senior complex where Helen lived. I picked Mom up after class.) Even when he grew ill Dad insisted they make the trip. I made it a point to call him before class and ask how he was holding up. He always asked if I had eaten and he ended every call with, "Take care of yourself."

Dad was definitely fatalistic in the sense of believing that what will be, will be. He was certainly fatalistic about his health and that influenced his reluctance to risk surgery. He was fatalistic about life and death. He took the deaths of other people calmly—his grieving for his parents and siblings was to sit by himself—and he took the possibility of his own death calmly. He said, "When the Man Upstairs calls, you have to go", and that was how it turned out for him. I suppose that's how it's going to turn out for all of us.

Chapter Seventeen

~

Sophia Bielawska Ford

My mother **Sophia Bielawska** is the daughter of Pawel Bielawski and Zofia Storta. I'm going to give Mom's age away—this is what is called a "plot spoiler". If you don't want to know, skip to the next paragraph. Mom always said that a lady never reveals her age, but she has reached the point when congratulations are in order. Mom was born 23 February 1926. She was baptized April 11 in St. Anthony's Church in Jersey City. Her godparents were Casimir Wasilewski and Stanislawa Lakiewska. Fr. A. Wisnieski officiated [47].

Mom and Dad met in Casino-in-the-Park restaurant in Lincoln Park, Jersey City. It was at a political function. Mom was with a girlfriend. She no longer remembers the girlfriend's name, only that she had expensive tastes. She once rejected a suitor because the engagement ring wasn't valuable enough. Dad was with Sonny Garrick. He asked Mom to dance, but she said she didn't know how. They exchanged phone numbers. Dad or Sonny drove the ladies home. The next day Mom called Dad asking if they found her friend's lost earring in the car. This is what is called a "likely story". The rest of the story was 48 years of marriage, three children, six grandchildren, and six great-grandchildren.

About six months later Mom and Dad were partying with Ray Weber and his girlfriend Frankie. They drove into Maryland—Mom believes it was to Baltimore—where a justice of the peace married them. The date this occurred was 14 February 1951.

Mom afterward regretted the way they married and Pawel was disappointed they didn't have a church service, but I think this is a romantic story. People fall in love, they party, they make their minds up, and they make a foolish decision that turns out to be the best possible decision.

Jeanne Lowe once told me that "There is joy in marriage and there is also heartache in marriage." Jeanne also said that "There is joy in the single life and there is also heartache in the single life," but I don't think she was right about the first half of this statement. Mom experienced both joy and heartache in her marriage. She found Dad fun to be with and good-looking, but she became dismayed at the amount of drinking and at the poverty. The drinking contributed to the poverty. It wasn't until we moved to Kennedy Blvd. that money became better—those were the years the drinking stopped.

On 8 November 1946 Mom was described as 5'4 in height, 140 pounds, with brown hair and hazel eyes. This was an idiosyncratic use of the word "hazel", as Mom's eyes are green gray. She always joked she had a *sibula* nose—*sibula* is phonetic Polish for "onion". It's probably a hereditary trait, though it's hard to say from which line. Mom's nickname was "*Zosia*". This is affectionate Polish for "Sophie". It's pronounced "Zur-sha".

Some of Mom's early memories include watching her sister Carol on roller skates so she wouldn't fall. Playing dolls with her friend Hattie and dressing a cat like a baby and wheeling it around in a carriage. Playing jump rope and hide-and-seek with her friends. Singing *Jingle Bells* on stage in grammar school. Mom remembered that a woman in the neighborhood had been struck by lightning inside her apartment—the woman wore metal curlers that caught on fire, singeing her hair. Mom has happy memories of her confirmation. Her sponsor was a friend of *Cocci* Anne's. After the confirmation they went to a Chinese restaurant on Journal Square—this is certainly the Canton. This is a memory of her young adult years—being so terrified by a dog as she walked in Keansburg she jumped into a car driven by strange men to be rescued. Mom remembers she went to the 1939 World's Fair with Henry and Helen. We went as a family to the 1964 World's Fair. She remembered that she worried that *Dziadek* would spoil me by holding me and rocking me in his arms and that he hesitated to hold my sister Felicia because she was so thin. Mom doesn't have many memories of her mother or of her mother's passing. She remembered a nun tried to comfort her.

As a child Mom loved to read and to visit the library. This is a tradition that continues to this day. Every two or three weeks I drive her to the Little Egg Harbor library where she checks out a few books. They're large-print books now. Mom often told us how scared she was reading *Dracula* as a child. She kept her feet near the coal-burning stove to stay warm—and to feel she stayed safe.

Mom listened to *The Shadow* on the radio and to the Jack Benny program. She remembered listening to President Roosevelt—these must have been to his fireside chats. On Saturday nights she went to the Palace Theater where the late movie was in Polish.

Mom was close to her siblings and liked to listen to them talk. She had arguments at first with Blanche, who became a surrogate mother, but they ironed out their differences later. Anne set the style for the family, especially with her luxurious hair, which she combed and curled every night even if it meant waking up late for work. Helen was a lot of fun to be with—Mom and Helen became very close in their old age. Henry was the only brother. As we might expect, he was spoiled and he played a lot of pranks on his sisters. Carol was the baby of the family. Mom and Carol were very close when their children were young.

Mom's best friend growing up was Veronica "Ronnie" Rakowicz. Ronnie was somewhat heavyset and her family was more affluent than the Bielawskis. She married a man named Pietrowski. Ronnie's sister Irene married a man named Stankiewicz. Mom believes these men were the sons of the partners of the tavern where Josef Bielawski died. It's possible Ronnie was the daughter of the man Pawel listed as "friend" on the ship's log. Mom and Ronnie stayed in touch until early adulthood and then lost track of one another.

Another of Mom's friends was Hedwiga "Hattie" Wisniewski. Hattie was the daughter of a widow who ran the butcher shop on the ground floor of the building where the Bielawskis lived.

Mom accompanied Pawel to Mass every Sunday. She belonged to the "Children of Mary" Society and walked in processions in ceremonies in the month of May. Mom believes she is a religious person. She believes in the existence of the soul and in a life after death. She prays for intercession to the Blessed Mother and to Sts. Joseph, Anthony, and Teresa. She believes there are guardian angels. She gets up early to say her prayers.

There was a custom in the neighborhood that a priest visited and blessed the homes of the faithful on Holy Saturday. Mom remembered when she was a child that on one Holy Saturday Monsignor Ignatius Szudrowicz visited their apartment. She was told to kiss the monsignor. To everyone's amusement she kissed his cheek rather than his hand. Mom remembered a vivid incident that occurred in St. Anthony's involving Monsignor Szudrowicz. During Mass he saw a man place a nickel in the collection basket. He left the altar, walked to the aisle, and gave the nickel back to the man, saying "You need this more than we do."

Our Lady of Grace Church in Hoboken was the church of the Ford family. St. Anthony of Padua Church was the church of the Bielawski family. St. Anthony's was founded in May 1884 to serve the needs of the Polish community in Lower Jersey City. At one point there were 11,000 congregants. The original church at Sixth and Monmouth Sts. was a small wood structure that was replaced in 1892 by the stone building that now stands. The church is a prominent landmark that's visible from the Turnpike on the approach to Jersey City. A grammar school opened in 1898. Like many Catholic grammar schools in Hudson County it has since closed.

The interior of the church was badly damaged by a fire in 1895. Only a crucifix—considered "miraculous"—remains of the original interior. Fr. Boleslaw Kwiatkowski (Order of Franciscan Friars Minor) was pastor of the church for 39 years. We note his name on many Bielawski events. Monsignor Szudrowicz served as pastor in the 1940s. Fr. Edward Majewski was pastor in the 1950s.

Mom—and Dad—lived through a tumultuous age. The Great Depression. The World War against totalitarianism. The Korean War. The Vietnam War. Men walking on the moon. Robots walking on Mars. The home computer. The Internet. Antibiotics. Google. Mom has seen enormous changes in technology and in social-cultural life—she thinks children grow up too fast and are exposed to too much media. In Mom's lifetime she's gone from rotary phones and party lines to cell phones that take pictures and provide Internet service, and from the iron range and wood icebox to microwave ovens and refrigerators that have cold water faucets on the outside doors, and from black-and-white television sets with thirteen stations to high definition flat screens with hundred of stations, and from a hand-scrubbed world of washboards and wringers to a push-button electronic world where everyone is connected to everyone and where every last scrap of information flows instantaneously at the touch of a finger. In Mom's lifetime she's gone from Jim Crow and racial violence to a country that elected a black man as president, and from the inequality of the sexes to a country where women are in positions of power, and from a world of polite manners and civil discourse to a world where the foulest language is heard and where children think nothing of standing up to adults and telling them where to go, and from a world where the priest and the local politician lorded over everyone to a world where authority in every order and guise has been scattered to smithereens.

It was a different material world when Mom was a child. The only connection that world has with our life now is the basic one—our human nature. Mom daydreamed as a girl of getting married and of having beautiful clothing. At one point in life she wanted to learn to fly a plane. She did fly in a two-seat propeller plane. The best time in her life was when her children were young. She believes the best part of being a parent was watching her children grow up. The worst part was worrying if she did a good job. As with every person, there are regrets. Mom wished she had been more outgoing and had more friends. She wants to be remembered as a loving, gentle, and kind person who never intentionally harmed anyone. She's surprised she's survived for so long.

Mom attended St. Anthony's Grammar School, graduating on 18 June 1939. Veronica and Hattie attended the same school. Mom remembered a homely boy named Jacob Kiszka was teased more for his name than for his looks. Mom recalled Sr. Fabiola, who may have taught sixth grade. This sister had a habit of putting a pencil in the corner of her mouth. Every Friday the students had to kneel and ask her forgiveness. And Mom remembered having Sr. Mary Philomilia in the eighth grade. Sr. Philomilia liked Mom and said she would get a prize for academic achievement. The prize went instead to Ronnie Rakowicz. This surprised and disappointed them. Mom thought Ronnie got the prize because her family donated to the church.

The sisters taught in both English and Polish. (The order was Felician.) The report card listed subjects in Polish. At the start of the school day the students sang the national anthems of America and of Poland.

Mom entered Ferris High School in Jersey City in September 1939 and graduated in the commercial course on 24 June 1943. Looking back over six decades Mom judged high school an unhappy experience. She remembered that she didn't have many friends and that, being one of the tallest girls, she always stood at the rear of the line. I wonder whether Mom isn't experiencing what psychology calls "mood-congruent retrieval". Mom's memories may be tinged by her current mood of isolation and loneliness. Mom is mentioned in the *Yearbook*—portions of it have survived. There are a number of signatures in the yearbook. In it she's called "Sal" and is described as "Receptionist N.Y.U." The caption reads "With her pleasant manner and smile / A receptionist she'll be for a while." Mom no longer remembers why she was listed as a receptionist.

Her favorite teacher at Ferris was Miss Deinish, "who made history come alive." A public speaking teacher—the name is not remembered—actively disliked her. Mom's closest friend in high school was Sabrina Citkowicz. Sabrina married soon after graduation and died at a young age.

The Ferris *Yearbook* tries to be upbeat. It writes about dances like the jitterbug and the lindy and has a humor section full of jokes so awful I might have written them. ("Wanted—Window Washer. Last one took a step back to admire his work.") But these are grim years. The World War is in horrific progress and it is not clear which side is going to win. Classmates and teachers have joined the service—they visit the school in uniform. A fair number of young men are graduating into places like Iwo Jima and Normandy Beach. There are blackouts in Jersey City and air raid drills and rationing. People watch for enemy planes from the roofs of the tenements on Henderson St. There are signs in the school corridors—"Buy War Stamps." The same command appears as an ad on page 49 of the *Yearbook*.

The *Yearbook* doesn't shy from events. It notes that the events of 7 December 1941 "shook the very foundations of our homes and school." The *Yearbook* concludes, "May we with the aid of the Almighty God help right this world and make it secure for the generation to follow." The graduates look serious and older than their ages. There are years of war ahead and places with names like Okinawa and the Hurtgen Forest. The young men are graduating into the service. The young women are going to become the girlfriends and the wives of soldiers. Some of the soldiers are not going to come home.

Mom herself went to be a soldier—she lied about her age to enlist. Mom enlisted in the Woman's Army Corps on 19 June 1945. She entered the service on 2 July 1945 and separated at Fort Dix, NJ, on 8 November 1946. She was given $200 mustering out pay and $3.90 travel pay. Her serial number was A223215. She was awarded the World War Two Victory Medal. Mom went into the service because she wanted to make a contribution and to do something for the country in the war effort.

Mom made the rank of sergeant in the year and a half she was in the service. She outranked Dad.

Mom spent basic training in Des Moines, Iowa (Co. E, 3rd Regiment, Lt. Harriett Hassell, CO.) She spent active duty in the 2511 WAC Detachment at Fort Myer, VA. For seven months she was the company clerk and mail clerk. She handled correspondence and duty rosters and kept files of all records. She was acting first sergeant for three months. For six months she was assigned to the personnel section of the post HQ. She handled morning reports and made entries on officers' records. She interviewed personnel about their job experiences and kept records up to date.

Mom resided in the barracks until she made sergeant, after which she had her own room. She remembered that she came down with measles at the same time she was promoted. She and her friends visited Washington, DC, on a number of occasions. We have photographs of her visit to the Tomb of the Unknown at Arlington Cemetery. Mom recalled they lost track of time on one visit and got locked inside the cemetery. They had to climb a gate to get out. One time they got in trouble for picking cherry blossoms.

Mom prospered in the service. She was on the fast track to success. She believed she was nominated to join Eisenhower's staff, but that an officer chose another sergeant. Members of her detachment were going to Japan, but Mom couldn't avail herself of the opportunity. She had to return to civilian life and take care of Pawel, as her sisters were married and Carol was too young to manage a household. Mom always believed this was one of the major turning points of her life. If she had gone overseas, I might be typing this in Japanese. Maybe she would have met a sailor named Joe Ford, who similarly took the opportunity and stayed in the service.

Captain Lorraine Bowers was the commanding officer of the Fort Myer detachment. She was a short, well-liked officer who was fond of the unit's mascot, "Bridget". "Betty" was the executive officer—it's possible her name was Eutha Reynolds. Mom's best friend in the unit was Dorothy Sealy, who came from Syracuse, NY. Mom remembered Muriel (last name unknown), who was from New York City and Jewish. Muriel spoke French fluently. Mom also remembered "Fergie", who was Irish, and Norberta Brown—"Brownie"—who was the oldest soldier in the unit and who did go to Japan.

Mom worked at a number of jobs. She worked part-time in a photography company while in Ferris High. Immediately after graduation she worked for the publishing house Dodd Mead on Fourth Ave. She was listed as a clerk-typist—and as a receptionist. Her boss was an Englishman named Mr. Mosher who took one drink at the start of every work day.

Mom worked part-time in a perfume or chemical company. Her sister Helen met Fred Ost there. Mom also worked in a candy store in the Port of Authority Bus Station. She got in trouble one time for taking candy home without paying for it.

Mom entertained a notion of becoming a dietician after returning to civilian life. She took courses at the New York Institute of Dietetics on Madison Ave. and graduated with a certificate on 19 August 1950. She recalled that an instructor looked like Spencer Tracy and that he had a problem with his throat. In one experience the Bunsen Burner Mom used flared up. So did Mom. She ran from the room to get water to douse the fire, which amused everyone as water was available in the classroom.

Mom may have derived the idea of becoming a dietician from the Institute's ad in the Ferris High *Yearbook*. The ad read:

> Work for Peace
> Plan for Victory
> When the War is over and peaceful living is resumed
> millions of war jobs will cease to exist. Plan now to
> be qualified for post-war living.
> Be a Dietician

Mom's main job in the civilian world was for Maxwell House in Hoboken—it was a block from our apartment on Hudson St. Mom worked as a Kelly Temp when she was hired for a full-time position in the order department. She transferred to Personnel and worked as a benefits clerk. Her job was to advise the plant staff about benefits and to assist them in filling out forms. The Personnel director was Jim Lucy. Mom's immediate supervisor was Murphy Gropher. Murphy's secretary was Lydia Gerloff. The second benefits clerk was Betty Holder.

Mom's best friend in Maxwell House was Jean Mulkenberg. Jean was a divorced woman who was tall and thin with black hair and a sharp tongue. Another friend was Gwen Essman, who was English and whose husband was a foreman in the plant.

Mom worked in Maxwell House from 1965 – 1982. She was proud that she got the position on her own and she enjoyed working there. She would still be working there, but the plant closed and moved to Jacksonville, where the mix roast and grind of coffee production could be done more cheaply on the banks of the Saint Johns River than on the banks of the Hudson.

After Maxwell House Mom worked briefly as a clerk typist in the publishing office at Jersey City State College. Mom's last job was in the purchasing office in St. Francis Hospital in Jersey City.

Mom and Dad moved to Hoboken around 1955 when Civil Service mandated that police had to live in the cities they patrolled. This was an unpleasant experience, as *Dziadek* refused to move with them. He preferred to stay in Jersey City and moved in with *Cocci* Blanche. Hoboken was Dad's hometown, but Mom didn't know anyone at first. She gradually met local ladies through Nana and through the network of kids going to school and playing in Columbus Park. Mom became friends with Mary Anderson, since I played with her sons George and Robbie.

Mom's closest friend and confidant in Hoboken was Kay Mahoney. They spoke frequently on the phone—Mom said she could tell Kay things she could never tell her sisters. I played with her son Michael. Kay was from a large family from Scranton, PA. She was married to Jeremiah "Jerry" Mahoney who worked on the Erie Lackawanna Railroad. They resided at 913 Clinton St. directly across the street from Columbus Park. After Jerry died Kay moved to 12th and Hudson in the Applied Housing apartments. She died unexpectedly on 17 April 1978 a week after Michael's wedding—maybe she didn't find it unexpected. A few days before she died Kay insisted I retrieve an article of clothing Mom loaned her for the wedding. When I met her in the hallway she reminisced fondly about Jerry and Michael.

On Halloween 2000 Mom and I moved to Little Egg Harbor in Southern Ocean County. It was a momentous occasion for both of us. We left Hudson County for good. For the first time we owned a house rather than rented. Since that day Mom has dutifully kept the house up. She jokes on the phone that she is "lady of the house" and, indeed, she is.

On 14 September 2002 Mom fell and fractured her hip. While in the hospital Mom discovered that she was a diabetic. Since that time she has been taking pills to regulate insulin. She watches her diet scrupulously. Recently, her legs have been giving her trouble. She uses a cane to get around—in Ireland we heard that Bridget Fitzmaurice used a "stick" to maneuver. Mom frequently refers to Francey Ford's observation that the "legs are the first to go" as a person ages and she mentions that old age does not bring the advertised "golden years". She claims the only aspect of old age that's golden is the money doctors make.

Despite diabetes and problems with her legs Mom became a world traveler in the last 15 years. As documented in *Genealogical Jaunts* Mom crossed the ocean three times to Ireland. She crossed the ocean three times to Lithuania as well. She's seen the fields where her parents grew up. She's seen the fields where her husband's parents grew up. Consider the twelve month period from June 2000 to June 2001. Mom visited Lithuania in June, Wildwood in August, Hershey Park in December, Disney World in May, and Pensacola in June. And consider that in August 2009 at the age of 83 Mom fulfilled a childhood dream and visited Jason York and his family in Washington State. She rode to the top of the Space Needle in Seattle and walked on the plateaus of Mount Rainer and Skagit Dam.

Pawel's family didn't celebrate birthdays in the same regal fashion we do. They didn't have the money to buy expensive presents or prepare extravagant meals. Our birthdays were always lavish affairs. When we were young cousins and aunts and uncles came over to our house and got treated to dinner and to cake. Our chums and school buddies were also invited. We have photographs showing rooms crowded with kids and the kitchen table crowded with food and beverages.

Birthdays are still important occasions. We try to visit one another on our birthdays and always make it a point to call and send cards and presents. Since childhood we continue the custom of singing "*Sto'lat, sto'lat, yez-ze-a-ze-a-nam*", which is phonetic Polish for "May you have a hundred years."

Christmas was the major holiday for Pawel's family. They fasted until after Midnight Mass. When they returned home they dined and celebrated with kielbasa, soup, and cabbage. They exchanged small gifts. Mom inherited the tradition of a Christmas Eve party from the time she and Dad lived at West Hamilton Place—the feast seems to have slipped to the hours before Midnight Mass rather than after. The tradition continued with the extended family into the 1970s. It faded as cousins grew up and families dispersed. Until the 1970s the Bielawski sisters resided in Jersey City and Hoboken. Everyone could be visited by riding the number five orange bus. Since that time people moved away, so that was no longer possible. Kathy and Joe Pecoraro continued the tradition in Hasbrouck Heights. Mom and I were part of the tradition until we left for Little Egg Harbor. Kathy and Joe's family have grown, so there are replacements.

Mom prepared a huge dinner—turkey and kielbasa, vegetables and salads of every kind, and a great number of sweets, including stolen and babka. The Bielawski relatives came over early in the evening to dine and wine for a few hours. A considerable amount of drinking went on during these occasions. Photographs show beer and hard liquor bottles on the table and many the uncle looking blotto.

Felicia and Kathy presented a little "Christmas Play" consisting of carols and dances. I acted as master of ceremonies. (We put this play on for Nana and Grandpa on Christmas morning.) I'm not sure how seriously the adults took these plays. The only adult I remember joining in was Uncle Fred, who sang and hummed his favorite folk song *500 Miles*.

Cocci Blanchie brought the *oplatek*, which was the Christmas wafer—it tasted exactly like the communion host. The custom was for everyone to exchange pieces of *oplatek* from relatives and to wish one another well. We weren't as competitive as our ancestors in the Old Country, so it didn't matter who got the smaller piece.

The party broke up sufficiently early for anyone who chose to—and was able to—get to Midnight Mass. In the early years Mass was at midnight. In later years as the neighborhood deteriorated Mass was celebrated in the early evening. I remember walking to Our Lady of Grace Church and back. On two occasions it snowed. On the first occasion it snowed heavily during the party. I was outdoors with Cousin Anthony and I lost my eyeglasses. There were angels in the snow that evening—I reached in a drift and found them. What a long shot—and what a disaster if I lost them. The other time Mom and Kay Mahoney came home from Mass. They had a lot of fun laughing as they walked in the snow.

After Mass our toys were placed beside the tree. When we were young Mom kept the toys hidden, so Santa always surprised us. As we got older we knew what the presents were. Sometimes they had to be assembled, which could be problematical at two in the morning. But waking up on Christmas morning and finding the presents was always a thrill.

Thanksgiving was also an important family holiday. In early years Mom prepared the turkey and everyone came over to our house for dinner. Today Kathy and Joe Pecoraro and their daughter Jennifer manage the Thanksgiving dinner. It remains as sumptuously extravagant as in former years. We honor God and country by eating ourselves sleepy.

My favorite meals Mom made were chicken soup and meatball soup. I could instantly smell either when I walked in the house. Mom often made meatballs and spaghetti in a pressure cooker. One time the lid exploded and we had meatballs on the ceiling and spaghetti on the walls. They had to be repainted. She frequently made "pigs in the blanket"—they are soft meatballs and rice packed in cabbage leaves. A favorite of everyone is kielbasa, cooked with sauerkraut or with potatoes. One of Mom's favorite foods is *kishka*, which is a dark sausage. During the school year I buy it for her in a butcher shop on Second Avenue in Manhattan.

If the books are right our nineteenth century ancestors were a superstitious lot. Mom's family wasn't. I recall only a few. If we spilled salt we had to toss a handful over the shoulder. We were never to put a hat—or shoes—on a table. If an extra fork was found on the table a visitor was coming. If our palms itched we would give money away. If the ears rang someone was talking about us. If our nose itched we were going to have an argument. If we got a chill someone was walking on our grave.

Mom has played the roles that anyone who lives a long and full life plays. Dutiful daughter. Alienated teen. Patriotic citizen. Devoted wife. Afflicted wife. Mother. Grandmother. Dad said it was the mother who "held the family together." He said that in reference to Nana. It's true in Mom's case as well. She was cook, housekeeper, disciplinarian, teacher, confidant, cheerleader. The fundamental image we have of Mom—of *Babci* (grandmother), as she's been called since 1975—is that of friend and playmate.

Babci sang us to sleep in 803 Willow Ave. She read the funny papers to us on Sunday mornings. She took us to Columbus Park and watched over us. She played with Jason York when he was an infant. He wobbled around in the crib in 60 12th St. waving a broomstick and holding the plastic statues of Laurel and Hardy. When Jason grew to be a preschooler they played "Spot". Jason pretended he was a dog and *Babci* talked to him for hours on end. *Babci* did the same for Joe and Kathy's kids. When she babysat for Jennie Paradiso they took long slow walks to Mosquito Park. I'd give them an hour's head start and they'd still be moseying along. Later she and Kathy took Kimberly, Matthew, and Danielle to the playground in Pershing Field. *Babci* played catch with each of the children—this frequently meant chasing after the balls they threw over her head. Luke Ford slept over regularly when he was a preschooler. He and *Babci* talked interminably—she did most of the talking. In the evenings we watched television. Luke sat with *Babci* until she dozed off. He'd get off the couch, look at her, and walk over and sit with me until the program ended and it was time for bed. I called him my "little lap dog", as he was three feet tall and 98.6 degrees.

Babci's been blessed to play with another generation of children—her great-grandchildren. When we visit Jacksonville she talks and sings to Shane, Evan, and Alex York the same way she did to their parents. And she cuddles the infants Anthony and Dante Paradiso and Jack Jones. She's been a friend and playmate to three generations of children, which is a wonderful accomplishment.

When she played with the children *Babci* mixed in a lot of Polish words. I'd like to mention them phonetically. I'm sure they are written differently. When she teased the children *Babci* called them "*dudda mowrahs*". When she asked them to hold hands she said, "*Die runski*". She tickled them and sang, "*Cuzza, cuzza, ben-gi-ba-chi, ste-di.*" And she sang, "*Ecuffa, ecuffa, enamina, kiskabeenah-boof.*" She called the children *sigons* or *sigonka*—this meant "gypsies"—and *scrimpka*—this meant "little piggies". The littlest children were "*shooka* babies". When they were bad they were "*bebber*" and they could be "*bibbied*" or gently spanked on the *duppah*. When they were crybabies they were "*bexa*". If they were nosey they were said to be "*jeekavah evah*". Babci told the children to look at the "*zuzzah*"—the ceiling light. At the mention of the word they invariably looked up—this was a version of classical conditioning. Babci frequently asked, "*Seta kaygu?*"—"What do you want?" Often the answer was "*Menscha* (milk)". And she asked, "*Yakshe mash?*"—"How are you?" The expected answer was "*dubsha*". *Babci* said about herself that she was "*Stadish neradish*" or "getting old", which the children hardly believed. She told them Grandpa drank too much "*pifka*". And she frequently exclaimed, "*Muy Buza*"—"My God." Reference was frequently made to an imaginary character named "*Mr. Papoofnic*". Sometimes he was "*Mr. Papoofnic Meyer*".

A song we heard over the years was, "*There Were Three Jolly Fishermen*." The first fisherman was "Jacob"—the name was broken up into a number of syllables, "Jay-a-cup-cup-cup." The second fisherman was "Babci"—this was broken up, too, "Ba-a-Ba-Ba-chi." The third fisherman was whichever child Babci played with. Their names were broken up, too.

We played the usual games growing up. Bingo. Checkers. Tic-tac-toe. Monopoly. We played a game called, "I've been fishing." The kids placed their hands flat on a table and *Babci* slowly waved her arms in a circular motion over their hands, intoning in a singsong, "I've been fishing, I've been fishing." Suddenly she lunged and tried to seize hold of their hands. If she did she pronounced, "And I've caught a fish." Usually, she didn't.

We played a game with preschoolers that might be called "Piggies" for want of a better term. We wiggled each of the children's toes in turn and told them where the toe was going. "This toe is going to the beach." "This toe is going to the office." "This toe is going to the store." "This toe is going to church." "This toe is going on a boat ride." We had to come up with five more destinations for the other foot. As one round was never enough we had to come up with twenty and thirty destinations.

We played the usual card games. Poker. War. Five-card stud. Blackjack. We played a game called "Toilet". In this game the deck is cut into three equal portions. Two portions serve as the legs of a triangle. The third portion is balanced atop the legs. Each player has to remove a card without toppling the deck. The top section is removed first and then cards from each leg. The player loses who causes the deck to topple. Usually, the losing player got a few gentle taps on the knuckles with the deck. The preschoolers who lost immediately wanted to change the rules of the game.

We played a card game called "Pig". The cards are arranged face down in a circle. One card is placed face up at the center of the circle. The task for the first player is to find a card in the circle with the same suit as the card faced up. The player picks up as many cards as necessary. He places the correct match on top of the face up and places a card from the ones he drew on top of it. The next player must find a card that matches that suit. And so on. If a player holds a card of the same suit he does not have to search the deck but can place the card on the face-up pile. The winner of the game is the first player to have no cards in hand when there are no cards left in the circle. The game continues until only one player is left with cards in hand. This player is the loser. When there are no cards left in the circle players must match the face-up card from their own hand. If a player cannot match the face-up card he must pick up the card. He does not have to put a card down. If a player has a card with the same suit as the card faced-up, he puts that card down and another card of a different suit the next player must match.

We also played a card game called "Stealing the Old Man's Bundle." Each player gets five cards. If a player has been dealt a pair she places it face up on the table so everyone can see it. A card is turned face up from the deck. If a player needs cards to form a pair she can take the one faced up or she can draw one from the deck. The player picks up as many cards as required to form a pair. She must return a card to the deck when her turn is complete. If a player has a card that matches a pair laid down by an opponent she can take that bundle during her turn. The object of the game is to form pairs and to steal other players' pairs. The winner is the first player not to have any cards left in hand.

Chapter Eighteen

~

The Strange Case of Honest Den Ford

So this is where my life has come to, this is where my life has led.

I'm the firstborn and only son of Joseph Ford and Sophia Bielawska. I was born in Margaret Hague Maternity Hospital at 8:11 AM on 23 January 1953. I was baptized in the church of St. Anthony on February 15. My sponsors were Ray Weber and Carol Bielawska. The priest was Fr. Edward Majewski. My parents resided at 48 West Hamilton Place in Jersey City. I was named after my father's brother. My confirmation name is Joseph, so I have my uncle's full name.

I find it difficult to objectify the particulars of my life. I think I've lived an interesting and uneventful life, so I'm doubly blessed. But there really isn't much to say. I'm a seriously introverted person, but I rarely mull over the details of my life or the lives of family and friends. Instead I've been preoccupied with fictional characters and events and with the kinds of thoughts that went into *Thinking About Everything*.

I may as well say it and get it over with—I never married and raised a family. This is the greatest hurt and humiliation of my life. I'm sure there are explanations, but I've never wanted to find them. Whatever explanations I come up with would be inadequate and beside the point—you can't explain a life. I think I would have been a good husband and father, but that's something that hasn't happened. I'm sure it has cost me severely.

A few early memories come to mind. A warm wonderful memory—my grandfather hoists me in his arms. A scary memory—we're climbing to the attic in a bungalow in Keansburg; we near the top of the stairs, but a noise scares us away. An odd memory—I'm locked in a bathroom or cloakroom and I can't open the door. This may be at *Dziadek's* funeral; I think *Cocci* Annie is with me. A patriotic memory—I'm seated at an end table watching President Kennedy's inauguration; it may be the part when Robert Frost had trouble reciting the poem. A painful memory—I chip a tooth playing on the serpentine rocks in Hudson Square Park near the river; Mom lets me ride home in the baby carriage. A scandalous memory—I wet my pants walking home from kindergarten; Mom lets me walk between her and the carriage so no one notices. A guileless memory—I see the toy robot I want for Christmas in the hall closet at 803 Willow Ave. I ask if it's for me. My parents say it's for another little boy. I believe them.

I attended Our Lady of Grace grammar school. Mrs. O'Sullivan was the rotund and ruddy-faced kindergarten teacher. Miss Loretta Healy was my first-grade teacher. I've known Loretta all my life, as she married Uncle Tony's brother, Basil. Sr. Agnes James was my second-grade teacher. (The order was Sisters of Charity.) Sr. Agnes was 100 years old—maybe not that old, but she taught my father in the 1930s and she taught me in the 1960s, so she was up there. Sr. Delphine was the strict sixth grade teacher. I was in her class when we heard President Kennedy was assassinated. The grim news from Dallas preempted the French show hosted by Madame Anne Slack on Channel 13. Three days later Mom rushed to Columbus Park to tell us Oswald had been killed. Considering what came later, those events may have piqued my interest.

There was Sr. Barbara Anthony in the seventh grade. She had a stick she used to whack students. She called the stick "Harvey". She must have thought she was being funny. In retrospect I consider this bizarre and abnormal. There was Sr. Dolorine and Sr. Anne Therese in the eighth grade. Mr. Harry Maus was the only male teacher in the school. He taught eighth grade and he suffered a lot of abuse from the students. The principal was a stern nun named Sr. Margaret Cecilia—she looked like a Margaret Cecilia.

I became a Knight of the Altar on 16 December 1962 and one of the chief altar boys in the Parish. We were taught the Latin responses by the older altar boys. I have vivid memories of being in empty classrooms and trying to memorize the responses by rote learning—I still remember some of the responses. Joining the Society I pledged "to live and die befitting one who has dedicated himself to the service of our Lord." I played priest at home and pretended I said Mass, but I never entertained the thought of becoming a priest.

I attended Hudson Catholic in Jersey City for the freshman year of high school. That was not a happy experience. I'm a shy and reserved person and I didn't know anyone. Fifteen is a rough age not to know anyone. And the Christian Brothers who taught there were more loony than the Sisters of Charity. Maybe the word "loony" is unkind. Maybe I should use the word "oddballs" instead, but only if it's in boldface.

It's almost impossible to believe, but I failed science. I think I missed by three points. Brother Pat must have thought the cardboard tablets of the Ten Commandments he wore in place of a collar would tear if he gave me the three points. I was supposed to attend summer school, but I never told my parents what happened. This led to some bad scenes when September rolled around—I was right to think I'd get punished for failing science. It also led to some scrambling to get me in Hoboken High School.

Hoboken High was an enjoyable experience. I knew a lot of people and thrived there socially and intellectually. My average never dipped below 90 for the next three years. The students were agreeable and the teachers were—well, they were normal people. My favorites were Mr. Zweig and Mr. Neville. Mr. Zweig taught journalism. If he gave you a grade of "sharp", you got 100 on the assignment. If he gave you a grade of "sharp, sharp", you got an A for the marking period. I got a lot of "sharp, sharps". Mr. Neville was son of one of the park caretakers. He was a genuinely friendly man and a fine teacher. I worked with him on the yearbook staff and became the editor. I got turned on by literature at that period and entertained the notion of majoring in English. I read heavily in American literature—Melville, Twain, Hawthorne, and O. Henry were my favorites. I graduated from Hoboken High in June 1970.

I attended St. Peter's College in Jersey City. The Jesuits were quite an experience. The chaplain actually told us not to pay attention to the Pope on the issue of birth control. He was running his own church, of course, but it was the correct advice. This issue demonstrates that the early 1970s were a tumultuous and contentious time. The young people of today little know the excitement of that period. I was 18 years old in a time of cultural revolution. I'm sure I was as messed up and confused as anyone. There were race riots and assassinations. The Vietnam War was in full horrible progress. There were riots in the streets over the War. I was caught in a riot in Lower Manhattan. There was Watergate and the resignation of a president. We actually brought down a president—Nixon should have been strung up like a bad Roman emperor and his body run along Connecticut Ave. and thrown in the Potomac for all the evil he accomplished. There were hippies and drugs and rock and roll music and frank sexual expressions in books and in movies and there was free love—if not free, then at bargain prices. The St. Peter's chaplain had it right on the last issue.

I started in St. Peter's as a literature major, but switched to psychology in the first year. We were a small and tight-knit group. The names Diane DePalma and John Dowd come to mind. The goal of the program was to get students admitted to graduate schools, so we had a rigorous training. Dr. Angelo Danesino was the chairman of the department. He was a clinician and was up in years. He had been taught in Italy by a student of Wilhelm Wundt, so I am two generations in a direct line from the man considered the founder of academic psychology. The department included Prof. William Burke, who I had for many courses, and Prof. Andrew Schein, who was instrumental in getting me into Fordham. There was a statistics teacher named Carter who used computers as part of his course work. I was heavily into computers at the outset of their emergence into society, but never followed up in this area. In that period we used spools of ticker tape in computers that were as large as bookcases.

I graduated *magna cum laude* in June 1974 with a B.S. in psychology. I was a member of the Most Noble Order of the Peacock, the honor society on campus.

My nephews and nieces reside in suburbia, which offers a lot of opportunities, but they will never know the advantages of living in the heart of a crowded city. The kids of my generation hung out in Columbus Park. This was a sprawling park that started at 9th and Clinton Sts. and ended somewhere in the factory section of town. There was a ball field used by the *Red Wings* of Hoboken High. There were tennis courts and basketball courts beside the field—we used these for slap ball and punch ball. Hitting the ball over the fence was a home run in punch ball. The ball field was adjacent to a bamboo factory that was the scene of an epic fire. It literally rained bamboo embers for days. When we were young we played on a small rock-strewn and grassy plot between the factory and the ball field. At one point we tried to build a clubhouse on the plot.

I was part of the 8th St. gang—this wasn't our name, it was the place where most of us lived. The gang included George and Robbie Anderson, Michael Mahoney, James Bulzis, and Ed Garland. Our competition lived on 10th St. The games were rough and intense. Looking back, I'm sure we were excessively competitive. But no one got hurt and we policed ourselves. No one went over the edge and harmed anyone. And we did this without adult supervision.

I didn't have any talent in sports. But I was tall and I was strong and fast, so that gave me some advantages, especially in two-touch football.

We were pretty poor in those days. At one point we didn't even own a car. We took vacations in Keansburg on the Raritan Bay across from Coney Island. We rented a bungalow for a week. We visited the "concrete boardwalk" and played chances and rode the few amusement rides. There was a small-size Ferris wheel and a small-size roller coaster—everything was small size there. The Raritan was overfilled with rocks and driftwood—I think the beach at Keansburg must have been the target for everything that floated ashore. (I still have loaves of quartz we carried from the beach.) We couldn't swim in the water, which was unguarded, but the beach was expansive and sculpt for sunbathing and hiking. Dad took us crabbing on Port Monmouth Road. There was an inlet where we could throw the crab cages in. If we caught any we gave them to the other crabbers.

We drove to Keansburg the morning Apollo XI landed on the moon on 20 July 1969. There was a real estate agency on Carr Ave. that rented bungalows. We reserved a place and drove back to Hoboken in time to watch the lunar landing in the late afternoon. Later in the evening Armstrong and Aldrin walked on the moon. I recollect sitting in front of the television set and seeing the grainy images as the astronauts descended. After four decades I still feel the thrill of seeing humans walk on the moon. The young people of today, bewitched by high definition and 3-D, little appreciate how thrilling black-and-white television can be.

There were only thirteen stations at the time. Twelve originated from New York City and one from Newark. The day of the first great New York City blackout in November 1964 Mom yelled at us for breaking the television set when all the stations except the one from Newark went blank. We lived at 1208 Hudson St. and could see Manhattan through the front windows. One of us discovered that the island across the river also went blank. The set wasn't broken, after all.

One summer we stayed in a bungalow on Carr Ave. near a putt-putt course. I lost a cough-drop box in the grass in the back yard. Dad and I sat for a spell at the front of the house drinking coffee and watching the people come in and out of the laundry across the street. I went back and found the cough-drop box and put it in my shirt pocket. Within a few minutes ants were crawling over me like I was a hillside. It seems the ants had colds, too, and liked the taste of Smith Bros. licorice.

In the 1970s we started taking vacations in Virginia Beach. I bought a paperback—*There Is a River* by Thomas Sugrue—in the A&P on Rt. 36 on one of our trips to Keansburg and discovered Edgar Cayce, the "Sleeping Prophet". I became intrigued by Cayce and joined the Association for Research and Enlightenment. We'd drive down Rt. 13 on the Delmarva Peninsula, cross the Chesapeake Bay Bridge, saving "ninety miles of driving". The Bay Bridge was one lane in each direction at that time—it was thoroughly nerve-wracking to drive across. We stayed at the Cherry Motel on 26th St. and Arctic Ave. The family went to the beach and I hiked the 40 blocks to the A.R.E. on 67th St. and Atlantic Ave. The original building was a vast old house that once served as a hospital. Later, a modern library was built. I copied notes from the psychic readings and rested on the porch before the walk back to the Cherry Motel. The Atlantic Ocean was across the street, so the view lent itself to cosmic speculations.

It may not be proper to mention unmentionables in this kind of book, but one time I got caught in a drenching rain walking back to the Cherry Motel. I had on white shorts that got soaked. I wore red boxers underneath that showed through in the rain—they had little black designs of boats imprinted with the sails unfurled. I tried to remain innocuous, but there were a number of accidents on Atlantic Ave. as I proceeded.

Intellectually, I've moved on from the "Psychic Sage", but I still have a lot of affection for Cayce and for Virginia Beach.

In the 1990s we started vacationing in Wildwood Crest at the southern tip of New Jersey. We'd go with Joe and Kathy Pecoraro. We stayed at the Madrid Motel on the beach at Miami Avenue. We always tried to get a corner room on the fourth floor, as Dad liked the privacy. We'd visit the incredible boardwalk. It's miles long with three huge amusement piers extending over the sand. The boardwalk is so long a trolley commutes from one end to the other. The boardwalk gets so packed on summer nights the trolley has a warning announcement that repeats itself like the timed notes of a horn on a buoy, "Watch the tramcar please, watch the tramcar." The warning is so famous, it's printed on tee shirts.

In the early years we went jet skiing on the back bay. I've since become too fragile for this kind of nauti-maniacal activity. One time my niece Jennie Paradiso and I got thrown. The bay was only a few feet deep, but we no sooner landed in the water than we were attacked by the relentless greenhead flies that waited for juicy human beings to capsize.

Wildwood Crest has the best combination possible in a resort—a vast beach and the gentlest ocean water. I'd hike to the low tide after lunch, unfold a chair, take out a book or some writing paper and get down to business. When I got tired of reading I'd take long hikes in the shallow water. Or I'd just sit and relax and let the sea breeze turn the pages.

This was strongly frowned on by the locals, but every tourist does it. On the last day of every vacation we fed the laughing gulls by hand. We tossed bread in the air and in no time a flock hovered at eye level. They swarmed hysterically in a matter of minutes. The joke in our family was that the only person who didn't join in was my niece Danielle. She stood in the group with 20 birds swirling overhead and ate the bread rather than toss it. I was the only other person not feeding the gulls—I had the pleasure of standing to the rear and filming the frenzy with my camcorder.

Later, when I got seriously involved with genealogy we traveled across the sea to Erin and to Lietuva and took our vacations in places like Ballybunion and Palanga.

I haven't had a lot of jobs over the years and I certainly haven't made a lot of money. The jobs I've had were very different from those of my grandparents and father. Pat Ford did physical labor in the holds of ships. Pawel Bielawski did physical labor for the railroad and for a meat-packing company. Both started life as small farmers and agricultural laborers—I really can't picture myself as an agricultural laborer. My father was a policeman. His profession may not have involved physical labor, but it could get quite physical at times. My occupations have mostly involved moving my fingers over a keyboard and using spell check on a frequent basis. And my occupations have involved moving my lips in front of classes of students.

My first job was working part-time for Merrill Lynch, Pierce, Fenner & Smith. My Aunt Blanche got me a job in Jeanne Lowe's proxy department at Maiden Lane in Lower Manhattan. In November 1969 I went with Jeanne to the preliminary prospectus unit she founded in investment banking. Blanche joined us a few years later. This was at 70 Pine St. and later at One Liberty Plaza across from the World Trade Center. I worked from 3:30 - 7:30 PM during the school year and full-time in the summers. My job entailed taking prospectuses to brokerage houses—Lehman Brothers, First Boston, Kuhn Loeb, Goldman Sachs, Goodbody & Co., to name a few—many are gone now, undone by greed and bad management. After 5:00 PM I replenished the shelves in Jeanne's office. This meant taking a rolling cart to the sub-basement where we stored the prospectuses and bringing a few cartons back to the 10th floor.

In summer I took lunch at the pier that became the South Street Seaport. The place is now a tourist trap. When I worked for Merrill Lynch the pier was vacant. There was one ship—the *Ambrose* Lightship. I'd sit at the edge of the pier with my back against a bitt. The full span of the Brooklyn Bridge was in front of me and Brooklyn Heights was across the East River. The great towers of Manhattan were behind me. There are said to be eight million people in New York City, but I couldn't tell that from where I sat. I was alone with my thoughts. Despite what Ambrose Bierce claimed, that wasn't a bad place to be.

One time I was in a riot when I was delivering red herring prospectuses. The date was likely 8 May 1970 when the "hard hat riot" occurred at the corner of Wall and Broad Sts. There were fist fights between construction workers and the college students who protested the Vietnam War and the killings at Kent State that had occurred a few days before. I came out of 120 Broadway and turned a corner to hike back to 70 Pine. A herd of people charged toward me screaming that the police were attacking. In actuality the police weren't attacking anyone. They were standing idly by while their union brothers battled the war protestors.

I faced a major decision in the summer of 1974 whether to stay with Merrill Lynch as a full-timer or to go to graduate school at Fordham University. I chose the latter. I don't know if this was the right decision. I had a lot of executive contacts at Merrill Lynch and I floundered in an academic career. I don't think I would make the same decision if I could do things over. Unfortunately, I don't have a second chance, so I'm rather stuck.

I worked in a number of jobs since I left Merrill Lynch. I've been an adjunct at Kean University since 1983 and at the Borough of Manhattan Community College since 1988. Sometimes I think I'm the poster adjunct for academic underachievement. Other times I think I've made a difference in the lives of students—by my estimate more than 4,000 students have been exposed to the wonders of psychology through my lectures. I worked part-time in the Eclair bakery in The Cellar at Macy's at Herald Square for six years. I worked as a security guard and, later, as a dispatcher for Gilbert's trucking in Secaucus. I taught for a year at Westside High School in Newark. My main employment for the past 18 years has been with Barnes & Noble. I think I have had a unique career there. I worked for a few years in the used books department at the Sale Annex at 18th & Fifth Ave. When that closed in January 1997 I went with the books to Paramus and founded the used books Distribution Center. In 2000 I transferred to the corporate Distribution Center in Dayton and, later, in Monroe. I worked there in rush customer orders and, since 2003, as an inventory planner for Bargain Books.

I attended Fordham University as a full-time student from 1974 – 1976 and as a doctoral candidate from 1976 – 1987. This meant traveling from Hoboken and, later, from Jersey City to the Rose Hill campus in the Bronx. I took the IRT train from 34th St. to 149th and Morris Ave and the BX55 bus that replaced the elevated tracks on Third Ave. When I started taking classes the trestles were still standing in the streets. An alternative route was taking the D train to Fordham Road and walking. The walk to campus was downhill. The walk back to the station was uphill and grueling. Whatever the direction, it was a two-hour commute.

The Rose Hill campus is a beautiful place. Once inside the gates you'd never know you were in *Da Bronx, New Yawk*. There are open fields beyond a tree-lined cobblestone lane. In autumn the leaves turn a beautiful gold color. When the leaves shed the tree trunks get encircled with haloes. Most of my courses were in Dealey Hall, a four-story blue-gray building that opened to the quadrangle. Keating Hall, the signature building of the campus, was across the grass from Dealey. The library was a cramped old building that hardly had room for books, still less for students. The building was distinguished by a large stained glass window. One time I took Jason York to the campus when he was a little fellow of four or five. When he saw the window he asked if we were in church.

I obtained a master's degree in 1976. My thesis was on the relation between extraversion and projection as a style of defense mechanism. The topic derived from Carl Jung's conjecture that extraverts use projection as the preferred style of defense. I didn't find a relationship—I was using, surveys, however, and had a small and non-clinical sample. My mentor was James C. Higgins.

In 1987 I obtained a doctorate in psychology. My dissertation was entitled *Evaluation Anxiety, Interpersonal Anxiety, and the Accuracy of Nonverbal Communication: An Experimental Study*. My mentor was James C. Higgins, but he died at the last minute and was replaced by David Ward. The topic came out of Harry Stack Sullivan's suggestion that anxiety, defined as a drop in self-esteem, disrupts cognitive processes. The procedure involved easy and hard anagrams. Solving the easy anagrams was conjectured to increase self-esteem or, at the least, not to undermine it. Failure to solve hard anagrams was conjectured to lead to a temporary drop in self-esteem. Immediately after the anagram task the participants watched

Robert Rosenthal's *Profile of Nonverbal Sensitivity Test.* The hypothesis was that the drop in self-esteem brought about by failure at the anagram task reduced sensitivity to nonverbal communication. Unfortunately, it did not. I found no difference between the experimental and the control groups. There were enough variables in the study to come up with a number of significant correlations, so there were some positive results.

The dissertation was well-received by the committee. Alan Gray, one of the members, suggested that the study was a model of the kind of research needed in personality theories. It was, after all, an *experimental* study. And Celia Fischer, another member, said that it was worthy of a prize. Unfortunately, they didn't have any to give. I asked if they could make one up, but they said they couldn't.

Very few people know that I have a doctorate in psychology. I never capitalized on the degree, other than getting adjunct jobs and impressing assassination researchers. And I've mostly worked in places where an advanced degree earned squints rather than kudos. I think one of the themes of my life is that I achieve something notable that fails to blossom into the opportunities it should. This is true of the doctorate. This is also true of my books. Most people like to talk about themselves and blow their horns. I have an aversion talking about my accomplishments—when it comes to my horn, it's a Jew's harp.

I look back fondly on my years at Fordham. We were a close bunch of students and we were not competitive. My closest friend was Jim McGee, a huge kindly bear of a man with a long blond beard that matched the color of his pet retriever. I visited Jim and his wife at their home in Astoria the night of the second New York City blackout in July 1977. Since the trains stopped running I had to stay the night, most of which was spent on their stoop drinking Remy Martin and kibitzing about psychology. I owe Jim a lot, as he was instrumental in getting me working on the doctorate. He got his doctorate the same time as I did, so we started together and we finished together.

I was fortunate attending Fordham when I did. The faculty were nearing retirement, so they were laid back and not particularly focused on grades. I was the assistant to Fr. Joseph Keegan, a former chairman of the department. He had already retired, so I didn't have much to do. Fr. Keegan mostly sat in his office reading and smoking. In those days smoking was permitted in class. One of my teachers was Fr. Richard Zegers. He was a heavy chain smoker—I think he smoked saying Mass. As he lectured he reached in his pocket and peeled out a new cigarette before the old one was done. One time he took the last cigarette in the pack from his left pants pocket. It was the midway point in the lecture. Good, I thought, we're getting out early. The joke was on me. When he was done with that cigarette he reached in his right pants pocket and pulled out a fresh pack. So much for getting out early.

The bigwigs in the department were Anne Anastasi, who wrote textbooks and had been president of the American Psychological Association, and Joseph Kubis, who did research for NASA and who had been at Fordham since the time of Archbishop Hughes. I didn't find Dr. Anastasi inspiring, but Dr. Kubis was a joy in class. I had him for The Interview and for the Analysis of Variance. The latter course was a fourteen week exploration of the mysteries of inferential statistics. The final exam went on for hours. I didn't learn a single thing except the trick to passing his course. This trick was to give him everything you knew about the analysis of variance in every single answer. I got a "B", so my answers must have been thorough.

My mentor at the master's and doctoral level was James C. Higgins. He was a gentle clinical sort who taught courses in personality and ego psychology. I never found out much about his family or private life or that he was ill with leukemia, which eventually dispatched him to the lecture hall in the great beyond. He was easy to work with and he was helpful with advice, which were the reasons he was popular as a mentor. I suppose I was his last dissertation.

I typed the 193 page dissertation on a portable typewriter. I think I was the last Fordham doctoral candidate to use a typewriter.

For a number of years in the early 1990s I became interested in Kennedy assassination research. I joined the elite squad of sleuths who intended to get to the bottom of things. I spent a small fortune in the process. I traveled to six conventions. I owned over 200 books on the assassination, some of them rare pieces—when I fell out of favor I gave the books gratis to the Paramus bookstore. I became a big fish in a brackish tributary of the big puddle. I wrote a number of papers that were published in the *Third*— later *Fourth*—*Decade*, the premiere assassination journal. One paper was coauthored with Mark Zaid, a prominent lawyer in conspiracy circles. Another was coauthored with Jim Folliard, who I first knew as a history professor in St. Peter's College.

My experience with the sleuths soured when I opted for the lone-gunman scenario. Like Colonel Boycott in a different era, I was shunned and promptly drummed out of the assassination business. Not a moment too soon. God only knows what the field became in the late 1990s. It was already psychotic when I was in it. In my ambition to crack the case I failed to realize who I was dealing with. I was the darling of the assassination crowd when I agreed with the sleuths. When I disagreed and became a dissenter I was a snake in the weeds. They turned out to be a poisoned and poisonous bunch, paranoiacs of the worst ilk. That said, I made substantive and methodological contributions to the field they proudly called "assassinology".

My focus on the case was the rooming house where everyone's favorite patsy spent the last few weeks leading up to November 22. I believed that if it existed we could find evidence of conspiracy in 1026 North Beckley Ave. I had the simple idea that if Oswald returned to the rooming house after the assassination then he was the assassin. I doubted the conspirators would let the patsy return to the rooming house to get a jacket and a pistol—the pistol that shot Officer Tippit.

At the outset I entertained the conjecture that Oswald never returned to the rooming house. This strikes me now as amazing and ridiculous, but I took it seriously at the time and the sleuths took it seriously. When I mentioned that I believed Oswald never returned to the rooming house one prominent sleuth responded, "Of course he didn't return. That was the imposter Oswald." I based the possibility that Oswald never returned on eyewitness testimony. Mrs. Roberts, the housekeeper, was an unreliable witness from the get-go. Mr. Whaley, the cab driver, dropped Oswald a few blocks away, so he didn't see Oswald go inside. And by admitting he returned to get the handgun Oswald directly implicated himself in Tippit's murder, which struck me as an odd maneuver.

I refuted the conjecture that Oswald didn't return when I located one of the roomers who was there in November 1963. This person graciously responded to my query with a long letter in which he stated that he returned to the rooming house shortly after the assassination. Mrs. Roberts told him that he was the second person to return and that O.H. Lee—Oswald's alias—had already come and gone. This independent validation of Oswald's return was one of the decisive factors that led me to question and, ultimately, to renounce, the possibility of a conspiracy [48].

I located Mrs. Roberts's mysterious "Officer Alexander". I did this by placing an ad in a local Dallas newspaper. Mrs. Roberts reported that she heard a car horn toot outside the rooming house while Oswald was inside. She claimed she saw a cop car at the intersection. She later named "Officer Alexander" as one of the officers. There was no Officer Alexander on the

Dallas force in 1963. The sleuths thought this was suspicious—but no one thought to place an ad in a local newspaper.

In 1963 Floyd Alexander was a retired Dallas policeman. Mrs. Roberts had done housekeeping for him and his wife some years before the assassination. The sleuths might think it conspiratorial that she mentioned a policeman who left the force in 1957, but there was nothing suspicious in what she did. Mrs. Roberts did what any civilian would do under the circumstance—when she was interrogated she dropped the name of a policeman she knew.

My methodological contributions focused on the appreciation of the factors that distort eyewitness testimony and on the importance of refutation in guiding research. The sleuths gave lip service to the former. They never really understood the latter—if they did, they applied it only to the lone-gunman scenario. My final methodological contribution was the one that earned me walking papers out of the "research community".

In a short paper entitled *Major Trouble in Conspiracy Land* I pointed out that the sleuths made a major mistake declaring important evidence to be fraudulent. The Zapruder film, the Nix film, autopsy photographs and X-rays, the backyard photographs, even Oswald himself, were considered forgeries. I predicted that this was a fatal development in conspiracy research. The sleuths didn't know for a fact the evidence was fraudulent. They only supposed it was. They supposed so for the most transparent reasons—the evidence contradicted their theories. They failed to realize that declaring evidence to be fraudulent destroys the possibility of proof and, more importantly, of disproof. It is not possible to proceed on the basis of fraudulent evidence because the true situation is not known. The sleuths were sure that the true situation involved multiple gunman and massive cover-ups, but the argument could be made—and could not be dismissed—that the evidence was falsified to strengthen the case for the lone-gunman in the Book Depository. Once major evidence was held to be fraudulent the empirical field of assassination research collapsed into fantasy land where anything and everything was possible.

I come from a religious tradition that's deeply ingrained in me. I was an altar boy. I attended Mass throughout high school. I've read the Bible. I take Jesus at his word. I believe everything Jesus said.

I also come from a scientific tradition. I've done a dissertation. I know how to evaluate research. I know the main theories of psychology inside and out. I know experimental design. I almost knew how to compute an analysis of variance.

I've never felt any conflict between religion and science because there is another element in my life. Without sounding immodest, I have a creative side when it comes to words and language. It is the dominant side. It treats religion and science equally and takes whatever it needs from them. And it's more than that. This side takes whatever it needs from me. It uses my personality and my experiences in the same way it uses the facts and theories of religion and science.

In *Limelight* Charlie Chaplin tells the ballerina he befriended that his family was so poor growing up they couldn't afford toys. He goes on to say that bothered him until he discovered the creative imagination. Once he discovered the imagination he didn't need toys because he had the greatest toy of all. That's been my experience as well. Nearly every day of my life I've written or jotted ideas down. From the time I played toy soldiers on the counter at 803 Willow Ave to this same day I've been consumed with the creative imagination—I should say the creative imagination has been consumed with me.

Since the early 1970s my writing coalesced into novels. *Disparate Destinies* was the first. This was a massive handwritten story of a Confederate who deserts and heads North. If I'm allowed to continue, it may see the light of day. The original *Landsman* was the second. I rewrote *Landsman* word-for-word in 2008 and published it in 2009. *The Watchman* and *World Without End* were next. These two are unpublished—like I say, if I'm allowed to continue, they'll appear in print. In 1987 I started *Red Star*. This was the first book I published, but the fifth I wrote. The origin of the book laid in what the creative imagination provided in the long twilight walks I took waiting for Jason York to finish baseball and football practice in Harrison Field.

I picked up the nickname 'Honest Den" in the Barnes & Noble Sale Annex for my diligence in returning every cent of change to customers. I kept the name over the years in the way a tall person becomes "Tiny" and an obese person becomes "Slim". I was a dishonest person I'm ashamed to say. Until *Red* Star came out in August 2007 no one knew what fundamentally mattered in my life. I've written a dissertation and have a doctorate from a reputable university, I've written humor and nonfiction and travel essays and history pieces, but I consider *Red Star* and *Landsman* the crowning achievements of my life. They are what I'm taking on board the ferry to the great beyond. My psychology career, my career in Barnes & Noble, my interest in the assassination, all the rest of it and everything else, is so much dunnage.

This is what my imagination is—a pool that never drains. I published *Thinking About Everything* in 2008. This was a medley of whimsical musings, some humorous, some serious, I worked on since 2000. Many of the musings originated in the long drives to and from the Barnes & Noble Distribution Center. *Genealogical Jaunts* was also published in 2008. *Jaunts* was a collection of travel essays about our excursions to Ireland, Lithuania, Florida, and Utah. There are other books, too, that await print, but they are not written and it's not good form to name books that aren't put on paper yet.

I don't know how it is for other writers, but I don't completely identify with my creative side. Everybody knows I'm an incompetent. I could never write such coherent and sonorous books like *Red Star* and *Landsman* without help. I hate to admit this, but Carl Jung was right. My ego and sense of identity are not the only things inside me. I rewrote *Landsman* longhand—I write the first draft of everything longhand—while seated on the living room couch. I never became Jamie or Anny or Lt. Wanesford while I was writing. Here's the point I'm trying to make—in the hours I was writing I wasn't exactly Dennis Ford. The best I can compare the process to is to a neutral intelligence that can become any identity or play out any scene in any way it chooses. It's like a higher power or authority that flows without help from me. It's like a voice—I don't mean a voice speaks to me. I mean it's a style of thought that's different than my ordinary style of thinking. The words and sentences don't flow in drips and dribbles like they usually do but in a rush of finished thoughts.

We say we write books, but I think it's the other way around. The books write us. Long before these books were written they shaped my life in such a way that the words and ideas and characters and scenes emerged when the time was right. Certainly I'm a changed person because of these books. They've rewritten my identity in the way the waves rewrite the coast. I've gone places in these books I wouldn't otherwise have gone. I've said things and done things I otherwise would never have said or done. I know things and appreciate themes that were not present at the outset of the books. I've learned these themes only when the books were completed, quite as if I were a reader and not the author. There is a river after all—it leads away from me to the truth of my existence. Honestly, the best I can say is because of these books I'm no longer just Dennis Ford.

Chapter Nineteen

~

Felicia Ford

My sister **Felicia Ford** was born in 1954. She was baptized in St. Anthony's Church by Fr. B. Moscinski. Her godparents were Thomas and Mary Grogan. Mom remembered a trade-off at the baptism. Mary Grogan was selected as godmother only if the baby was named Felicia. Mom liked the name, although when we were little we couldn't pronounce it correctly. We called her "Deecee".

Felicia married twice. Her first husband was Mark York, who she met in the Navy in Norfolk, VA. They married in a civil ceremony in North Carolina. Their witnesses were Dennis Ford and Kathleen Ford. Mark was born in Indiana, but lived as an adult in Georgia. He was the son of William York and Marjorie Anne Berry. After their careers in the Navy Felicia and Mark lived for a time in Hoboken and then in Marietta, GA. They divorced after three years of marriage. At the time of their marriage Mark worked as a golf pro in a country club.

Felicia's second husband was Charles Hirsch. They married in a civil ceremony in New Jersey. Their witnesses were a man named Red—last name not known—and Kathleen (Ford) Pecoraro. Charles was born in New Jersey. He was the son of Abraham Hirsch and Dorothy—last name not known. Charles was an older man, well-off and settled in his ways at the time of the marriage. He had a variety of businesses, including check-cashing, scrap metal, and a pharmacy. After their marriage they lived in Roseland in Essex County, NJ. When Charles's health turned bad they moved to Tuckerton in Ocean County. They divorced after a few years of marriage, but then reconciled and lived together as husband and wife, although they never remarried. Charles died of lung disease in 1999. He was buried in the William C. Doyle Military Cemetery in Wrightstown, NJ (plot N O 5843).

Felicia attended Our Lady of Grace grammar school. She has happier memories of Sr. Barbara Anthony than most other students. She ran afoul of Sr. Mary Brien who slapped her and accused her of stealing a glove. Sr. Mary had to apologize publicly when the glove turned up. Felicia's friends in childhood were Doris Hounkin, who lived around the corner from her at 8th and Park Ave., and Michelle, Mary, Jenette, and Ellen. Their family names are not remembered.

Felicia attended Hoboken High School. She did not think it a happy experience. She was a rebellious person in that period and she was not interested in learning. Her best friends in high school were Pat and Carol Jacques.

Felicia took college courses sporadically, attending class at Essex County College and at Ocean County College. She earned a certificate in gerontology from Caldwell College.

The Irish proverb that we make our lives in the shelter of one another was true in our family. Felicia and Kathy have always been close and I was told I was solicitous of Felicia when we were children, always wiping her face when it was dirty.

Felicia wanted to be a Broadway dancer—this was a dream that never materialized.

Felicia's stormy years in late adolescence and young adulthood quieted when a friend advised her to join the Navy. This was a way to settle down—the same crises was faced by her son Jason in later years. She worked in communications in Norfolk. She had a few friends in the service—Wanda, Kathy, Barbara. An important influence in her life at that time was Robert Green, an African-American chief petty officer.

Felicia remembered that she bought her first car while in the Navy.

After her stay in the service Felicia worked at a number of jobs. She drew blood in a clinic in Marietta. She worked as an operating room technician and in respiratory therapy in Medical Center in Jersey City. She worked briefly for Merrill Lynch in the proxy department on Houston St. in Manhattan. She tended bar. She was a substitute teacher in New Jersey and later in Florida. She worked as a job coach for the mentally handicapped and as a hospice caregiver. She believes these two jobs took a toll on her psychologically. In Florida she worked as a hostess at an Inn and as a receptionist in an architecture firm.

In June 2003 Felicia made a major move. She sold her home in Tuckerton and moved to Mount Dora, a pleasant community in Lake County an hour north of Orlando in central Florida. The move benefited her son Luke, who prospered in a program for gifted students, but Felicia learned the hard lesson—to paraphrase Oscar Wilde—that the only thing worse than not moving to a place you want to go is moving there. Felicia's health took a turn for the worse in Mount Dora and the partnerships she inherited from Charles evaporated through mismanagement. Her financial standing plummeted at the same time the nation's economy collapsed.

Broadway never summoned, but Felicia accomplished one of her life's dreams after she moved to Mount Dora. She published a book entitled *Quiet Desperation*. (The original title was *Out of the First Person*.) *Quiet Desperation* described Felicia's lifelong struggle with alcoholism and with sobriety. The addiction began in high school and continued in secret for twenty years. Felicia describes in moving detail how the addiction poisoned her life physically, socially, and spiritually. *Quiet Desperation* ends happily as the book describes Felicia's twenty-year period of sobriety. She wrote the book to heal herself and her sisters in recovery. Her dearest friend in adulthood died from alcohol abuse. Felicia saw the necessity of offering her life story as a model of hope to women struggling to remain sober. Felicia discovered a secret that is not frequently whispered in the rooms of Alcoholics Anonymous—staying sober is more difficult than getting sober. AA insists that recovering alcoholics let their Higher Power guide and govern their lives. Felicia discloses with examples from her experiences in sobriety that it is not easy to let a Higher Power rule our lives.

Jason Eugene York is Felicia's first son. Jason was baptized in Our Lady of Grace Church by Fr. Wilfred Yeo. His godparents were Dennis Ford and Kathleen Ford. Jason married Anna "Ginny" Pfeiffer in a civil ceremony in Hawaii. Their witnesses were Chad Barshsinger and Tracy Aquino. Ginny is the daughter of James "Michael" Pfeiffer and Karen Forrest of Jacksonville, FL. She and Jason have three sons—**Shane Ethan York**, **Evan Nicolas York**, and **Alexander James York**.

Jason attended kindergarten in Our Lady of Grace school and first grade in Our Lady of Mount Carmel in Jersey City. He completed grammar school in Our Lady of the Blessed Sacrament in Roseland. He attended West Essex Regional High School in North Caldwell. He believes football coach Ron Aniello was the main influence on him in high school. Jason's friends in Roseland included Thomas "Bumper" Rodriguez, Chris Critchet, Adrian Young, Sean Cronin, Steven Cole, and Robert Selvaggi.

I'm a fan of all my nephews and nieces, but owing to the circumstance of our lives I was especially close to Jason and to Luke Ford as they grew up. I can't conceive how bleak my life would have been without them. I had a regular routine with Jason when he was in grade school—the routine continued right into high school. I watched him mostly on Wednesday's, which allowed Felicia and Charles the chance to socialize and to enjoy a late meal out. After playing and doing homework—mostly after playing— we watched *The Dukes of Hazard* and *The Greatest American Hero*. Jason always tried to stay up past 10:00 PM to watch *Dynasty*, but he was too little to make it so late.

The years in Blessed Sacrament and in West Essex centered on sports. Jason learned to play ball in Mosquito Park on Manhattan Ave. in Jersey City and he never stopped learning. The 8th St. gang always played rubber ball when we were kids in Columbus Park. With Jason it was always hardball. We played catch in the grassy pit and in the parking lot in front of his home in Roseland. I was the catcher. When Jason started to learn to pitch catching was mostly a matter of chasing after wild throws. By the time he was in eighth grade catching was mostly a matter of trying to stay alive and in one piece as the ball screamed toward me at 70 plus miles an hour.

I watched Jason play ball from the top deck of the tiny bleachers in Fernwood Field on Eagle Rock Ave. I always wore my red Hawaiian shirt for luck. My usual cheer was "Rock and roll" for encouragement. When he was twelve he struck out 88 batters in one season. Later, I watched from the stands in Harrison Field as Jason pitched for the *Knights* of West Essex and for the American Legion Team. Jason continued to pitch when he entered the service. In one game in Hawaii he struck out 20 of 21 batters—I'm not sure what that says about his ability or about the ability of batters in the Navy League.

I wanted to motivate Jason as he went into the senior year of high school so I asked him what the school record for wins was. It was eight wins, no losses. On a rainy Friday evening in August I had a shirt made up in a store on the Wildwood boardwalk. The shirt read "8 and 0." I should have been more enthusiastic of what Jason could accomplish. He went 9 and 0 his senior year, establishing a school record. The ninth win was a two hitter against Dover High School. Jason struck out five. Brian Ehrhardt drove in two runs with a single and sacrifice fly and Greg Ochojski doubled in a run. John Lindner retrieved the ball. I have it in my display case. I feel very proud every time I see it.

Jason played quarterback for the Roseland *Raiders* when he was in Blessed Sacrament. Some of the players on the local teams were Brian Wilson, Joey Spina, and Doug Rogers. When he was in high school I drove him to football practice at Harrison Field and walked to the Fairchild Deli where I bought hero sandwiches and daydreamed about the plot of *Red Star*. After practice we drove home, ate the sandwiches, watched TV, wrestled, and did homework—tried to do homewok, that is. Jason was never a fan of homework in those years—it's amazing what he became in the Navy.

We played a game back then that was like "tag", only we played it seated on the couch. We poked each other with a finger while saying "You're it!" and leaning briskly to the side to avoid being poked in turn. We also started a custom of tapping our index and middle fingers and saying, "High two" when we met or parted. I think we copied that from professional players, but there's no copyright infringement involved. And we asked at bedtime, "Where's your truck parked?" This meant "Where are you sleeping?" It was never the bed we were on, but some elaborate place far away on the open road.

Jason started out as the freshman quarterback for the high school team. Coach Aniello converted him to tight end. He played that position on the varsity team for three years. One of my fondest memories was watching him on the field as a junior when the Wessex *Knights* defeated their arch-rivals, the mighty West Morris team, 20 – 0. Local papers called the win the "perfect game" and they were right.

It wasn't always sports. When Jason was young we played a game called "scuba diver". We pretended the couch was a boat. I asked Jason, the scuba diver, if he had his cap on and his snorkel and his mask and his oxygen tank and his knife and his watch and his fins. After checking that nothing was amiss he jumped into the ocean—this was the rug. After he swam for a minute I cried, "Get back into the boat! I see a great white shark! Hurry, hurry!" He scampered back on the couch in great fear, stabbing at the shark with his knife. "Wow, that was a near miss," I said in a relieved voice. "You just about made it."

After high school Jason drifted for a while—he was not psychologically ready for college. He followed his Uncle Joe Pecoraro's advice and joined the Navy and found his niche. His naval career has been a story of success with no setbacks. His parents and grandparents would have to salute him if they were in uniform. I'm proud to say that he's a "Mustang"—he progressed from enlisted man to the rank of chief petty officer and then to a commissioned officer. He is currently a lieutenant junior grade in rank.

Jason completed basic training in Orlando, FL. He served in a VP-30 fleet replacement squadron based in Jacksonville. He next served as an acoustic warfare officer based in Oahu, HI. He logged more than 1,500 hours of flying in a P3 Orion. He vividly remembers the first time his plane tracked a Delta-class Russian submarine out of Vladivostok.

Jason transferred to Pensacola, FL, as an acoustic instructor. He then returned to Jacksonville where he revised and created nine acoustic lessons totaling more than 2,000 pages. His proudest moment in the Navy as of this writing was finishing first of 558 teachers and becoming "Instructor of the Year." Captain Tom Keeley stated in the base newspaper that, "He is unquestionably my most motivated junior instructor and a proven leader with the ability to create a positive learning experience in any environment." That Jason became instructor of the year is an accomplishment that could convert atheists to a fundamentalist creed. It's a long way from the little boy who whined and cried and used every possible stratagem to avoid doing homework.

When he became a commissioned officer Jason transferred from naval air to the blue water navy. He also changed coasts, moving from sunny Jacksonville to snowy Seattle. Shane, Evan, and Alex saw their first snowfall in their home in Arlington, WA. Jason reported for duty as a tactical warfare officer aboard the nuclear-powered aircraft carrier USS *Abraham Lincoln*. *The Abe* was commissioned in November 1989. It is 1,092 feet long and 206 feet tall. It displaces 97,000 tons and can do more than 30 knots. It has a complement of 5,500 sailors when the air wing is aboard.

Jason has earned two Navy Marine Corps Commendations and three Navy and Marine Corps Achievement Commendations. One of the Commendations was for his service in the War in Iraq. It reads:

> "Chief York superbly led a highly successful tri-site deployment in support of Operations Iraqi and Enduring Freedom ... his watch team was instrumental in the planning and execution of 445 combat sorties ... in support of troops on the ground in Iraq and Afghanistan.

Chief York established MOCC's training, operations, procedures which … is now the training standard being utilized for all MOCCS worldwide. Chief York's distinctive accomplishments, unrelenting perseverance and steadfast devotion to duty reflected credit upon himself and were in keeping with the highest traditions of the United States Naval Service [49]."

All my nieces and nephews—and now my great-nephews—gave me the opportunity to re-experience the world and to grow up again from infancy into adulthood. I've cheated life and loneliness because of them. Jason gave me the opportunity to experience the world in a literally geographical sense. Jason joined the Navy and I've seen the world. I've made several trips to Jacksonville, three trips to Pensacola, and two trips to Oahu. There was one rainy week in Washington State—there was snow in the mountains in August—and one blistering hot day in San Diego. The highlight was crossing the Pacific on the *Abraham Lincoln* on a Tiger cruise sailing from Pearl Harbor to San Diego. I vividly remember walking on the hangar deck and seeing the ship race by one of the Hawaiian islands. It's incredible that something so huge can move so rapidly. It was fantastic to be given the run of the ship as a civilian. As I promised I didn't touch a single button, especially those marked with bright red X's.

Luke Joseph Ford is Felicia's second son. Luke was baptized in Our Lady of the Blessed Sacrament Church in Roseland. His godparents were Andrea LaRusso and Carmel Holmes. Felicia is as proud of Luke as she is of Jason.

Luke attended the George Mitchell grammar school in Little Egg Harbor. In Florida he attended Round Lake Elementary School for a year and then the Eustice Middle School, where he entered a program for gifted students. As of this writing Luke is in the senior year in Mount Dora High School. He wants to study physics when he graduates and work in the electronic games industry. Felicia finds it incredible that the years have passed so rapidly.

Luke is different temperamentally from Jason. He has a black belt in karate, but he was never interested in organized sports. We hardly ever went outside to have a catch. Tossing a football with Luke was unthinkable—I don't believe it ever happened. When we went outside it was on nature walks to find "specimens". When Luke was a child this was to Holly Lake, where we poked for insects under rocks and logs. In his teen years we strolled the beach at Osborn Island at the tip of Little Egg Harbor on the bay looking for snails and hermit crabs in the low tide.

Luke is a serious young man who's extremely knowledgeable in virtually every topic involving science and technology. I'm sure he knows more science than most of the students in my psychology courses. He knows more science than I do, although that's not a fair comparison since I've been in intellectual decline for a number of years. Luke hasn't stopped that decline, but he has slowed it. Doing homework with Luke and talking with him about science gave me the opportunity to remember things I had forgotten and to explore new facts and ideas in novel ways.

Luke's third-grade teacher wrote that:

> "Luke is a cooperative and conscientious student who wants to succeed in the classroom. Luke always gives his best effort in all assignments. Luke is an inquisitive, insightful, and thoughtful learner. He is also a thoughtful and caring boy regarding his fellow students and teachers."

When Luke entered the gifted program his intellectual skills were assessed. In the fifth grade he read at the college level. In the sixth grade his math skills were at the college level. It's gotten better since.

It hasn't been all schoolwork. Luke has a keen musical sense—he is the only one in our immediate family who knows music. He played xylophone in Little Egg Harbor and trombone in the school bands in Mount Dora. In his senior year he was the drum major for the marching band. He learned to play the ukulele. He has an organ in his room and a mandolin. One of the highlights of our visits is Luke serenading us. It's a joy to hear *Band* songs performed live in the living room.

When Luke was a little boy of two or three we played a game in which I entered a room and pretended to scare him. He'd run behind his mother or behind a piece of furniture and hide. After a few seconds he'd peek out warily. I'd say "Boo!" and he'd hide again. This went on for quite a number of repetitions.

When he was older we played a game in which I crouched on the floor on my hands and knees. Luke crouched under me. We pretended to be dogs—Luke did the panting, I did the growling. Sometimes Luke hid under the table. I couldn't fit there, but I gave instructions warning him to be careful not to get attacked by the neighborhood cats and not to chase cars too far into the street.

The highlight of the games we played was Tex L. Rogers, the "two-fisted meanest varmit in the whole dern West." Tex was ringleader of a posse of bank robbers and cattle rustlers. "Yee-hah!" The members of the posse were Tex's brother Nevada Rogers, Clem Labine, Mad Mike, Shorty (who was short because he smoked too many cigarettes), and The Chief, who was 137 years old, but still in good health owing to his knowledge of nature and herbal lore. Each of these figures was an inch tall and made of the cheapest plastic, but that didn't matter. They captivated Luke. We didn't need any other props. We sat side-by-side at the bare kitchen table and held the little men and talked for an hour—when a character talked we lifted the little figure off the table and moved him up and down. Charlie Chaplin was right—imagination is the greatest toy.

I should say I did most of the talking. I elaborated stories about a bank heist Tex was planning or about a trip to a ranch to round up cattle. I related Tex's orders to his posse and I made up healing powers of ordinary plants and flowers. No matter what happened to any member of Tex's gang, The Chief found a healing salve to restore him to health. No matter how precarious the situation or how many lawmen were chasing them in the badlands, things always worked out for Tex and the boys. These stories went on for so long Babci had to remind us to stop. She had to chase us off the table. Luke didn't say much, but he listened with the keenest concentration. I'm convinced his bright intellect derived from making sense of these tall tales.

Luke's world is currently an expensive world of computers and electronic gizmos. I'm not disparaging these things—Google and the Internet are marvels never before known. Luke's world in childhood was a world of poorly chiseled plastic toys one inch tall. Tex and the boys cost a few pennies in the dollar general store. It's not possible to count their effect across the years.

Chapter Twenty

~

Kathleen Ford Pecoraro

Kathleen Ford was the third and last child of Joseph Ford and Sophia Bielawska. Kathleen was born in Hoboken in 1955 and baptized in Our Lady of Grace Church. Her godparents were Roman Rog and Blanche Szustek. Dad wanted Kathy to be named Catherine after his mother, but Mom preferred another name. They settled on Kathleen as a compromise.

Kathy made First Holy Communion on 11 May 1963. By luck, her brother Dennis held the communion plate. He vividly remembered how nervous he was holding the plate for the children one step ahead of Fr. Meehan. The last thing he wanted to do was to step on Fr. Meehan's foot or strike a communicant in the throat with the plate.

Kathleen married Joseph Pecoraro in Our Lady of Grace Church. Their witnesses were Arthur Corvo and Felicia Ford. Fr. Frederick Eid officiated. Joseph was the son of Francis Pecoraro and Florence Ciancibello. He was born in the Bronx, New York. He worked as an executive in information technology for Prudential Insurance Co. Joe has a black belt in karate. He has been heavily involved for many years in the Shorin Ryu Shidokan style of karate that originated in Okinawa.

Kathy met Joe in the following manner. Joe was a sailor stationed in Norfolk. He was friends with Mark York, Felicia Ford's future husband. Kathy visited Felicia and partied in the Trade Winds, which was a club on base where the enlisted men and women danced, drank, socialized, made small talk, fell in love, and spent the next 30 years together. After a late-night party Joe volunteered to walk Kathy and Felicia to the barracks. As they walked Kathy whispered to Felicia, "He's cute." Kathy no sooner returned to Hoboken than she booked another flight to Norfolk. She claimed the trip was to visit her sister, but people suspected otherwise.

Kathy found Joe funny, smart, and good-looking—she still thinks he is. He has always been a hard-working and family-oriented person.

After their marriage Joe and Kathy lived in Wallington, NJ. They subsequently purchased a house in Hasbrouck Heights and, later, in Emerson. They have a second house in Little Egg Harbor. Our family had a lot of fun in their home in Hasbrouck Heights. Everyone visited during holidays like Memorial Day and Independence Day. There was a pool in the backyard where the kids swam and played games like "Marco Polo", a watery version of "hide-and-seek". Everyone, including Felicia's husband Charles Hirsch, pitched in and helped construct a second pool when the first one got used up. There were swings and a monkey-bars like toy on which the kids climbed up and slid down. Kathy kept a garden in the corner of the yard for a few years.

Kathy attended Our Lady of Grace grammar school and Hoboken High School. She believes Mrs. Fusco, an English teacher and drum majorette instructor, made an impression on her. She took a few courses at Jersey City State College. Growing up, she traveled in the same circle as Felicia and had the same friends. She sees Felicia as her best friend. Mom remembered that Kathy was always solicitous of Felicia—she made sure to do the household chores Felicia avoided so neither of them would get into trouble.

Kathy entertained the thought of becoming a veterinarian. She has always been good with animals—except with fish, maybe. Mom remembered that everyone else was squeamish but Kathy had no compunction jabbing hooks through bait when they went fishing.

After graduating from high school Kathy worked for a few years in the corporate headquarters of Marine Midland Bank on Broadway in Lower Manhattan. In the late 1970s she made a major career change and became a Licensed Practical Nurse, graduating a nursing program run by the Medical Center in Jersey City. She remembered that an instructor named Mrs. Griffin made an impression teaching the practical aspects of nursing. Kathy worked in Medical Center for ten years, mostly on 14 Medical. This was a floor that specialized in renal cases, but there were other disease categories treated. Kathy found her years in Medical Center exciting and challenging. She saw life on the other side, since many patients were desperately poor and often narcotic addicts. She left nursing to raise a family.

Kathy loved horseback riding when she was young. She rode a trail in Staten Island on a regular basis. She liked to swim and to exercise. In Hoboken High School she was a majorette in the school band. Her favorite pastime is reading.

Kathy has a lot of happy memories of our vacations in Keansburg and of our day trips to Coney Island and to Palisades Park. She recollects that when we went to Palisades Park we always stopped for hot dogs and fries at Callahan's, a roadside stand that featured a huge selection of condiments. Callahan's also featured a shortage of indoor seating. Most of the time we had to eat in the car, holding boxes of food on our laps. She and Joe started a tradition of visiting Hershey Park in Pennsylvania. Initially, they visited in summer, but then they started visiting in winter during the Christmas break. They made it a point to visit the chocolate factory and the amusement rides. Of course, the temperature was bitterly cold. We have pictures to prove how cold it was. Everyone was bundled up and bravely trying to smile for the camera, but the pained grins on red faces gave the temperature away.

Warmer memories involved Wildwood and our August vacations at the Madrid Motel. Kathy and her family loved the ocean and the pool. As her children got older they climbed the sliding pond in the pool and ventured beyond the gate into the deeper water. They always played miniature golf the first night in Wildwood. Two or three nights everyone ventured to the fabulous Boardwalk and "watched the tramcar" as they maneuvered baby carriages from ride to ride. Kathy tracked the growth of her children in the rides they went on. In the early years the rides were "baby rides" of slow-moving swings and cars and boats that dipped a foot or two. To preschoolers the dips must have looked as perilous as the edge of Niagara Falls to a man in a barrel. In later years the rides were "grown up". This meant upside-down roller coasters and rides that revolved at shotgun velocities. Danielle's favorite ride was the Tilt-a-Whirl. She gave instructions on which direction to turn to maximize the whirls, but we never managed to coordinate tilts. Trips to the Boardwalk included chances and visits to the arcades where a bucket of tickets earned a trinket.

The Pecoraros took a New Year's holiday cruise in 2005-06 on the Norwegian liner *Dawn*. The eleven-day cruise included stops at Jamaica, Belize, Honduras, Cazumel in Mexico, and the Cayman Islands. Highlights of the cruise included swimming with wild dolphins in Honduras and tubbing in white water on the White River in Jamaica on Christmas Day.

Kathy and Joe had the following children: Jennifer Paradiso; Danielle; Kimberly Jones; and Matthew.

All their children are special and very dear to Kathy and Joe, each in their own way. They are alike in many ways, but there are differences among them as well. These differences make them who they are. They have grown up to be amazing people.

What Kathy and Joe find gratifying is that their children stayed close to one another as they grew up. Jennifer and Kimberly always shared and guided one another as children. They do the same as they experience adulthood and motherhood. And they have cared for and have been solicitous of their special sister and of their brother, even as he entered manhood and towered over them in height. Matthew can eat the proverbial apple off their heads, but he is still his sisters' little brother.

Jennifer Pecoraro was baptized in the Church of Corpus Christi in Hasbrouck Heights. Her godparents were Nicholas LaPolla and Felicia Ford. Jennifer married Anthony Paradiso, the son of Antonio and Marie Paradiso. They have two sons, **Anthony Paradiso** and **Dante Paradiso**.

Jennifer attended Lincoln Elementary School in Hasbrouck Heights and Hasbrouck Heights High School. In high school Jennifer was in the National Honor Society and in the French Honor Society. She was a member of the Student Council. In her senior year she was voted Prom Queen.

Jennifer graduated Rutgers University with a bachelor's degree in political science and a minor in woman's studies. She earned a certificate in elementary education from William Paterson University. She taught sixth grade for six years in Lakeside Middle School in Pompton Lakes, NJ. She was head of the sixth grade staff. One year she became "teacher of the year"—becoming "teacher of the year" may be a hereditary trait in our family. Jennifer left the world of education to raise a family.

Jennifer was a beautiful and pleasant child, strong-willed, bright, and dramatic. She has grown up to be a beautiful and pleasant young woman, strong-willed, bright, and dramatic. From the earliest grades she liked to be involved in school activities. She loved to dance and attended dance school for a while. She was in the dramatic society in Hasbrouck Heights High School. Jennifer portrayed a munchkin in *The Wizard of Oz*, Charity in *Anything Goes*, Bunny in *California Suite*, and Mary in *The Pajama Game*. Jennifer's theatrical talents included staging a family pageant on Christmas Eve when she was young. She and her siblings danced and sang carols to the delight of her parents and grandparents.

Jennifer belonged to the Hasbrouck Heights Color Guard and performed in the flag twirling section of the high school marching band. At Rutgers she was an active member in the Gamma Phi Beta Sorority and president of the Pan-Hellenic Group, which was an organization of campus sororities. One of Jennifer's favorite hobbies is reading—this may be another hereditary characteristic she shares with her mother and grandmother.

One of my stock sayings to Jennifer growing up—I said this to all Kathy and Joe's children—was, "Don't take any wooden nickels." I said this teasingly whenever they were going home or for a stroll on Central Ave. in Jersey City. It was a joke—and it's not bad advice. I also teased Jennifer and her sisters, calling them "Voluptuous." I said that in jest when they were kids. It has turned out to be an astute observation.

Danielle Pecoraro was baptized in the Church of Corpus Christi in Hasbrouck Heights. Her godparents were Dennis Ford and Felicia Ford.

Danielle attended Villano Elementary School in Emerson and Emerson High School. She attended Bergen Vocational Technical School for two years. She currently works in the Hoehne Center in Hackensack and participates in the Broadway Medical Program in Fair Lawn. The former is a vocational center that employs people with disabilities to assemble products. The latter is a recreational program.

Danielle was born with Down Syndrome, so she has faced—and has overcome—many challenges. Danielle attended remedial programs from infancy to adulthood so she could express the best her abilities allowed. She has an easy-going and pleasant personality that makes the challenges easier to solve. Danielle has grown up to be a bright and giving young woman.

Danielle has participated in the Special Olympics for many years. She has won trophies in the 50 meter dash and in softball pitching. She plays basketball in a league. Her team, the *Killer Bees*, has been state champions. Danielle also enjoys bowling. Her average is now 110, which is 110 points higher than what her godfather could achieve. She appeared as an extra in two episodes of the television series *Law and Order*.

Danielle loves family and is always happy to hang out with her sisters, brother, and cousins. She is now the best aunt to her nephews. Danielle always accompanies Kathy when she visits Babci in Little Egg Harbor. She's affectionate with her grandmother and is always sensitive to the state of Babci's health. During these visits we often sit at the kitchen table and have coffee and dessert. It's a delight to have Danielle join us in conversation. Danielle is a sensitive person. She dislikes when the conversation turns to politics or to the state of the economy. She teaches us to talk kindly about people and events and not to complain.

Danielle is a joy and a beautiful young woman who has taught her family many surprising things. To be sure, she has taught us more than we have taught her. Her parents are very proud of her.

Kimberly Pecoraro was baptized in the Church of Corpus Christi. Her godparents were Joseph Fabian and Joann Fabian. Kimberly married Matthew Jones, the son of Michael and Laura Jones. They have one son, **Jack Jones**.

Kimberly attended Lincoln Elementary School and Emerson High School. In high school Kimberly participated in the Teens for Diversity Program and took a course on TV production. She was voted "Class Icon" in the senior year. Kimberly has an associate's degree from St. Thomas Aquinas College. She is taking courses at William Paterson University to obtain a degree in English and elementary education. In addition she has a certificate in Cosmetology from Artistic Academy.

Kimberly was a bright and beautiful child. She was very curious and inquisitive. Kathy called her "My busy child." She was always active and in motion. She was a Girl Scout, she played soccer, and she even practiced karate like her father and brother. Growing up, she had a collection of dolls and pocketbooks that she organized and re-organized on a regular basis. She had so many pocketbooks she was called the "bag lady". She was a take-charge kind of person and was always willing to help others and to extend encouraging words.

I can attest to Kimberly's organizational prowess. One year in Wildwood we stayed on the second floor at the Coliseum Motel across Miami Ave. from the Madrid. Dad wanted coffee from the first-floor shop. Kimberly volunteered to get it—she was a child, probably four or five years old. As a reward Dad gave her extra money to buy French fries. Kimberly went downstairs and ordered at the counter. This is impressive in itself—I don't know many four or five year olds who have the nerve to order coffee and fries at a take-out counter. Ordering proved the easy part. Kimberly now had the task of carrying a coffee container, a carton of fries, and the change. She could have used a third arm. Her return to the second floor was methodical. It was also comical to watch. She placed the coffee container on the first stair, walked up a few steps, and set the carton of fries down. She went back, retrieved the coffee, and ascended a few steps past the fries. She placed the coffee down, descended, and retrieved the fries. She walked a few steps past the coffee and set the fries down. Then she went back and retrieved the coffee. She systematically did this on the first flight and then on the second flight. She didn't spill a single drop of coffee. She didn't lose a single fry. I think she got to keep the change. Watching Kimberly, I realized how humanity became the superior species.

When she was three Kimberly exhibited one of the clearest examples of conditioning—it was one of the cutest statements anyone in our family ever uttered. To show the birthday candles off we always closed the houselights when we carried the cakes into the parties. One year we held the birthday party in the backyard of Joe and Kathy's house in Hasbrouck Heights. Everyone waited at the picnic table to sing "Happy Birthday" followed by *"Sto'lat, sto'lat, yez-ze-a-ze-a-nam."* Kathy carried the cake outside. The candles were lit, but the sunlight stayed on. Kimberly hastily insisted, "Put out the light!" when she saw the cake. It was an adorable statement and one we'd have to wait a few billion years to carry out.

Matthew Pecoraro was the fourth and last child of Joe and Kathy Pecoraro. Matthew was baptized in the Church of Corpus Christi. His godparents were Jason York and Jennifer Pecoraro. Matthew attended the Lincoln and the Villano Elementary Schools. He graduated Emerson High School. Currently he is matriculated at Rutgers University. He is majoring in communications with minors in sociology and in psychology.

Matthew was a handsome, happy, and cooperative child. Mom remembered he walked around with a bouquet of pacifiers tied to his shirt. His favorite holiday as a child was Halloween—one year he wore a cape for days. He received a lot of mothering growing up. With three sisters, he has four mothers and that was often three too many. Matthew was a diligent child throughout grammar and high school—this is a quality that continues to serve him well in college. Matthew loved to draw and to play Legos. Without any formal training, he's demonstrated artistic talent. One of his paintings was displayed at a Bergen County Teen Arts Festival. In high school Matthew was chairperson of the yearbook staff—this may be another trait that runs in our family. In Emerson High he displayed a dramatic flair that took everyone by surprise. He stared as Ryan Evans in *High School Musical* and as Max Detweiler in *The Sound of Music*. In these plays Matthew showed he could sing and dance with aplomb—and he showed a definite talent for comic acting. He had the audience laughing in both plays.

Matthew was a Boy Scout. He played soccer in grammar school. Since the age of five he has been heavily engaged with karate. Matthew has a second-degree black belt—this helps him to be a big brother to his sisters. For many years Matthew and Joe traveled to Michigan to compete in the national conference of their school of karate. In 2006 Matthew accompanied Joe on an once-in-a-lifetime journey to Okinawa. The flight was a half-day trip from Newark Airport to the airport in Naha, capital of Okinawa. They wanted to explore firsthand the culture and history of the people who originated the form of karate they practiced for ten years and better. They arrived during the Uchinanchu Festival, which is held every five years to welcome home Okinawans who immigrated to other countries.

Matthew and Joe trained in several Shorin Ryu Shidokan dojos in Naha. They had the privilege of demonstrating their martial arts prowess under the personal direction of the Shikokan Master Seikichi Iha, Hanshi, 10th Dan, in the martial arts pavilion in Naha. The local media covered the event and to their surprise Matthew and Joe were featured on the evening news. The following day during their tour of Shuri Castle local girls approached Matthew and treated him as a celebrity. They recognized him from the newscast and were astounded at his six-foot-three height. The castle in Shuri was the traditional home of the Ryukyu kings who ruled Okinawa from the fifteenth to the nineteenth century. The building that now stands on the site was built in 1992 from images of the original in photographs and in artwork. The original castle was shelled into oblivion in World War Two by the battleship *Missouri*. On 27 May 1945 a Southern soldier raised the Confederate flag over the ruins. The flag was ordered removed by General Simon Bolivar Buckner Jr., son of the Confederate general who unconditionally surrendered to Ulysses Grant at Fort Donelson in February 1862.

During their visit Matthew and Joe performed with an Okinawa dance troop as *Taiko* or traditional Japanese drummers. They practiced for several months to be able to perform at the Okinawa Convention Center in front of several hundred people. The response of the audience was overwhelmingly positive. They were approached by many natives and thanked for their commitment to Okinawa culture.

Chapter Twenty One

How We Did This Research

In this last chapter we look at how we did the research. We address the questions of how and where we accumulated the information that went into the preceding twenty chapters. Then we examine what we knew when we started a long journey that commenced at Houston and Varick Sts. on a bitterly cold day. We had little information at the outset. We started with a blank slate that, I'm proud to say, has been ably filled in. Our immigrant grandparents said little of their lives in the native lands. They were too busy struggling to hold jobs to croon of Erin or Lietuva. And their children were too busy trying to fit in American society to inquire about life on the ancestral farms.

We had direct access to primary material on the Forde, Freeman, Hunt, and Fitzmaurice lines. The Tuam Archdiocese allowed the Mormon Church to film the nineteenth century Parish registers. To our great good luck the microfilms were on permanent loan in the New York City Family History Library. We were able to view the handwritten baptisms and marriages of our Mayo and Roscommon ancestors. It was possible to extract generations of Parish records for specific surnames—this is what Bernie Freeman found so useful when he read the Freeman file. It was also possible to extract records for specific townlands, as I did for Derrynacong and Laughil.

We weren't so lucky on the Kerry side. The church records for Ballybunion Parish have recently become available on-line, but the records were "closed" when we did the research in the mid-1990s. The records could be viewed if you made a contribution to the bishop and traveled to the National Library in Dublin. They could also be obtained on a pay-as-you-go basis with a "heritage center"—ours was the Killarney Centre. These were organizations that were permitted to research Parish records and forward information. We got the information we needed, but it was an expensive and time-consuming process.

Everyone is on-line today, but in the mid-1990s e-mail wasn't as popular. We used the "snail mail" with great success on both the Irish and Polish sides. I obtained from the South Mayo Heritage Centre a list of heads of household in Derrynacong and forwarded a copy of the research I was doing to each of them. I also obtained the name of the current holder of what was the Forde farm—this was Mr. Ronayne. A few residents of Derrynacong wrote back with regrets. They had no information. But the reply from Mrs. Kathleen Fitzharris was extraordinarily informative. She knew Aunts Delia and Kate and she even remembered Tom Forde, her next-farm neighbor. And she directed us to Pat and Kathleen Hunt of Carrick. Mr. Ronayne forwarded my letter to the Eatons of Ballyhaunis, who kindly replied with a photograph and stories about Aunt Delia.

The majority of baptism and marriage records on the Polish side were provided by the Vilnius Archive. Formally, it is the *Lietuvos Valstybes Istorijos Archyvas*. This is a state-run organization that provides church records for a fee. The time period is early nineteenth century forwards. Unfortunately, the records for the Girdziunai vicinity end around 1880, after which we had to deal with the government of Belarus. The Vilnius Archive provides photocopies of the Parish records and an English translation of the Polish and Russian information.

We were able to provide a general time period and specific locale—Girdziunai—for the Storta family. We had nothing to supply on the Bielawski family. The Archive searched a number of registers by hand, focusing on the general time period of Pawel's birth. Once Kalniskes was identified, information came rapidly on the other Turgeliai families.

We engaged successfully in letter writing on the Polish side. There is an organization in Lithuania that lists surnames by locales. I forwarded letters blindly to any Bielawski within a few miles of Kalniskes. I also sent a letter addressed to the *Storta rodziny* of Girdziunai. It took a while, but the letters made their ways to the correct parties and we received replies. Later, we had the great fortune to meet Mom's first cousins.

In America we obtained census data at the National Archives and at the New York City Research Library on Fifth Ave. The Mormon Church filmed Parish records for Our Lady of Grace Church and for

St. Anthony's. These registers, unlike the ones in the Old Countries, are perfectly organized and legible.

What information did we have when we commenced researching our family history?

We had a lot of details about the personality and life in America of **Pawel Bielawski**. And we had a number of photographs—he is the most photographed of my grandparents. We had little information about his life in Europe. We had what we believed to be his birthday. As it turned out, the year was correct, but the month was widely discrepant. We didn't know the name of Pawel's father. We knew the name of his mother—Ursula Milosz—and the details that she died young and that her husband remarried. We knew Pawel was from Vilnius—actually, he was from a tiny village 20 or so miles to the south. And we knew he had a brother, Josef, who didn't make it in America. We didn't know when Pawel or Josef immigrated.

We were lucky to find Pawel's naturalization papers. These records were kept in the Courthouse on Newark Ave. in Jersey City. The records were in deplorable condition at the time I used them. They were in huge ledgers on shelves exposed to the open air. The clerk in the office kindly let me peruse the ledgers book by book until I found the right year. It was literally a needle in the haystack style of research.

We found Pawel's entry on the ship's log at the National Archive with little difficulty. The surname was spelled "Bulawski". Because of the Soundex system used at the time, that did not make much difference. The Soundex system, created by the WPA during the Great Depression, developed an index card file that recorded every name on all the ships' logs and organized them by similarity of surname pronunciation—Bielawski, Bulawski, Belopski, and so on—and then by personal name. It was easy to match up Pawel—a relatively uncommon personal name—with something that sounded like Bielawski.

The entry on the *Patricia*'s logbook disclosed the name of Pawel's father, which was a great find, but it also threw us a major curve. His last village of residence appeared to be *Skalmierz*—that's how it looks and how it's listed in the on-line Ellis Island records. There is no village by that name in Lithuania. There is a village by that name in Central Poland. It was very unlikely that Pawel lived in Skalmierz. I now believe the attendant on board the *Patricia* had an unusual handwriting. I can't explain the "*mierz*" portion of the word, but I think the attendant wrote the letter "K" so that it looked like "Sk".

We had little information on the life of **Zofia Storta** when we started this research. We didn't know the names of her parents or where she was from. We didn't have her correct birth date. We knew her brother Stanley immigrated and that a second brother lived in Poland. It was easy locating her record on the ship's log—both "Zofia" and "Storta" are not common names. The ship's log provided the name of her father and a misspelled version of Girdziunai.

Research on Stanley Storta proved to be helpful on the Storta and Juchnewicz lines. He demonstrated the value of collateral research and why it's useful to research more than one family member at the same time. Stanley's WWI registration listed a better spelled version of Girdziunai and the district he came from—"Wilenska". His Social Security registration disclosed the surname of his mother. With this information the Vilnius Archive produced records expeditiously.

We had a number of details on the life of **Catherine Griffin**. We knew the names of Nana's parents and the names of her brother and sisters. We knew the area of Ireland they were from. We knew the names of her brothers-in-law. And we knew the names of Nana's aunts and uncles. They lived in Hoboken and were known by my father. Allen, Keane, Lovett—these were names I frequently heard growing up.

It proved surprisingly easy to find Nana on the ship's logs. We knew the general time period she immigrated and the place she was from. It was a simple matter of checking the logs ship by ship until we found the right person.

Patrick Ford proved the most difficult of our grandparents to locate in the Old Country. We knew he was from County Mayo, but we didn't know where. We suspected Grandpa was an only son, which made his grandfather's name "Pat" if the naming pattern held. But the name "Patrick Ford" is not particularly rare in Mayo. It's not possible to proceed unless a specific townland or Parish is indicated. To our dismay the marriage record in Our Lady of Grace Church listed a townland that didn't exist—Ballyhaunis was badly misspelled. We didn't know the names of his father and mother. We knew his father remarried and that a wicked stepmother inspired him to immigrate, but we didn't know her name. We knew he had sisters, but we didn't know their names or where they lived in America.

The break came when I was at the Family History Library and described my predicament to a sympathetic missionary. Another person overheard my dilemma and suggested I find out if Grandpa registered to vote—I'm sure this person was an angel sent to guide me. If he registered, they would know when he was naturalized and I could get the name of the ship that way. I called the voting office at the courthouse in Jersey City and got this information within a minute or two of holding. Yes, he registered to vote. I went to the naturalization office at Newark Ave and found the date he arrived and the name of the ship. The next stop was Houston and Varick Sts. I found the ship's log and the names of his father—Thomas—and townland—"Dernacong". I still recall the intense happiness I experienced catching the 1/9 train on Varick St. on my way to work at the Sale Annex. It's true—there is a joy in finding things out.

If this person—this angel—didn't mention voter registration, we might never have found Pat Ford's ancestry. His name was recorded on the ship's log as "Gord"—the "F" was turned in the other direction and inside out.

In some things we were lucky—an informed person with good hearing in the Family History Library the same day as I; Mary Linnane listing the specific month and year of her birth on the 1900 Census; Girdziunai being on the border in Lithuania and not inside Belarus. I found the family of Martin Griffin of Connecticut by sheer accident. When I learned that William Lovett, the son of Pat and Mary Lovett, was born in New Haven I obtained a number of microfilms from the Mormon Church for that vicinity. I supposed that people traveled in groups and that there might be another ancestor in New Haven in that time period. Sure enough, I found the marriage record of Martin Griffin and Catherine Lovett and the baptism records of two of their children.

One of the films the Mormons provided listed Griffin burials in a cemetery named St. Bernard's. I called St. Bernard's. The lady on the other end was very helpful. She checked—there was no one named Martin Griffin buried there. I was set to hang up and to say hello to another dead end when she said to hold on. She would check records of an affiliated cemetery—St. Lawrence in West Haven. I held on. Sure enough, Martin and Catherine were buried there, along with a number of children. The family was far larger than I anticipated.

You don't have to leave home to do genealogical research today. A vast number of records are on-line. The ship's registers are on-line. When we were doing research in the 1990s we had to travel to Varick St. to view the microfilms. And the 1911 Census of Ireland is now on-line. When we were active in research we had to travel to Salt Lake City to view the census. It's a great boon to have so much information literally at one's fingertips, but in a strange way this instant access to treasure troves of data undermines one of the goals of genealogy. It's great fun to find things out. It's equally great fun to go places to find things out. We traveled to places we never heard of, places like Derrynacong and Kalniskes and Ballyegan and Girdziunai. And we traveled to places we most likely would never have visited or visited for purposes other than for reasons of blood. We traveled to Ireland—three times—and to Lithuania—three times. We traveled to Salt Lake City. We traveled to cemeteries in the Bronx and in Hawthorne, New York, and to a library in Orange County, and to the National Archives in Maryland. There were a few places we visited on a number of occasions—the Old Records Room in the Courthouse on Chambers St. in Manhattan, the Genealogy Room in the New York City Public Library, and the New Jersey Room in the Jersey City library.

There were two places we visited regularly—the National Archives on the twelfth floor of the vast building on Varick St. and the Family History Library on the second floor of 125 Columbus Ave. near Lincoln Center.

The National Archives was one of my favorite places in New York City. The microfilms were kept in vast file cabinets. Readers were in a dark room on the other side of the cabinets. Microfilm is an obsolete technology in a digital age, but grainy images and squeaky hand cranks somehow feel appropriate when dealing with people who lived a century age. People like Bridget Fitzmaurice and Magdalena Asakewicz somehow don't have the same human resonance in a Google search as they do on the scratched boards of a hand-operated microfilm reader.

After research we'd stop for coffee at the café next to the Archives. The windows of the café commanded a great view of Midtown Manhattan and of the Hudson River. So much of my life and the lives of my ancestors opened in the view from those windows.

The Family History Library is part of a "stake" or church. Mormons are obligated to pursue their family history as a religious requirement. Non-Mormons are free to use the vast resources accumulated there—at the height of my research I was visiting the Library once or twice a week. I think I visited the Library at a unique moment. Records were open and available and everyone was cooperative to the extreme. We became friends with the very professional and good-willed missionaries at the time—Gene and Maurine Lyons; Richard and Joyce Long; Sister Gardner; Director Wes Landon.

I owe a debt to the always courteous Mormon missionaries and to the archivists at the National Archives on Varick St. and in Vilnius. I owe a debt to the many relatives who were kind enough to tell us things about the people who came before us. And I owe a special debt to my Mom, who was enthusiastic about family history and who was an active partner in this research. Mom frequently accompanied me to the Archives and to the Family History Library. As I wrote in *Genealogical Jaunts* she became a world traveler in her senior years. Mom crossed the sea to visit Ireland and Lithuania where she walked on the ancestral farms where her grandparents and great-grandparents made their lives.

I remember Mom's first visit to the Family History Library. She was nervous and unsure what she would encounter inside the reading room—these people were Mormons, after all, and who knows what they are like. She insisted on taking a few moments and combing her hair before going inside. I joked at the time that she was a vain person. I've since come to realize that I do the same thing before entering work or any official place. Surely, it can't be vanity on my part. It must be a trait that runs in the blood.

From the computer room in the Family History Library I could look out and see the bustle of the crowds at the intersection of Broadway and Columbus Ave. So many people from so many places rushing on so many chores. I wondered where they were from and whether they were rooted in the soil of their family histories in the way I was becoming rooted in mine. Like those people I live—my family lives—chaotically busy and hectic lives. We're on the go all the time, like the avalanche of colorful pedestrians when the signal turned to green. That hushed room on the second floor bestowed a peacefulness and a sense of gratitude removed from the noise and the crowds and the traffic. I have no idea what the future will bring—that troubles me. I know where I'm from in the world in the broadest sense and I know where home is—this comforts me. As it encompasses all the people and places we retrieved from the oblivion of forgetfulness, this knowledge transcends my individual experience. It allows me to share in history and in family history and to be someone greater and someone different than I could ever be on my own. We got the chance to know our people of the long ago—to know them a little, anyways—and for that I'm deeply appreciative.

End Notes

[1]. The full title is *Irish Land Commission Return According to Provinces and Counties of Judicial Rents Fixed by Sub-commissions and Civil Bill Courts.* The subtitle is *Cases in Which Judicial Rents Have Been Fixed by Sub-Commission under Land Law (Ireland) Act, 1887.*

[2]. Bernie Freeman was the great-grandson of Thomas Freeman and Mary Glavy of Gorteen townland in Annagh Parish. His parents, who immigrated to New Jersey, were Thomas Freeman and Mary Anne Rafferty.

[3]. The townland is the smallest geographical unit in Ireland. Rooted in the Medieval period, townlands consist of a cluster of family farms called *clachen*. In the older period residents would likely be related as extended families. This is less true today. The Poor Law system commenced in 1838. It was an attempt to establish workhouses—poorhouses—on a local scale to assist the sick and the destitute.

[4]. Twenty shillings add to one pound. Twelve pence add to one shilling.

[5]. Griffith's Valuation of properties was periodically updated in what are called "Closed Valuation Books". They are an important genealogical resource as it is possible to trace the names of renters of specific properties.

[6]. *Statistical Survey of the County of Mayo with Observations for the Means of Improvements Drawn up in the Year 1801 for the Consideration and Under the Direction of the Dublin Society.* I read an orginal copy of this book in the New York City Public Library reading room on 42nd St.

[7]. The blight was worldwide, extending from America to Russia. It was only in Ireland that people died on a mass scale.

[8]. Fr. Coyne's letter appears in *Ireland Before & After the Famine* by Cormac O Grada, Manchester University Press, 1993. The Skibberin comparison appears in *History of the Great Irish Famine of 1847* by John O Rourke.

[9]. Despite the horrendous conditions of the Famine, farmers were required to pay the annual rent on their holdings as if nothing was amiss. Unscrupulous landlords used the Famine as a means to clear out small

farmers in order to maximize profits in larger farms. Forcible evictions conducted by police and hired thugs led to grim consequences. Evicted families had few options. They could emigrate. They could proceed to the despised workhouses. They could live in the open—hence, the number of people found dead on roads.

[10]. Pat Hunt may have been from Derrynacong. A man named James Cox married Bridget Hunt of Derrynacong and replaced Mary Hunt in property #10 in the Closed Valuation Books. Individuals named James Cox and Bridget Hunt stood as godparents to Pat Hunt's children. It is possible Bridget was his sister and Mary his mother and the widow of Hugh.

[11]. It was not uncommon for two men to serve as witnesses in a wedding— we frequently see the same practice on the Polish side. The modern notion of a wedding party was unknown in that period.

[12]. The known children of Pat Fitzmaurice and Bridget Kyne were: Mary, born 1861; Thomas, birth year not known; Michael, 1866; Catherine, 1867; Bridget, 1869; Ellen, 1871; Sarah, 1873.

[13]. It is flattering to believe we are descended from the son of a Norman warlord, but the connection extends nine centuries and is tenuous at best.

[14]. Edmond Connell and Bridget Costello had the following known children: Margaret, born in Lackaboy townland in 1832; Honora, born in Lackaboy, 1833; Joanna, born in Ballyegan, 1838; Robert; 1841. Robert Connell married Mary Moriarty. They resided in Ballydonohue and had two known children, Denis and Bridget. It is likely Julia Connell was another daughter of Edmond and Bridget. Julia Connell married John Purtill in January 1845. They had a large family. Their son Edward appears to have been close to Martin Griffin's children. Two of Edward's daughters—Mary and Julia— traveled to America with John Griffin (see Chapter Eleven). Edward was married to Margaret Diggin. The writer John B. Keane was descended in part from Edward and Margaret.

[15]. There is a marriage record for Patrick King and Margaret Flahavan dated 24 August 1856. It cannot be proven, but this fits the time period of John's birth.

[16]. Three descendents of Martin Griffin and Catherine Connell died in June, 1999—Mr. Neville, Michael Lynch, and my father. A fourth cousin, Tom Allen of Ballybunion, died the same month.

[17]. Jeremiah Lynch and Elizabeth Kennelly married in Ballydonohue on 9 February 1864. Their witnesses were John Gearin and M. Keane. They resided in Inch townland and later in Affouley. Their known children were: Hanora, born 1865; John, 1868; Margaret, 1871; Jeremiah, 1874; Mary, 1877; Edmond, 1880; Michael, 1884.

[18]. Every man born between 1873 and 1900 had to register for the draft. There were three registration days depending on age. The draft cards provide addresses and, frequently, a brief physical description of the individual.

[19]. Timothy Linnane of Tarbert married Catherine Weeks on 9 February 1872. Witnesses were Timothy McEssey and William Walsh. They had two sons, both of whom immigrated. John William was baptized on 17 January 1874, Timothy on 25 February 1877. John William married Ellen Sullivan and resided in Hoboken. He was close to my grandmother. Timothy was twice married and resided in New York City. His wives were the wonderfully named Margaret Sweeney Quinn and Margaret McManus O'Rourke.

[20]. There is a civil record dated 15 May 1864 of the marriage of Thomas Purtill and Elizabeth Gallivan. Witnesses were John Gallivan and Nicholas Mulvihill. Thomas's father was James, Elizabeth's Michael.

[21]. William Lovett married Catherine Gallivan on 24 June 1866. They resided in Tulla More, Galey Parish. Their known children were: Patrick, born 1867; Mary and Catherine, twins, 1872; Honora, 1874; Joanna, 1876; John, 1878; Margaret, 1881. There is a baptism record for William Lovett dated 1 July 1832. He was the son of John Lovett and Catherine Walsh.

[22]. There is a baptism record in the Our Lady of Grace register for Mary Costello dated 7 July 1897. She was the daughter of James Costello and Margaret Halligan.

[23]. Thomas McCarthy married Mary Leonard 9 June 1896 in Our Lady of Grace Church. Witnesses were Patrick Allen and Mary Allen. Thomas was the son of Patrick McCarthy and Mary O'Connor. He resided in New York City. Mary Leonard was the daughter of John Leonard (Linnane) and Mary Lovett. She resided in Hoboken.

[24]. The known children of Edmond Ferris and Norah Moran were: John, born 1866; Mary, 1869; Margaret, 1870; Mary; 1872; Ellen, 1876. Another son was Edward, who married Mary Donahue in February 1905

in Our Lady of Grace Church and who may have been a police officer and tavern owner.

[25]. Lawrence Keane married Margaret Behan in Carrigaholt Parish on 6 February 1869. Lawrence was the son of Charles Keane and Mary Cullinan of Baltard townland. Margaret was the daughter of John Behan of Tullaroe townland. After their marriage they resided in Shanganagh townland located on the Shannon River in the County Clare. They had the following known children: Charles, born 1870; Mary Anne, 1871; Thomas, 1872; Anne, 1874; Bridget, 1876; John, 1877; Catherine, 1878; Michael and Patrick, twins, 1880. Lawrence Keane died in 1890, Charles Keane in 1876.

[26]. *Genealogical Jaunts*, Dennis Ford, iUniverse, 2008, pp. 38 – 39.

[27]. Policarp Storta immigrated in 1913 to Jersey City under the surname "Stord". He was accompanied by Osif Stord. Policarp was the son of Franciszk Storta and Marianna Kartanowicz. His village was Rybacki, presently located in Belarus to the south of Girdziunai. He married Clara Mackiewicz in 1915. They resided in Jersey City and had two children, one of whom was Joseph, a decorated WWII veteran. Policarp died in 1950. His age was given as 57.

Joseph Storta of Dobrowlawny immigrated in 1911. (Dobrowlawny is located in Belarus to the south of Girdziunai.) He was married to Emily Raksa and resided in Bayonne. It appears he returned to Europe. It is likely he had a brother named Franciszk, who resided in Bayonne. Franciszk was the son of Vincenty Storta and Agatha Mikszan. He married Stanislawa Chadkiewicz in Our Lady of Mt. Carmel, Bayonne, NJ. Franciszk was baptized in Subotninki. He died 1946, aged 61.

Maryanne Storta immigrated 1912 and resided in Bayonne. It is likely she was Joseph's and Franciszk's sister.

[28]. There is a marriage record in St. Anthony's Church dated 22 August 1907 for Thomas Juchnewicz and Marianna Undrawke. Thomas was listed as the son of Motiejus Juchnewicz and Maryanne Jackiewicz. Maciej Storta stood as godparent to a son born in 1910. It is possible Thomas was descended from Motiejus and Kristina Juchnewicz.

[29]. Doran's report is included in *On the Verge of Want*, James Morrissey (Ed.), Crannog Books, 2001.

[30]. *Irish Distress and Its Remedies, The Land Question, A Visit to Donegal and Connaught in the Spring of 1880*. James Tuke.

[31]. The usual naming pattern does not appear to hold in John's case. The first and second sons were named after grandfathers. The third son was named after the father. The fourth son was named after the father's oldest brother.

[32]. Edward Lyons married Catherine Bones in Bekan Parish on 11 March 1866. Witnesses were Edmond Grogan and Bridget Waldron. Edward was the son of Pat Lyons. Catherine was the daughter of Michael Bones and Bridget Connally of Brackloon townland. She was baptized in Bekan Parish on 21 November 1840 or 41. Edward and Catherine were alive in Larganboy in 1911. Their known children were: Bridget, born 1866; Mary, 1869; Catherine, 1870; John, 1872; Mary again, 1874, Michael, circa 1880.

[33]. Relative to the pulp, the peel has fewer calories and carbohydrates, but more protein, calcium, iron, and fiber. The peel is not generally eaten. It is removed by knives and fingernails. We saw Michael Lynch of Affouley hold a potato on a fork and use a knife to shave the skin.

[34]. Timothy McNamara of Ennis, County Clare, married Margaret Lynch of Daugan townland on 13 February 1876. They had the following known children: Michael, born 1877; Mary, 1878; Elizabeth, 1880; Patrick, 1884. In the 1901 Irish Census Timothy was described as a "herdsman".

[35]. Michael Connor and Alice Campbell had the following known children: Patrick, born 1871; Olive, 1873; John and Mary, twins, 1876; Bridget, 1879; Anne, 1881; Catherine, 1885; Michael, 1888. We do not have their marriage record.

[36]. We can't identify with certainty the children of Alexander Banda and Annetta Pelreal. In addition to Charles and Hanna the following individuals are buried in the Banda grave: Alexander Banda, June 1965; Agnica Banda, November 1965; Romeo Bender, June 1988; Irma Bender, January 1974; Rose Fersterman, August 1975; Florita Santana, January 1979.

[37]. A marriage record dated 30 October 1893 exists in Baltimore for Charles B. Klinak and Regina Bothe. They had the following known children: Adam, born circa 1894; Tillie, 1895; Milton, 1896; Jerome, 1899.

[38]. Here are the directions for Josef's grave. It is in the poor section of the cemetery. Find the grave of Victoria Johnson (3-G-Q-33). Walk toward the fence. There is a large tree on the same line as the grave near the fence. Josef's grave is six or seven feet to the left of a marker to "Helen" as you face in the direction of the large yellow house.

[39]. Salcininki is the major city in Southeastern Lithuania. It's about thirty miles from Vilnius. It was first mentioned in historical accounts in 1311. It was the scene of fierce fighting in World War Two and in the partisan activities against communism. The current population is 7,000. There is a glass factory, paper mill, and distillery. *Genealogical Jaunts* describes our visits.

[40]. The *President Grant* was ceded to England after World War One and rechristened the *Republic* in the White Star line. Agnes Forde sailed on the ship under that name. The Hamburg-American Line used the names of presidents to attract American passengers.

[41]. Maciej had company on the return home. Approximately 30% of Polish immigrants went back to Europe.

[42]. We don't know why Stanley was in Trieste. However, Trieste held a sizeable number of Polish people. James Joyce taught English there to make a living while writing fiction. It's fun to consider that Stanley might have had Joyce as a teacher.

[43]. The naturalization process involved three steps. The first step was a "declaration of intent". This was followed by a "petition for naturalization" and, later, by a swearing in ceremony. The documents in the naturalization process list the ship and date of entrance to the United States and include important genealogical information.

[44]. Jeanne Lowe was one of the founders of the proxy department at Merrill Lynch. Later, she founded the preliminary prospectus unit in which Blanche and I worked. Jeanne was originally from New England. She had two daughters—she was estranged from one for many years. Shortly before I met her Jeanne converted from Catholicism to Seven-Day Adventism. She was very active in that church. Jeanne died in March 2002 at 88 years of age.

[45]. According to his enlistment papers Dad worked for Bethlehem Steel from April 1943 to April 1944.

[46]. A "deck log" is a daily contemporaneous record of events on the ship. It includes accidents, changes in personnel and command, expenditures of weaponry, incidents at sea, moorings, ship movements, and weather conditions. The four volumes we reviewed were in excellent condition. Most of the entries were typed. Some of the officers handwrote their notes—Ensign Ditmars always used green ink.

[47]. We don't know who Stanislawa Lakiewska was. Casimir Wasilewski is buried in Holy Cross Cemetery near Pawel and Zofia. His dates were 1889 – 1951. His wife is with him, as is their son Edward. Wasilewski is a name we associate with Girdziunai.

[48]. If you ask, I'll tell you his name. I promised I would never reveal it in print.

[49]. MOCC is an acronym for Mobile Operational Command and Control. They are forward units who direct the activity of fighter planes.

Printed in the United States
By Bookmasters